The
Garland Library
of
War and Peace

The
Garland Library
of
War and Peace

Under the General Editorship of

Blanche Wiesen Cook, *John Jay College*, C.U.N.Y.

Sandi E. Cooper, *Richmond College*, C.U.N.Y.

Charles Chatfield, *Wittenberg University*

Not By Might

Christianity:
The Way to Human Decency

and

Of Holy Disobedience

by

Abraham J. Muste

with a new Introduction
for the Garland Edition by
Jo Ann Robinson

Garland Publishing, Inc., New York & London
1971

Library of Congress Cataloging in Publication Data

Muste, Abraham John, 1885-1967.
    Not by might; Christianity.

    (The Garland library of war and peace)
    Reprint of 2 works first published in 1947 and
1952 respectively.
        1. Peace (Theology) 2. Conscientious objectors.
3. Pacifism. I. Muste, Abraham John, 1885-1967.
Of holy disobedience. 1971. II. Title. III. Title:
Of holy disobedience. IV. Series.
[BT736.4.M88]   261.8'73   70-147628
ISBN 0-8240-0403-5

Introduction

The reader will discover for himself that Not By
Might *is a religious statement. Its chapters are laced
with biblical allusions. Its arguments proceed from a
religious assumption: "Unless men are prepared. . . to
accept the laws of God and the spirit of Christ as the
way of life for nations as well as for individuals, there
is no hope for us" (p. 133). The book clearly
expresses, too, the anguish, outrage, and fear of its
author. Anguish is plain in his analysis of World War
II (pp. 8-19). Outrage punctuates his consideration of
the possibility of World War III (p. 7). Fear is
admitted openly at the outset: "I think of my two
grandchildren and of millions of other grandchildren
in all the lands and then I think of the atomic
armament race. . . and of the atomic war which will
surely grow out of it if it goes on − and I am afraid"
(p. 2). But a word about Muste's emotionalism, and
some explication of his assumptions and the deeds
they generated may be in order.*

*Abraham John Muste (1885-1967) was 62 years
old when this book was published. He had been
reared in Michigan in the relative innocence of
pre-World War I America. In these pages one may
glimpse the simple patriotism of his Dutch-immigrant
heritage (pp. 130-131). In his repeated warnings that*

5

INTRODUCTION

*"God is not mocked" can be felt the stern teachings
of his Dutch Reformed upbringing (pp. 14, 48, 213).
But Muste was not anchored to the origins whose
traces his writings bear. His concept of God, always
influenced by his Reformed heritage, evolved beyond
Calvinist bounds. In 1947 it was defined in language
that "even the reader who reacts against the term
God" could accept (p. 49). Muste identified his
religion with a pacifist viewpoint which, he wrote,
"the greatest religious teachers and saints have
virtually all in one way or another arrived at and
preached" (p. 74). He universalized his faith beyond
any one age or tradition and drew out its implications
for modern political and military policy, its relevance
to the atomic age.*

The religious message of Not By Might *had
practical applications, then. But what purpose is
served by the freely bared emotions which repeatedly
break forth in the book? Do these not signal
sentimentality or lack of control in the author?*

*Seventeen years of labor organizing (1919-1936),
years marked by violent strike experiences, trips to
jail, and bitter factional fights, had purged Muste of
sentimental responses. His outbursts of feeling here
are not maudlin. He consciously emulated the
unsparing biblical prophets: "Out of their insight and
anguish," he insisted, "is wrung the cry which so
often dismayed the privileged, the arrogant and the
complacent" (p. 66). Muste's own cry was meant to
unsettle an "age of mechanization, regimentation and*

6

authoritarianism" (p. 150). By uttering it he enacted his assertion that "there must enter into every relationship something of that emotional intensity. . . which gives depth and rapture to our most intimate relationships." By sharing his emotions he addressed each reader not "as a thing, an object," but "as truly a human being" (p. 68).

To the prophetic tradition A. J. Muste attributed not only his open and impassioned form of direct address but also certain assumptions about human creatures and their creator. " 'God manifests his own love toward us,' " he wrote, "by confronting us with a moral order," requiring justice and brotherhood (p. 65). It is "an inexorable spiritual law," he insisted, that whenever these requirements are violated "disaster. . . overtakes men and civilization" (p. 52). Traces of Dutch Reformed predestination are evident in this stress upon divine confrontation and inexorable law. Life experiences had shaped the emphasis as well. Late in his labor career Muste had affiliated with the Trotskyist American Workers Party (December, 1934-July, 1936), briefly denying that individuals "cannot escape the obligation to be supremely good" (p. 50). But in July, 1936 his denial was dramatically overturned by a conversion of the same sort to which he called individuals and nations throughout this book (pp. ix, 37, 74, 115, 117, and chapter III in its entirety).

The 1936 experience is not recounted in Not By Might, *but the parallel between his writings about it*

7

INTRODUCTION

elsewhere and the description here of "the moment of moral decision" will not be missed by those familiar with his autobiography.[1] Clearly, the event also was the basis for his interest in and interpretation of Rosa Luxemburg's experience (p. 44).

When Muste wrote that "at its central core the universe is love" (p. 86), then, he was reaffirming an insight that had been burned into his consciousness eleven years earlier. The course of history since that time, he indicated, had substantiated both that insight and its corollary that "we cannot escape the consequences of our denial of love, our refusal to be good" (p. 87). Look, he demanded: look at "the awful price we have paid for World War II" — more of the same international chaos that started the war, terrible human suffering and death, and in Hiroshima and Nagasaki the ultimate consequences of "the logic of atrocity" by which Americans setting out to destroy a monster had been transformed by their choice of means into monsters themselves (pp. 8-19). "We have to get away from the wisdom and realism which have brought us where we are. . ." (p. 89).

A. J. Muste thus took the offensive against those who had unleashed massive violence in the name of reason and realism. Now, he argued, under the threat of atomic annhilation pacifism may be seen not only as a sensible position but also as man's sole surviving hope. Muste was particularly anxious in 1947 to seize

[1] See "Sketches for an Autobiography," in Nat Hentoff, ed., The Essays of A. J. Muste (New York, Bobbs Merrill, 1967).

INTRODUCTION

*the initiative from Reinhold Niebuhr, whose skillfully
argued "crisis theology" had lent significant justification to the Allied effort in World War II and had
stamped pacifists with a public image of naïveté. Two
chapters of Not By Might (VI and IX) are devoted
primarily to discounting Niebuhr's thought.*

*Muste probed the core of Niebuhr's analysis when,
in Chapter IX, he discussed the meaning of justice. He
did not `question Niebuhr's devotion to this central
value of crisis theology, but he did deny that it had
actually been served. Dresden bombings, Hiroshima
and Nagasaki, calculated flirtation with World War III
— Muste was certain these did not square with any
conceivable definition of justice.*

*Theologians following Niebuhr's line in support of
the necessity of these deeds had started from false
premises, he suggested. When many of them broke
with the pacifist movement in 1934 they lost sight of
"what holds society together. . . what is the source
and nature of authority" (p. 96). Seduced by the
modern trend toward focusing "almost entirely upon
the outer rather than the inner, upon the surface
rather than the depths" (p. 49), they had been
unduly impressed by "naked power and belligerency." They had concluded that human beings are
"held together. . . by clubs and guns," he wrote (p.
97).*

*Since 1936 Muste had been convinced that love is
the "source and nature of authority." The failure of
"realists" to gain justice by other means seemed to*

prove his point one more tragic time. They were mistaken to equate obedience to love with naivete, he declared; love is "primarily a demand upon us. . . love is judgement" (p. 65). Love is bound up with the very justice championed by Niebuhr. The great theologian, Muste charged, had attempted to escape from "the complexities of the love ethic" by drawing "a sharp line between justice and love," had become bogged down in "moral relativism" (pp. 108-109), and had obscured the calling of the church: "Men are waiting to have the church tell them . . . whether making . . . war is right or wrong," Muste insisted, "simply that." Christian leadership must give "a clear and un-equivocal" pacifist answer (p. 169).

What practical consequences follow from such an answer? They are outlined in Chapter VII. Recognizing that his readers could easily regard the warless and humane world he envisioned as "utterly fantastic," Muste developed pragmatic as well as religious defenses for his unilateral approach to peace. Still, there was the haunting question: "Suppose the plan does not work immediately, and other nations do not follow the example of the United States — what then?" His answer followed the uncompromising character of the love-ethic with which he challenged the reader: "If the fearful choice has to be made, it is better to have atomic bombs dropped on us than to drop them on others" (pp. 126-27).

By comparison, a few years later, after the United States lost its monopoly on atomic power, Reinhold

INTRODUCTION

Niebuhr wrote, "If the bomb were ever used, I hope it would kill me, because the moral situation would be something that I could not contemplate. At the same time you cannot disavow its use prematurely — without bowing yourself out of responsibility for the whole generation."[2]

But in 1947 Muste was hopeful that nuclear tragedy could be averted. He pointed out that politicians, the mass media, and even the physical scientists were speaking as once only "impractical idealists" had spoken. Widespread opinion reflected awareness of a crisis "in the mind and spirit of man" that was "deeper than politics" (p. 37).

Accordingly, Muste devoted the last four chapters of Not By Might *to strategies which would sharpen that awareness and lead toward pacifist action. He identified target constituencies that might become the nucleii of a mass movement for peace — scientists, educators, churchmen. The pacifist leader thus foreshadowed some of his own future endeavors. Partly at his prompting scientists concerned about their moral obligations would establish in 1949 the Society for Social Responsibility in the Sciences. With his help educators and intellectuals opposed to atomic stockpiling would coalesce between 1960 and 1965 into the Council for Correspondence. Between 1950 and 1962, in response to his declaration that "a great mission to the churches must be organized" (p.*

[2]*Quoted in Nat Hentoff,* Peace Agitator, The Story of A.J. Muste *(New York: Macmillan, 1967), 180.*

11

216), he would lead the Church Peace Mission, a coalition of denominational pacifist groups, religious pacifist organizations, and traditional peace churches.

It is clear, then, that this book provides some guide to action and is not entirely theoretical. Yet it is not so easy to judge its fundamental assertions — that one must risk the destruction of himself and his country rather than become an instrument of another nation's destruction, and that atomic weaponry has brought us to the point where we have only one more chance to save ourselves by taking this risk.

Muste was prescient in some of his predictions, notably in his warning that the United Nations in its original form would be ineffective (p. 9), and in his forecast of Russian-U.S. relations (pp. 24-33). But what of his repeated warnings that "time is short," and his reduction of foreign policy choices to either immediate unilateral disarmament or the destruction of mankind in World War III? Did he underestimate the significance of deterrence and the possibilities of "cold" and "limited" wars? His later writings indicate that he did not overlook but rather rejected these developments as permanent safeguards against catastrophe.

Five years after publishing Not By Might Muste penned Of Holy Disobedience. The United States was then engaged in its "limited police action" in Korea. Deterrence and cold war terminology had become an accepted part of the modern vocabulary. But the essay conveyed the same time-is-short urgency as the *book. The main difference between them derived from the audiences to which they were addressed. In* Of Holy Disobedience *Muste was speaking to pacifists rather than recruiting them. Accordingly, detailed explanations of anti-war assumptions and the threat of nuclear destruction were unnecessary. The essay explored instead certain implications, complexities, and problems of the pacifist movement.*

By then the acknowledged pacifist leader, Muste posed three basic questions: 1) Can a Christian ever allow temporal circumstances, including war, to interrupt or change his vocation? 2) What responsibility does the pacifist movement have toward young conscripts? 3) Is it possible for pacifists to oppose war without resisting conscription? Muste's answer to the third question is implicit in his comments on the first two.

Essentially, he argued that war can be uprooted only by eradicating conscription. "If peace time conscription should be enacted in this country," he had written in Not By Might, *". . . it would be part of an unmistakable militarist and fascist pattern for American life" (p. 151). When he wrote* Of Holy Disobedience *the peace time draft had been in effect for four years, along with the increasing pressures for conformity and regimentation that are known as the McCarthy Era. In response Muste singled out another target constituency for pacifist organization, the group directly affected by conscription — American youth. With reference to Christian young people he*

13

raised again questions about "vocation."

The considerations which Muste examined under this heading are those with which he had struggled during his own conversion to pacifism in the era of World War I. Then he had felt the impulse to find new work that would seem personally meaningful and socially significant. He had felt obligated to demonstrate that a pacifist can face hardship and danger. Accordingly he had resigned from the Christian ministry in 1919 and accepted a life of physical and financial insecurity. Yet, in 1952, he was very critical of giving in to those very impulses which had initiated his own activist career (p. 11). The basis of his criticism was the difference between his situation in 1919 and that of draftees in 1952. In the World War I period he was already beyond draft age and, besides, he was exempt as a minister. He could change his vocation voluntarily. The young men whose position he examined in Of Holy Disobedience were changing theirs under government compulsion.

A. J. Muste had learned some hard lessons about government compulsion through his experiences with the National Service Board for Religious Objectors during World War II. What was undertaken as "a service of love" turned into service to the state. Virtually everyone involved with the NSBRO effort to cooperate with the conscripting state eventually concluded that collaboration was, as Lawrence Wittner has written, "an integral part of military authoritarianism."[3] *Muste held firm to that conclusion in* Of Holy Disobedience. *Conscription, he argued, is tantamount to authoritarianism, and authoritarian power exercised by a state must not be granted legitimacy by its citizens. Certain individuals, such as those from "traditional peace churches," might feel obligated to cooperate with conscription in a spirit of "nonresistance to evil," but, Muste pointed out, the very terms of their cooperation make it clear that the state is indeed evil.*

The question of whether or not to counsel draft age youth to resist conscription agitated pacifist circles in 1952, as it would for decades afterward. It was an especially poignant issue for A. J. Muste, whose son, John, had enlisted in the Navy during World War II (his father interpreted it as a response to pressures from his prepschool peers). Then, as in Of Holy Disobedience, *the elder Muste consistently announced his own absolute opposition to the draft system and his equally genuine respect for those youth who differed with him on grounds of conscience. Muste's discussion of conscription and of draft resistance would be relevant twenty years later, when there were still inequalities between "religious" and "non-religious" conscientious objectors, and when disillusioned Vietnam veterans would bear out his prediction that "accessions to the pacifist movement. . . will come mainly from young people who have gone through the experience of life in the*

[3] *Wittner*, Rebels Against War *(New York: Columbia, 1969), 76.*

armed forces" (p. 25).

For fifteen years after he wrote Of Holy
Disobedience A. J. Muste continued to exemplify the
resistance to which he called others. He had begun
federal tax refusal in 1948. Nine years later he was a
key figure in establishing the Committee for
Nonviolent Action, and he participated with CNVA
in the experiments with civil disobedience and radical
confrontation which made it "the radical action arm
of the traditional pacifist organizations."[4] In the
sixties Muste played an important role in the
accelerating protests against American military policy
in Vietnam. His writings at that time reflected less
optimism than either Not By Might or Of Holy
Disobedience. Three months before his death Muste
commented that the world might be turning into a
"wasteland." If so, he pleaded in that prophetic vein
which characterized so many of his utterances, at
least let there be "voices crying in the wilderness."[5]

Jo Ann Robinson
Department of History
Morgan State College
Baltimore, Maryland

[4] Ibid., p. 257.

[5] *Muste, "Cleveland And After,"* The Mobilizer, *December 19, 1966,*
n.p.

Not By Might

A. J. MUSTE

Not By Might

Christianity:
The Way to Human Decency

"Not by might, nor by power,
but by my spirit . . ."
ZECHARIAH 4:6

NEW YORK   Harper & Brothers Publishers   LONDON

NOT BY MIGHT

Copyright, 1947, by Harper & Brothers
PRINTED IN THE UNITED STATES OF AMERICA

K-W

To My Grandchildren
JOHN AND RICHARD
And to Everybody's Grandchildren

*With the prayer that the peoples may renounce
the sin and folly of war so that we may not sacrifice our grandchildren as we have our children
to "this Moloch of our supreme and suicidal
devotion."*

Contents

Acknowledgments

The author wishes to express his appreciation to the following publishers and authors for permission to quote from their copyrighted works:

The Federal Council of the Churches of Christ in America for the quotations from *The Relation of the Church to the War in the Light of Christian Faith* and *Atomic Warfare and the Christian Faith.*

Random House, Inc. for the lines from *Letters from Iceland* by W. H. Auden and L. MacNeice.

Reynal & Hitchcock, Inc. for the lines from "The Intellectual," which appear in V-*Letter and Other Poems by Karl Shapiro.*

Howard Spring and Harper & Brothers for the quotations from *And Another Thing* by Howard Spring.

Aldena Carlson Thomason for the poem "History Teaches Us."

Introduction

"New Ways I Will Not Try"

In a communiqué issued on November 15, 1945, the President of the United States, the Prime Minister of Great Britain and the Premier of Canada said: "We are aware that the only complete protection for the civilized world from the destructive use of scientific knowledge lies in the prevention of war. . . . Every nation will realize more urgently than before the overwhelming need . . . to banish the scourge of war from the earth."

War must go. There must not be another war. The practical politicians—also the high priests of modern culture, the physical scientists—are now saying what the pacifists and impractical idealists used to say, only to be smiled at, sometimes indulgently and often not so indulgently.

To abolish war it is not enough to say that war must be abolished. War is so much a part of our culture and of our economic and political and spiritual being that to say war must go is obviously the equivalent of saying that a revolution must take place in ourselves and in our world. Something has to occur in the political and spiritual realm which is comparable to the fission of the atom and the release of atomic energy in its realm. "The beginning of wisdom" for us in this extremity is to try to grasp this fact and because we grasp it to divest ourselves of preconceptions and of faith in methods and forces which belong to an age that no longer exists. We have to "become as little children," eager and ready for fresh revelation.

The point I am trying to make is admirably set forth in a humorous

poem which was brought to my attention a short time ago. It is entitled "Times Have Changed" or "History Teaches Us":

> Said Life Force to Amoeba,
>   As she wiggled in the tide:
> "It's time you're evoluting,
>   So get busy and divide."
> But Amoeba, from tradition
>   Argued, "It is plain to view
> Where there's been one organism
>   There can't suddenly be two!"
>   But there were.
>
> Said Changed Environment to Amphibian
>   As he floated o'er the sand:
> "You'll have to change your habits,
>   Go bone-dry and live on land."
> Wet Amphibian, by Zoology,
>   Law of Fittest-to-Survive,
> Demonstrated out of water
>   He just couldn't keep alive!
>   But he did.
>
> Said Instinct to the Anthropoid,
>   "If you're to slug and roar,
> It's time you learned to balance
>   On two feet instead of four."
> Mr. Anthro proved by Physics
>   That if he should leave his rut,
> He'd lose his equilibrium
>   And bump his cocoanut!
>   But he didn't.
>
> Said Experience to the Cave Man,
>   "This rough stuff's going flat;
> You'll have to rule your roost and clan
>   By subtler means than that."
> The Cave Man cited Nature's law
>   To prove he'd be a dub
> For flabby Law-and-Order
>   To scrap his solid club!
>   But he did.

Said Intellect to Modern Man,
   "You settle this affair
Of stab and starve and slaughter,
   Or you'll soon be rather rare."
Said wise, sophisticated Modern Man,
   "It's up to me to die;
Old ways are suicidal,
   And new ways I will not try!"
   But he will.[1]

The lesson of these verses is as clear as it is profound. The universe, life, human history are dynamic things, not static. There is, therefore, no set of rules or prescriptions which is eternally valid. Circumstances change and the organism must adapt itself to them or perish. Furthermore, there are turning points when circumstances change profoundly and perhaps swiftly. Then the organism has to make a swift and radical adaptation to the change which has occurred. It must make the great leap of faith.

At such times adherence to the "wisdom" that has meant survival in the past means suicide. That which seemed or even was eminently sensible no longer makes sense. Something new, which on the basis of past conditions may seem to have little or nothing to commend it, is now the only thing that makes sense. In the Apostle's words, the wisdom of men is foolishness with God. Some divine foolishness has to be tried.

What this "foolishness" is which must at last be tried is illustrated by an incident that occurred during the recent war to two pastors of the French Reformed Church who were also Christian pacifists, leaders of the Fellowship of Reconciliation. Before the war they had established, in connection with their church in the city of Le Chambon, a school which was interracial and international both in its faculty and in its student body. Shortly after the Germans invaded France and the Vichy regime was set up, the two pastors got into trouble with that regime because they would not desist from sheltering, feeding and instructing the Jewish refugee children in their school. They were accordingly thrown into a concentration camp.

A great furor arose over their arrest, partly because it was the first

[1] By Aldena Carlson Thomason. Used with special permission of the author.

time that ordained ministers of any church had been put by the
regime into a concentration camp. As a result of the stir created, they
were informed that they would be released after a brief imprisonment
of about a month. But they were asked, as part of the formalities connected with release, to sign a statement in which they swore allegiance
to the Pétain regime and promised to obey its laws. They read the
document and then said they were sorry, they could not sign it. They
hoped to be law-abiding citizens of their country but there were some
laws, such as the anti-Semitic ones, which they could not in conscience obey. Accordingly they were returned to the concentration
camp.

A large number of their fellow inmates were Communists, and
when the pastors first returned to the barracks, the Communists
laughed at them. "Why should anyone stick at signing a piece of
paper? So-and-so," meaning a former inmate, "signed the paper a
month ago and two weeks later blew up a bridge killing a couple
hundred Germans on a train passing over it." But after a while the
Communists began to reflect on what it meant that in the kind of
world in which they were all living there were still people left who
would not sign a little piece of paper which told a lie. Even though
that meant going back into a concentration camp and perhaps never
getting out. Even though the lives of loved ones might be placed in
jeopardy.

Thereupon the Communists sat down for several hours each day
to study the New Testament, including the Sermon on the Mount,
with the two pastors. After an interval the latter were released—
without signing the oath of allegiance. Shortly before that a spokes-
man for the Communists who had been studying the Bible with
them said: "We admit that your religion is superior to ours. This
way of life that Jesus taught and lived is the way all men ought to
live. It is the way all men will live—after the Revolution. But, of
course," he concluded, "it isn't practical now."

All that I try to say in this book is really a preachment on the text
that the trouble with the world, especially our Western world and
our own country, is that the position stated by this Communist spokes-
man is exactly the position taken by the vast majority of church
members, by the churches themselves and by the so-called Christian

nations. Our Christian, democratic way of life is, we are convinced, far superior to any other, including the Communist. Some day, in heaven or on earth or both, everybody is going to live as Jesus taught. But for individuals and more especially for nations to do so now is not practical. It is unrealistic and utopian.

My thesis is that, whatever might have been true in the past, this seeming "wisdom" is now most certainly "foolishness." For modern man to adhere to it is to say: "Old ways are suicidal and new ways I will not try." It is to refuse to make the radical adaptation which is now the only sensible thing to do. Men and nations now have to try the way of uncalculating and sacrificial love or perish. God and history will not let them buy deliverance at a cheaper price.

Before we attempt to state concretely what this approach involves, two preliminary steps are required. First, we must briefly consider the situation in which we find ourselves at this moment in history. Secondly, we must survey the measures which are being taken or proposed and consider why they are inadequate to meet the crisis.

Chapter I

Has It Come to This?

War must go because, as President Truman said to his neighbors at a country fair in Caruthersville, Missouri, on October 8, 1945: "We can't stand another global war. We can't ever have another war unless it is total war, and that means the end of our civilization as we know it. We are not going to do that."

If we have another war, it will be atomic war. Professor J. R. Oppenheimer, who was in charge of the manufacture of the atomic bomb at Los Alamos, New Mexico, was asked in a hearing before a committee of the United States Senate whether it was a fair estimate that in one raid on congested United States centers in a few hours forty million human beings could be killed. He answered that this was a fair estimate. Remember, this was not an author of horror tales, or a cub reporter or a glib "popularizer" of "science" trying to make a sensational story out of scraps of information given him by an expert. This was one of the world's greatest minds, a person accustomed to speaking in exact, measured, conservative language. And he did not say that four thousand, or forty thousand, or four hundred thousand, or four million people might be killed in an atomic raid in a few hours. But forty million.

Some night the people of Boston, Providence, New London, New Haven, Bridgeport, New York, northern New Jersey, Camden, Philadelphia, Wilmington, Baltimore, Washington, Norfolk go to bed and they never wake up again. Some night the people of the British Isles, as helpless a target for an atomic bombing as a sheep before the tiger crouched in the tree above its head, go to bed and they just never wake up again.

It is possible that none of them will know, that indeed no one will ever know, where the winged death came from. For this is the terror by night, the arrow that flyeth by day, the pestilence that stalketh in the darkness, the destruction that wasteth at noonday. This is the abomination of desolation, the great tribulation such as hath not been from the beginning of the world until now. This perchance is the Beast of the Apocalypse, who seemed to the ecstatic seer to be leopard, bear, lion and dragon in one, after whom the whole earth wondered and worshiped in terror, crying, "Who is like unto the Beast? and who is able to war with him?"

My friends sometimes remind me that fear is not a very exalted motive. They are right, of course. Jesus taught such as have ears to hear that they ought not to fear those who can kill the body but that which can destroy the soul. It is not that which goeth into a man, not even the bullet which plows into his brain, that corrupts him but that which cometh out of him, including the bullet which his hand sends into his brother's heart. By the same token Americans would do well to be less concerned about atomic bombs which may be dropped on them than about what the bombs they dropped on Hiroshima and Nagasaki did to them and about the bombs they may in future send on their way to God knows where. We shall have occasion to return to this problem.

Yet fear may have its uses. People are mad not to be afraid of infection, of impure water, of dropping out of airplanes without parachutes—of what atomic bombs may do to them. I think of my two grandchildren and of millions of other grandchildren in all the lands and then I think of the atomic armament race which is already under way and of the atomic war which will surely grow out of it if it goes on—and I am afraid.

Consider for a moment the position the United States has gotten into. We are unquestioned victors in the greatest war in history. Our cities and countrysides have not suffered the ravages of war. Our natural resources and industrial establishment are vaster than those of any other nation in all history. The same is true of our military establishment. On top of all this we have the atomic bomb. Surely, we are now at long last safe, secure! Whom or what have we to fear?

The veriest child knows that we are not safe and secure. Every adult with an I.Q. above the moron level knows that Americans are afraid today, afraid as Americans have never been before in all the years of the nation's existence. In the moment of our power and victory we are utterly insecure and weak. Our actions demonstrate what we feel. Our diplomacy is largely a diplomacy of appeasement. Before the soldiers are home from the war—though God knows no soldiers were ever in such a desperate hurry to come home from a war as the American troops of World War II—we are engaged in feverish discussions of preparations for the next war. The fact that brass hats, politicians and American Legionnaires call it "preparation to prevent war" fools no one, perhaps least of all themselves. We are building a stock pile of atomic bombs. Our military and political chieftains are demanding that we train huge conscript reserve forces.

By our own inventions—radar, the bomb and the rest—we have wiped out frontiers, our own and all others. There are no barriers any more against armed and winged magical destruction. By holding on to the atomic bomb for ourselves, and as long as we hold on to it, we force other nations into an atomic armament race. As long as the bomb exists at all, in no matter whose hands, there is no security for anyone anywhere.

In a political and military sense we stand about where Germany stood in 1939 as a result of the advances in armament which she had achieved, where every nation in all history which has achieved preponderant military might has stood. We have introduced a profound tension into international relations. We are suspected and feared, and we are ourselves suspicious and afraid. Presently we shall be hated—in some places we are already—unless we reverse our course.

It is extremely hard, for many Americans at least, to realize that this is so. Who could possibly be afraid of or suspect the United States? What could possibly induce any nation to feel anything but great satisfaction and joy that God should have given the atomic bomb just to Uncle Sam? General Eisenhower in his first public statement as chief of staff addressing the American Legion convention in favor of peacetime compulsory universal military training—conscription—said on November 20, 1945: "Based upon numberless contacts with many people of other nations, I hold the conviction that no other country fears a strong America. No decent preparations of our own will be regarded suspiciously by others, because we are trusted."

If everybody is perfectly happy about America's possession of the atomic bomb, why all the controversy about whether we shall keep it or not keep it? Did General Eisenhower compare notes with his commander in chief, Mr. Truman, who about this same time was in conference with Prime Ministers Attlee and King seeking a way in which atomic weapons could be completely abolished?

Russia, all too obviously, is not happy about the situation. Certainly Argentina is not, and the other Latin American nations are not exactly enthusiastic. As much can be said of Oriental peoples.

Why if our consciences are so clear and our powers so vast are we ourselves suspicious and afraid in the very hour of our greatest victory? If a vast military establishment and an arsenal of atomic weapons constitute such a force for security and peace, why not equip all nations with them? If this does not sound reasonable, should we not try to achieve a modicum of objectivity and humility and stop thinking that we and our preponderant might constitute an exception among all nations and in all history? That, in other words, we are the master race, the *Herrenvolk*, whose supremacy all men will, and must, hail with delight?

As a matter of fact, General Eisenhower did not believe his own words. I am not accusing him of insincerity or conscious duplicity. He just fell into the common human error of thinking one thing with one part of his brain and the opposite with another part of his brain, and not establishing any connection between the two. In the same speech he told the Legionnaires: "We come then to this. We dwell in a world in which the possibilities of destruction are so great as to terrify peoples everywhere." Terrify what people? Those who are blissfully happy about the existence of these destructive weapons, the most destructive of which are in America's hands? He goes on to advocate still greater forces "that may have to stand between our country and a thousand Buchenwalds." Who will seek to visit this evil upon us—which of these countries none of which "fears a strong America"?

"We must arm because we are unsafe and may be attacked" is what the military really mean. We can be assured that nobody will worry, indeed everybody will be very happy, over a heavily armed America; that is to salve our consciences and to throw a veil over horrors that we will not squarely face.

A thousand Buchenwalds—or shall we say a thousand Hiroshimas? —that is the fate in store for us. We have wiped out frontiers. We have also wiped out defenses. Those in the best position to know tell us there is no defense against atomic weapons. No one even pretends that the best defensive measures could prevent widespread destruction of life and property. If defensive weapons can be improved, what is to prevent offensive weapons also from being improved?

The bombs can be planted while "peace" prevails by an ostensibly "friendly power." General Arnold concludes: "We mustn't fail to strike down any future aggressor nation before it gets dangerous" and "A country's major cities might be destroyed over-night by an ostensibly friendly power." Dorothy Thompson correctly points out: "The logical deduction from this is that since aggression must never be allowed to start and an ostensibly friendly power may be a potential aggressor, *security consists in striking down all our friends.*"

Many well-meaning and otherwise intelligent people in effect reason as follows today: "The prospect of an atomic war, which is bound to result from an atomic armament race, is appalling. Certainly the most serious efforts to secure abolition of atomic weapons, international inspection and so on must therefore be made. But if we fail in this, we will however reluctantly support conscription and the building up of an arsenal of atomic weapons, because if there is to be a final war for survival, we want America to survive."

In the first place, the leaders who advance this argument ought to be frank and warn people that they are advocating a great gamble. It is by no means guaranteed that the United States would be the nation to survive. The concentration of her population and industry render her peculiarly vulnerable to the ultramodern type of attack. Even a little nation, we are told, might be the victor. Any nation can solve the technical problems. Professor Urey, whose discovery of "heavy water" made the bomb possible, has pointed out that one of the leading physicists on the bomb project here was a Dane who is now in Denmark, and another a Frenchman now in France. If it is a question of vast natural resources, Russia has them. She has also one of the half-dozen greatest atomic physicists in the world. Even without her satellites, daily increasing in number, she has much more manpower and womanpower to conscript than the United States, and a birth rate with which we shall not compete. As a matter of fact all historical precedent is against the survival in such conflicts of the more highly "civilized" nation. "The barbarians" take over. (Needless to say, we are not here employing ethical categories.) As someone has suggested, the United States may presently furnish the instance of the nation which achieved greater power than any other and also lost it more swiftly and spectacularly.

As a matter of fact, those who are disposed to think that the issue is likely to be decided by the arbitrament of arms, and who in the final analysis will embrace the doctrine of seeking survival at the price of atomic war, should probably support those who argue that now is the time for us to take steps once and for all to establish American hegemony over the world, say at the price of a war with Russia, which would not be nearly so costly and hard now as five, ten or twenty years later. Otherwise their children will pass upon them the same judgment which they pass upon those who waited too long before striking down Hitler and Mussolini and the Japanese militarists. In the end, it will "save many lives" if we act swiftly and inexorably. . . .

That sounds familiar; and it leads to the second observation about this line of reasoning. The object is that the United States, the American Empire, shall survive. And people assume that this will be the United States of today, the values associated with American life today. Certainly they do not steadily contemplate the fact that there would not and could not be the slightest resemblance between that America and the America of today. A war now would be a monstrous thing? Verily, it would. But obviously a war following on a protracted atomic armament race and between one or more nations equipped with the weapons of the future will be far more monstrous in its methods and in its devastations. In order to be equipped for it all American life will have to be militarized, industry regimented, large sections of industry and of the population moved underground. Think of Europe and Japan today, of Warsaw, Dresden, Berlin, Kiev, Tokyo—the cities in which a hundred thousand, a quarter of a million people were killed in one night. Then think of a New York, Chicago, Detroit, Los

Angeles, in which several million have been killed in one night. Think of the dead after that war. Think of the survivors in that hell. Think of the Fuehrer who will rule over America in the hour of that victory —of the Fuehrers perhaps who will rule over the dismembered fragments of the great republic. Think of what will happen to minorities, what will have happened under the totalitarianism that will have been established in preparation for that war. Think of the atrocities we shall commit. Think, for God's sake.

Did the Romans who fought in Rome's wars fight for the Rome which emerged out of those wars, the Rome of the late Empire, of the Dark Ages? Would they have fought had they known? They did not know, so the question is inconsequential. We do know, know that we shall be brought, if we survive at all, down to the level of that which we most abhor. No one in his senses can say with certainty that the gamble is worth the price that will be exacted. Surely few, if any, steadfastly contemplating the realities, ridding themselves of illusions, will contend that any alternative could be worse, any defeat more utter.

This, then, is the pass to which we have been brought. We have seen a demonstration of what might be called the logic of dependence upon material power, military might. Raise this power to the nth degree and you have weakness, impotence, utter disintegration. In the hour of our greatest triumph, we are undone, slain by our own creation, the creature of our own brain.

Here also the prophet long since discerned and proclaimed the truth. Sadly he pronounced woe upon the children of Israel, of God, who thought to "strengthen themselves in the strength of Pharaoh and to take refuge in the shadow of Egypt. Therefore shall the strength of Pharaoh be your shame and your trust in the shadow of Egypt your confusion. . . . Ye said, No, but we will flee upon horses; therefore shall ye flee: and, We will ride upon the swift; therefore shall they that pursue you be swift."

Since war in the future will take the hideous shape and bear the poisonous fruits we have described, it is from one viewpoint superfluous to dwell upon the wars of the recent past and the international situation in which we find ourselves as a result of them. However, no factor which may contribute to building up the case for the abolition of war must be neglected, and that case is strengthened by an understanding of the outcome of World War II, its failure to achieve any good, the grave evils which follow in its train. Furthermore, it is in the environment thus created that the atomic armament race has been launched, and to stop that rivalry the environment must be understood. We shall, however, limit ourselves to a brief sketch.

The toll of the dead, the wounded, the mentally disordered, the starving; the destruction of resources, goods and machinery, in this war surpasses that of any other conflict. The toll mounts daily. It will for decades to come. The human imagination cannot really picture it. It is well known that long since the nervous frame has stopped trying to react to it. Horrors against which the whole world would have cried out a few decades ago pass unnoticed. What do we have to show for this awful price we have paid?

The threat of war has not been removed or lessened. After World War I there was an interval when men cherished some hope in this respect. This time, as we have already noted, before the troops have been returned home from one war, feverish preparations for the push-button war are under way.

The struggle for dominion among the great nations has not abated, though one contestant after another is eliminated. At the beginning of the present century there were ten leading powers: Great Britain, France, Germany, Russia, Austria-Hungary, Holland, Belgium, Italy, the United States, Japan. World War I witnessed the breakup of Austria-Hungary, and the relative strength of Holland and Belgium was greatly reduced. The same was true of France, though that did not become immediately apparent. Japan moved into a stronger position, having taken advantage of the internecine strife among the Western powers. Russia was momentarily weakened. The future of Germany and Italy was problematical. The United States attempted to withdraw into its traditional isolation from the European power struggle.

World War II has eliminated most of the contestants. Only Great Britain, the United States and Russia remain as first-rate powers which can pursue a foreign policy of their own backed by the strength to make war under modern conditions; and a point has to be stretched to include Britain in this category. The basic pattern of seeking to arrive at unification over larger areas, and eventually on a world scale, by the elimination of certain nation-states by others in an incessant contest for power which flares up from time to time in large-scale war, remains.

Even the most enthusiastic protagonists of the United Nations Organization do not venture to claim that it provides assurance that this pattern will be altered. At most, they admit, it holds out a hope. And even this is open to serious question. For it is admitted that the success of the organization depends upon the continuance of the alliance among the Big Three and that there is in the organization no power to keep them from going to war against each other. But a military alliance of victor powers is notoriously unstable and highly unreliable as a basis for enduring peace. Since it is evident that the power struggle among these super-states is continuing, it is hard to escape the conclusion that the United Nations Organization is in reality both a camouflage for and an instrument of this titanic conflict. It is necessary that at certain stages of development—and especially after an exhausting war when the regimes have to take stock, consolidate their gains and regroup their forces, and the peoples must be given a rest and lulled into security by the feeling that the war has achieved some substantial good—the power struggle should be masked. This is just as much a part of the struggle as the feinting of pugilists in the arena. Hence Holy Alliances, Leagues, United Nations Charters and so on.

The effort thus to achieve world dominion is an old one. The tragic outcome has been rehearsed many times. Civilizations commit suicide, A. J. Toynbee concludes in his monumental *Study of History*. How? Two things invariably occur during the melancholy process of suicide: One is submission "to a forcible political unification within the framework of a 'universal state.'" The other is fratricidal, large-scale, continuous war!

We were told before World War II began that unilateral action by a big power altering the frontiers, partitioning the territory and violating the autonomy of little nations could not be tolerated. Today Russia engages in altering frontiers, partitioning territory and setting up puppet regimes in Poland, Germany, the Balkans and elsewhere. When sufficient pressure has been applied and a suitable formula has been found, Great Britain and the United States recognize and sanction the *fait accompli*. What has altered is that in the old days those regarded as liberals and progressives protested against such proceedings; today they are apt to advocate or at any rate defend them—an ominous change indeed.

The economic grievances and disequilibrium which were among the major contributing causes of war have been intensified, not removed. Before World War II, Dr. Alfred Salter, M.P., pointed out that Britain, France, Russia, Holland and the United States between them exercised economic and political control over more than thirty million square miles including much of the richest, most fertile and most mineral-laden lands on the globe, while all together Germany, Italy, Japan, Poland and Hungary controlled one million square miles, much of it poor in quality and remarkably deficient in minerals and raw materials. The territories controlled by the first-named group accounted for 85 per cent of the world's total minerals and raw materials, leaving 15 per cent for the rest of the world. The role played by the economic distress to which the German people were subjected in bringing Hitler to power is universally admitted. As for prewar Japan, if all the inhabitants of the whole earth were concentrated in the United States, we would have been in about the same position as the Japanese people. It does not require argument or a rehearsal of the tales of starvation and malnutrition which fill the pages of each day's papers to enable one to see that the colossal destruction of a major war aggravates economic pressures. As for disequilibrium, the annual income of the United States is three times that of the other fifty United Nations combined!

The plight of the Jews stirred millions. They accepted the war "to save the Jews." What might have happened if the Allies had not gone to war is perhaps largely a matter of speculation. It is a fact that millions of Jews have perished miserably and a large percentage of the survivors in Europe and Asia are in dire distress. Jewish leaders believe that Jews for an indefinite period will not be able to live in Germany and several other European countries. Anti-Semitism is not decreasing, nor will it so long as the threat of war and internal economic tensions exist. And the government of the United States is hailed for taking a highly commendable step when in the face of this appalling mass of misery it arranges to admit a quota of three or four thousand refugees, including some Jews, into the country each month but is unwilling to extend that number by as many as might have been admitted under its very strict immigration laws during the war years when of course the gates were closed. Thus have the Jews been saved.

We were horrified at the Nazi policy of forced displacement of peoples. Six to eight million Germans are being driven from their homes, territory which for generations has been German. The wandering of the peoples continues.

We had to destroy totalitarianism. The Nazi regime in a sense and for the present has been ended. But the power of the Russian regime has been immensely increased. Whatever else may be said of it, it cannot be denied that it is totalitarian and monolithic. It can be and has been as ruthless and as indifferent to human life as the Nazi regime. Its power is much more extensive than Germany's ever was and it has a machinery for propaganda and expansion much more competent than the Nazis ever had. In the nature of things the Russian dictatorship will not be eliminated or relaxed so long as the threat of war continues. It is the threat from without that enables this, as any other, dictatorship to justify itself in the eyes of its subjects, even in the eyes of its victims.

There are those who frankly admit this indictment and do not deny that it is a serious one. Some of them allege that they fully understood the nature of the gamble they were taking when they urged or acquiesced in resort to war and did not expect things would be better than they now are. "But," they contend, "the Nazi effort to dominate the earth had to be stopped. Everything would have been lost"—permanently, they tend to assume—"if their military plans had succeeded. War, it is true, has accomplished no positive good; but it has stopped this evil. At least we have a chance now, though admittedly a slim one and subject to great handicaps, to build a decent world."

Let us examine this argument. In the first place, it tacitly assumes that war was the only way to "stop the Nazis." This we still deny. The political and economic policies of the victors in World War I were decisive and indispensable factors in the emergence and triumph of Hitler. If we had been willing to spend one-tenth or one-twentieth of the money, energy and brains we put into the war on the economic rehabilitation of Germany and other countries, there would have been no war—could have been no war. If we do not face up to this fact, we shall drift into another war. Or rather, we are almost totally disregarding this factor in our dealings with Germany and Japan and are thus already sowing broadcast the seeds of another war. Even the supposedly extreme suggestion that as late as 1939 it would have been better to refuse to fight Germany and to offer passive resistance, as pacifists advocated and as was actually done to a quite remarkable extent in some occupied countries, surely can hardly be regarded as utterly fantastic in the light of the price we paid in the war and what we got in exchange. It is difficult to see how any alternative could have been more risky or absurd.

This leads to a second observation. The argument we are examining assumes that had the Germans not been resisted by arms the Nazis would have gone on to conquer the world and to rule it for an indefinite period, say for Hitler's "one thousand years." So far as I am aware, few people if any have paused to note what a truly colossal, "totalitarian" assumption this is and how complimentary to the Nazis in many respects. It is implied that they could have achieved military feats beyond the farthest reach of other conquerors. They could have organized the world politically. They had the ability and the means to organize a world economy adapted to the requirements and possibilities of modern science and technology. No form of sabotage and passive resistance would have availed against them. No titanic struggles for power would have broken out among them once external foes had been subdued. They would not have been surfeited with conquest and softened by indulgence as all other conquerors have been—not any of these figures in the dock at Nuremberg and others like them in the Nazi high command and the lower ranks! The deceit, the pervasive espionage, the utter lack of mutual trust which is inherent in such a regime would never have undermined it as termites eat the pillars of a house. On the one hand, time would not have mellowed them as it has other imperial regimes. On the other hand, their suppression of the free mind over long periods of time would not have interfered seriously with their ability to run the world or with the supply of powerful and trained minds to run it on their behalf. Well, dear reader, I simply do not believe this fairy tale about these supermen, utterly immune to all the forces that affect other men. Do you? The Nazis were not such supermen as this supposes. As for the rest of the human race, they may be foolish and weak but not as foolish and weak as this argument assumes. For the moment we leave God out of this except to note in passing that by the mouth of one of his prophets, an ancient Jew, God said of these pretenders and swashbucklers: "Yea, they have not been planted; yea, they have not been sown; yea, their stock hath not taken root in the earth." It never has. "The tumult and the shouting dies; the Captains and the Kings depart." Always. Even when they are Nazis.

In the third place, in a certain obvious and superficial sense the war achieved its objective of "stopping the Nazis." But have we destroyed or made impossible or even unlikely the resurgence of the tendencies and forces which fascism in its various manifestations represented? Have we achieved "the object of the war" any more than we did through World War I? Recall that on Armistice Day, 1918, in announcing the termination of hostilities to the Congress, Woodrow Wilson said: "We know that the object of the war is attained, the object upon which all free men had set their hearts, and attained with a sweeping completeness which even now we do not realize. Armed imperialism such as the men conceived who were but yesterday the masters of Germany is at an end, its illicit ambitions engulfed in black disaster. Who will now seek to revive it?"

Who indeed but the Nazis? Get rid of the Kaiser by the method of war and you get a Hitler instead.

Of course, the militaristically minded argue that German military potential was not sufficiently crippled after World War I, its industry not thoroughly destroyed, and they are determined to do a better job this time. We shall not pause to rehearse all the difficulties and perplexities they are encountering in trying to carry out their plans and how the old controversy between those powers to whose interest it is to have a relatively strong Germany and those to whose interest it is to have a relatively weak Germany has already re-emerged. The military themselves confess that "the object of the war" has not been definitely achieved and that having to do the job over again is more than a remote likelihood. It is the reason they assign for their nervousness about the future and the need of much more powerful military establishments than ever before. And I know of no political leader today who dares to speak with the superb—and alas, how misplaced—confidence of Woodrow Wilson in 1918.

The liberals, on the other hand, argue that World War I was necessary and justified and came out "right"; only then we did not put into effect that ideal combination of stern punishment and of sound social measures calculated to rebuild a prosperous but peaceful Germany which we had, they allege, a golden opportunity to do. The liberals of various kinds, "pacifists between wars," never face the fact that their objectives are not the ones for which the state and its effective leaders wage war. Nor do they realize that "the mentality of war-making is the precise opposite of the mentality of peace-making," to quote a leading sociologist, and that the end of a war is the worst of all times to make a sound and durable peace. Some of them do comprehend this fact intellectually and justify their support of each war as it comes along by arguing that war can no longer be prevented but there is at least a tiny chance that the nation will turn over a new leaf and pursue a radically different policy once it has won the war, i.e., destroyed more goods and life than its enemies. This is the doctrine, "Tomorrow, the day after we win the war, is the accepted time; then we shall repent." But God and history are not mocked. Certainly all this is being demonstrated to the hilt in the present situation, when months after V-E and V-J days not a peace treaty has been adopted; a titanic power struggle is being waged among the Big Three, on whose continued alliance "the peace" is said to depend; and millions in Europe are undernourished or actually starving with no living options except Stalinism or some new ultrareactionary regime. What monstrosities will emerge out of this macabre dance of death to succeed Hitler and Nazism? Their as yet indistinct but ghastly shadows strike a chill into men's hearts as they celebrate—or try to celebrate— another "famous victory."

One other factor in past experience, upon which people who cannot bring themselves to a clean-cut renunciation of war fall back, must be referred to briefly. It is the argument that if Hitler had only been stopped in time all would have been well. The inference is that if now we will just stop Stalin by force—"in time"—the threat of another world war will surely be averted. It is quite possible that a show of force would have halted for a time Hitler's invasion of the Saar, for example.

There is no evidence that this would have solved any fundamental problem. The conditions which produced Nazism would have broken out in another place and form, as surely as an overcharge of steam will blow out a boiler at one spot if not at another. The assumption that the imperialist nations, if they had stopped Hitler in the Saar, would have proceeded to remedy the evils which begot and nurtured Nazism finds no support in history. What about the present behavior of the powers that gained a complete military victory over the Nazi regime? With the proposal to be "firm" with the Russians we shall have to deal at some length in another chapter. Suffice it here to observe that, save perhaps for a couple of years during World War II, this has been the policy Western powers have pursued vis-à-vis the Russian regime. That regime seems to thrive on it!

One last consideration, the gravest of all. A moment ago we were saying that if we permit the atomic armament race to continue and are dragged into the war which must then ensue, the America we have known will perish even if some Americans survive and we shall be brought down to the level of the bestiality we abhor. But, alas, we are already there. The war and the atomic bomb have given us, as we suggested, a demonstration of the logic of material power and military might: raise them to the nth degree and what you have is weakness, defenselessness, man reduced to impotence and threatened with extinction by the creature of his own brain. But with the emergence of the atomic bomb we were also given a demonstration of what might be called the logic of atrocity.

We set out to defend and extend democracy and peace by means of war—reluctantly, because we knew that modern war is an atrocious thing. We were stirred by the atrocities against the Jews, and the Chinese, and others. Surely these things must be stopped, if not avenged. And how could you stop mad dogs and hyenas and monkeymen except by the means of modern scientific warfare, atrocious as that admittedly was?

Now where are we? We who preached day in and day out against atrocities turned thousands upon thousands of Japanese soldiers into blackened corpses with flame-throwers. A veteran addressing other veterans writes: "You have watched a man regulate his flame-thrower so that he could set a soldier afire rather than killing him outright. . . .

From your own experience you know that Americans shot prisoners in cold blood, strafed life-rafts, mutilated the bodies of enemy dead. . . . You have seen that many such 'crimes' are military necessities." But we did not stop with the use of flame-throwers on combatants.

It was we and our allies who according to the president of the International Red Cross killed two hundred and fifty thousand people, mostly civilians, in one night in Dresden. It was we—United States bombers—who destroyed all but one or two Japanese cities of any size, who burned a hundred thousand people to death in one night in Tokyo. But we did not stop there.

We dropped the atomic bomb on Hiroshima. And that was not enough. A few days later we dropped a bigger and better one—though it is said not to have been so well aimed—on Nagasaki.

There was no clear "military necessity" to "justify" these crowning atrocities. There is good reason to think that peace with Japan might have been made months before, but it did not suit Russian designs or our own. However that may be, at the time the bombs were dropped negotiations were under way, Japanese power had been crushed. According to such authorities as General LeMay, the Secretary of War and the Secretary of State, the war would have been over in a week or so anyway. Louis Fischer in the *Progressive*, October 22, 1945, refers to a speech made shortly before by Admiral Chester W. Nimitz at a celebration in his honor at Washington, D.C. Said Admiral Nimitz: "The atomic bomb did not win the war against Japan. The Japanese had, in fact, already sued for peace before the atomic age was announced to the world with the destruction of Hiroshima and before the Russian entry into the war. In saying that the atomic bomb played no decisive part, from a purely military standpoint, in the defeat of Japan, this is no effort to minimize the awful power of this new weapon."

The public has generally been led to believe that a land invasion of Japan was imminent in August and thus the launching of the atomic bombs saved the lives of thousands of American troops who would have perished in that operation. But a land invasion was in any case still many weeks away. The United States Strategic Bombing Survey, supplementing Admiral Nimitz' statement and supporting it with evidence, has effectively disposed of all such "justifications" for the use of the atomic bombs on Japanese cities. In its report, as summarized in the New York *Times* of July 14, 1946, the following passages occur:

It seems clear, however, that air supremacy and its exploitation over Japan proper was the major factor which determined the timing of Japan's surrender and obviated any need for invasion. Based on a detailed investigation of all the facts and supported by the testimony of the surviving Japanese leaders involved, it is the Survey's opinion that certainly prior to Dec. 31, 1945, and in all probability prior to Nov. 1, 1945, Japan would have surrendered even if the atomic bombs had not been dropped, even if Russia had not entered the war and even if no invasion had been planned or contemplated. . . . The Hiroshima and Nagasaki atomic bombs did not defeat Japan, nor by the testimony of the enemy leaders who ended the war did they persuade Japan to accept unconditional surrender. The Emperor, the Lord Privy Seal, the Prime Minister, the Foreign Minister and the Navy Minister had decided as early as May of 1945 that the war should be ended even if it meant acceptance of defeat on allied terms.

Discount every one of these considerations, assume for the sake of the argument and for the sake of our sensibilities that they do not exist and still there is no scintilla of justification for the refusal of the plea of the scientists who had made the diabolical instrument that it should be demonstrated on some uninhabited Japanese island before being unloosed on hundreds of thousands of babies, women and helpless old people. Mr. Henry L. Stimson, Secretary of War during World War II, suggests in an article in the February, 1947, issue of *Harper's Magazine* that the United States had only two atomic bombs ready in August, 1945. If Japanese leaders had been summoned to observe an experimental detonation and the bomb proved a dud, Japanese war morale would have been stimulated and this would have resulted in the loss of more American lives. The obvious question occurs, Could representative Japanese not have been summoned to witness the effects of a bomb after its explosion? In that case the invitation could have simply been withheld if the experiment had fizzled. Elsewhere we shall show that on quite practical and nonidealistic grounds many atomic scientists believed at the time that some such course would have been far wiser.

It must be noted also that the war with Germany was over and that by this time it had long been known to our military and political leaders that the Germans had not been able to develop the atomic bomb and share their discovery with the Japanese. No one believed that the Japanese had the bomb or would shortly have it. Even the contention that some American lives were saved—and it was the claim that undoubtedly large numbers had been saved which reconciled Americans to the use of the atomic bombs or caused them to rejoice in it—rests on the slenderest foundation.

If we in such circumstances could launch this apocalyptic horror upon the world, what can we say to any nation which may launch atomic bombs, or biological warfare, against us under the conditions of frightful, unbearable tension which will presently exist in the world unless the threat of atomic war is extinguished? But not only have we left ourselves no moral ground on which to protest against whatever atrocities may be perpetrated against us. How can we possibly persuade anyone else or ourselves that if we have atomic bombs at all we shall not use them if we deem it expedient? There is not the slightest guarantee even that we shall not launch bombs first, take the offensive, if a sharp international crisis develops. The military will have an overpowering argument for doing so: "Who but an insane man or an agent of the enemy would wait until some enemy"—or one of General Arnold's "ostensibly friendly nations"—"first destroys forty million Americans?" After what has happened, who can imagine a President standing in Roosevelt's or Truman's place refusing in such an hour to sign the order to shoot?

Thus it has fallen upon this "Christian" nation, incessantly declaiming against the perpetrators of atrocities, and still doing so, to perpetrate the ultimate, atomic atrocity—needlessly—and so to remove all restraint upon atrocity. That is the logic of the atrocious means. With fatal precision the means in war become more destructive, both of physical life and of moral standards and spiritual values.

Has it come to this? Yes, it has come to this.

And it is necessary, it is indispensable, that we should contemplate all this steadfastly, relentlessly, until it has burned its way into our consciousness and in doing so has burned away all illusions about war, including World War II. Oh yes, there was heroism and patience and unselfishness and honor and gentleness displayed by those who fought in this war, on both sides. On their own plane these things are always what they are and precious in the sight of God. But we have to face it: War is what we have said it is and nothing else. It has brought us where we have said it has, not any place else—to weakness, to fear, to bestiality, to shame. Those who died in it died in vain. Yes, that also must be faced and must burn itself into our consciousness. We murdered them, our own war dead. With the same good and, in the case of some of us, pious intentions as an ancient people threw its babes and its youths into the flaming arms of the god Moloch. And to the same end. It is hard to face that, but as one of our contemporary poets has said: "That world can only be better which knows they have died in vain."

This must burn itself into our consciousness until we would rather perish than not act to end war, knowing that if we do not so act, we shall perish and in perishing become the murderers of our grandchildren as we are the murderers of our children.

Chapter II

You Have This Dilemma

Unquestionably, then, war must be abolished. Furthermore, we must not lose sight of the extreme urgency of the situation. The decisive steps which put us on the slippery slope toward the precipice or start us up the ascent toward a stable peace will certainly be taken in the next five years; they may be taken in the next few months.

From this standpoint, the recent observation by Chancellor Hutchins of the University of Chicago is perfectly valid: "There is only one subject of really fundamental importance at the present moment, and that is the atomic bomb. Although it is not a cheerful subject, we must consider it, for the issue is that of survival, to which all other issues are secondary. If we do not survive, there is no use discussing what we are going to do with our lives."

When the house has caught fire, people are mad or irresponsible if they do not hurry to get the fire department out at once.

Primarily, this ultimate issue of survival for themselves and for mankind is in the hands of the people of the United States. For a moment in history we—President Truman; the congressmen from Rochester, Kalamazoo, Medicine Bow, Oshkosh; the senators from Texas, Mississippi, Wyoming, Iowa, Vermont; American lawyers, businessmen, labor leaders, editors; American movie magnates and stars—Orson Welles, Greer Garson, Bing Crosby, Veronica Lake, Sonny Tufts; America's religious leaders—Archbishop Spellman, Bromley Oxnam, Harry Emerson Fosdick, John Mackay, Stephen Wise, Abba Hillel Silver; all of us everyday Americans—garbage collectors, bus drivers, coal miners, spinners, weavers, stenographers, manicurists, college students, bobby-soxers, soldiers, sailors, fathers, mothers—all of us together hold in our hands a power such as no human beings ever possessed before. I see a picture of Uncle Sam, legs apart, in his self-assured and easygoing way tossing into the air and catching in one hand a little object the size of a golf ball—symbol of a force that can blow the world (and him too) to smithereens or open up untold riches and beauty and glory for mankind—while the rest of the world looks on holding its breath, spellbound.

Have the elder races halted?
Do they droop and end their lesson, wearied over there beyond the seas?
We take up the task eternal, and the burden and the lesson,
Pioneers! O Pioneers!

Thus sang Walt Whitman. But the task, and the burden and the lesson of the Founding Fathers of this nation, and of the pioneers who followed them, seem Lilliputian when compared to those with which we are now confronted. Never in all history has a people been faced with such a responsibility and such an opportunity as the present generation in the United States. It may well be that, no matter how long man's stay on earth, no crisis of the same magnitude will ever again confront a people. Are we going to be pioneers, leading mankind into the day of peace and brotherhood, or are we going to use this terrible weapon to push the race backward into "complete destruction in one burst of universal fury?"

The nature, risks and effects of modern war being such as we have pictured, the people of the United States might well, on the basis of what might be called Yankee shrewdness and common sense, now speak to other peoples, including the Russian, in some such terms as these:

We are through with war and preparation for war. We hope you are too and that we may therefore have universal disarmament. But whether you join us or not, we are through. War simply does not make sense any more.

Some of our top scientists who ushered us into the atomic age met with Albert Einstein not long ago and said they were agreed on certain

facts. One of them was that in the usual military sense there is no de-
fense against atomic attack. Another, that the effort to prepare a defense
would "destroy the structure of our social order." By that they meant
that our industries and population would have to be dispersed, we
would have to engage in a power conflict and armaments race with
some other great nation, and under such circumstances our democratic
way of life could not survive, our economy would be subjected to an
intolerable strain, and some form of totalitarianism would be imposed
upon us.

We would, in plain language, be committing suicide, which does
not make sense. If we refuse to yield to this death-urge and therefore
renounce war and war preparation, we hope the rest of you will do like-
wise. But if not, if the worst has already come to pass and mankind is
doomed to destruction, then we are not going to waste our substance
in these few remaining years on manufacturing poison to feed our-
selves. We are not going to spend our time in a frenzy of war prepara-
tion. We shall do the best we can to devise other than warlike means
to secure ourselves against attack. Knowing how desperately poor the
rest of the world is, we shall be prepared to share with others a good
deal of the resources God has given us and which—on the present
hypothesis—there is no sense in hoarding. Anyway, we prefer giving it
away to spending it on atom bombs and death rays. What is left for
ourselves we shall enjoy in peace and quietness during the few years
that remain to us and our children.

I say again, if we could get over our present attack of the jitters, if we
could keep cool, use a little hard common sense, this is what we might
well do. Assume that there was just one chance in a hundred that it
might "work," prove contagious. By what logic would it be better to
choose the 100-per-cent certain material and spiritual destruction which
the continuance of the armaments race entails? Suppose the one
chance does not materialize, what have we lost? The chance to show
that we can be tough, can give as good as we can take, in a brawl among
the inmates of a madhouse? That Americans have the physical courage required in war does not need to be demonstrated again. It would
show more courage and poise and maturity, and would be more in

keeping with what is called the practical strain in us, if we did not follow war to its logical conclusion of utter insanity.

The course we have just outlined is, however, not the one which the United States is following at the present time. It is not even the one advocated by the great majority of individuals and organizations working for world peace. Even those among them who personally believe that this course probably holds out the one hope of salvation are inclined to assume that not much is to be gained by advocating it, since it is bound to seem utopian and perhaps silly to the masses of the American people. The rest are firmly convinced that something more moderate, more practical, more down to earth is needed.

There is also among peace workers general agreement as to what this something is. It involves some kind of world organization—world government. This world government would have a "police" force which would be able to restrain offenders, keep "aggressors" from ganging up on peace-loving folks. And under this setup, national military establishments would be at first radically reduced and presently completely dismantled. There would be universal disarmament by agreement.

What indeed could be more sensible? Why should this proposal not commend itself to peoples and governments as wise and indeed necessary and urgent? After two world wars the whole of mankind is in a desperate condition. Even the two leading powers, Russia and the United States, have been subjected to terrific expenditures and the former has been horribly devastated. As World War II neared its end, the atomic bomb was added to the implements of war; subsequently also biological weapons on a vast scale. The scientists agree that there is no defense against atomic weapons. There is no possible guarantee that a given nation will win an atomic war. If it emerged as victor, it would be a "victor in hell" after fearful losses and suffering. It would be hated and feared as no other nation ever has been. On the other hand, if these nations will lay down their arms, establish a reign of law and co-operate in developing the peaceful fruits of atomic energy, there seems to be no limit to what they may, both in a material and in a spiritual sense, achieve. Why should they not jointly and simultaneously lay down their arms? What do they have to lose? What, in fact, can possibly keep them from doing so at once?

There are criticisms to be made of the concept of "enforcing peace" in its various current forms. It is based upon a conception of the nature of man and society which itself must be rejected or substantially modified and supplemented if peace is to be achieved. To this problem it will be necessary to return. For the present it will be most helpful if, in seeking an answer to the questions posed a moment ago, we note that the discussions about world organization and disarmament are not taking place in a vacuum or in heaven but in an actual historical context.

The key to the contemporary political situation is that two great nation-states, Russia and the United States, are locked in a tense power struggle all around the world. The struggle does not take the form of large-scale shooting war—yet. But neither leaders nor publicists of the two countries make any real effort to conceal the fact that the conflict is there and we need not pause to document that fact.

Each of these nations is powerful, heavily armed, dynamic, expansionist, self-righteous and afraid. A brief survey of the discussions about disarmament, and especially about atomic weapons, in which the United States and the Soviet Union have engaged clearly reveals the dilemma with which those who work, in this context, for world order and peace are confronted.

In making this survey I shall devote myself largely to an effort to interpret "how the Russians get that way." Let me emphasize, therefore, that I am trying to state facts, not to justify Russian behavior. The great majority of Americans believe that the present Russian government is aggressively expansionist. They believe that the Russian regime is totalitarian and in many respects brutally so. They hold also that at essential points there is a conflict between Stalinist communism and the democratic or Christian way of life, and that the domination of the world by the Bolshevist regime would be a calamity. All these views I share. Nor do I believe that international understanding and peace will be promoted by soft-pedaling the evils of the Russian regime and the Bolshevist way of life. I was opposed to war with Germany and I have already stated that I do not believe the war achieved the ends for which it was allegedly fought. But it never seemed to me in the interests of peace and freedom to gloss over the evil nature of Nazi totalitarianism; nor that these ends could be advanced by collaboration of peace workers or pacifists with unrepentant and unconverted Nazis and Fascists. Though I do not believe it is possible simply to equate Russian and German totalitarianism, I am opposed to the former as to the latter. If I do not dwell upon its dangers and evils here, it is because it has been done by others, not because I think it does not need to be done. Furthermore, the American people generally see that side of the picture. What is important is that they should also see the other. If they do not, they will inevitably settle down to the conviction that there is no choice but to get ready to wage an atomic war against Russia sooner or later, perhaps preferably sooner. And that is precisely the catastrophe which, it is generally agreed, must be avoided if it is at all possible.

If we then try to see the recent discussions about disarmament and related matters through Russian eyes, it will help if first we recall certain factors in the background of these discussions.

One is that the Russians, like the rest of the world, are very poor while we in the United States are very rich. Half of the wealth of the world is here in the hands of one hundred and forty million people. The other two billion may get along as best they can with the other half.

The Russians suffered terribly in the war, we very little. Someone has suggested that if we want to get an idea of what the Russians are up against we should imagine what it would be like if this country had been invaded and devastated all the way from the Atlantic coast to a line running through the middle of Kansas.

After the 1917 Revolution, the Russians passed through a period of painful weakness and humiliation. They were attacked. They were barred from the League of Nations. For a considerable number of years their government was not recognized or admitted to the family of nations by other governments. For people who belong to the majority group here in the United States, who for many decades have been habituated to success and victory, to looking down on other peoples, it is almost impossible to enter into the souls of humiliated and defeated peoples. But the effort must be made. If we make it, we may perhaps not justify but we shall to some extent understand why the Russians, now that they are co-victors in the greatest war in history, may be trying to "compensate" and in so doing become over-aggressive.

There is one more of these background factors to be noted, namely, that militarily the Russians are still backward and weak compared with the United States, though the Russian potential is formidable. Numerically the Russian Army is indeed greater than the American. But in this connection I recall a remark made by Mr. John Foster Dulles in the spring of 1946. Mr. Dulles, in his dual capacity of Republican party brain trust in foreign affairs and leader in the Federal and World Council of Churches, exerts very great and, in the opinion of the present writer, increasingly unfortunate influence. In June, 1946, Mr. Dulles wrote two widely advertised articles in *Life* magazine. In these articles he stated: "If we neglect our military establishment that may lead to a dangerous misjudgment of us by the Soviet leaders. They believe in force. They take it for granted that those who have precious things will, if they are able, maintain a force-in-being to protect them. . . . So long as the leaders of the Soviet Union feel that way about the significance of military establishments, so long must we maintain a strong military establishment." The Russians believe in force, so we are compelled to be strongly armed.

I was present at a discussion shortly after these articles were published during which Mr. Dulles was asked whether the Russians had not suffered great losses and whether there was not in some quarters a tendency to exaggerate Soviet military strength. Mr. Dulles unhesitatingly replied that this was true: "It is a matter of common knowledge that if when the American and Russian forces met last summer they had taken to fighting each other, the American mechanized forces would have gone through the Russians like a knife through butter."

So much for the respective land armies. When it comes to a navy, the Russians have hardly any; the American Navy is greater than all the other navies in the world put together. The Russian Air Force is relatively primitive; the American the greatest in the world. The Russians presumably have no atomic weapons; the United States has a growing stock pile of atomic bombs.

Let us imagine for a moment how Americans would feel if the shoe were on the other foot. If the Russian Army could go through the

American like a knife through butter, and there were Russian forces in Canada and Mexico, as there are American forces in Germany and Korea and Japan; if the United States had almost no navy and the Russian Navy were greater than all other navies put together, and there were Russian warships off New York, New Orleans and San Francisco, as there are United States warships off the Dardanelles in the Mediterranean and in the Sea of Japan; if Russia had a stock pile of atomic bombs . . . the people of this country would be afraid. They would be convinced that Russia had warlike intentions. Multitudes of them think these things now when the situation is reversed. Reflecting on that should help us to understand how the Russians feel and why they behave as they do.

The reference just now to atomic, to which we might have added biological, weapons is a good point from which to take off for a little further exploration of United States-Soviet relations. From the standpoint of good relations with Russia, making the Russians feel that we trusted them a little and wanted to consult and work with them at crucial points, we got off very much on the wrong foot in our initial use of the atomic bombs. The dramatic launching of the bombs on Hiroshima and Nagasaki came shortly after the Potsdam Conference. Great emphasis had there been placed upon three-power unity. But it is clear that the atomic bombs were a complete surprise to the heads of the Russian government, though not to the British. It is pointed out that the Russians were pretty secretive about their weapons and military plans too. There can be no doubt about that, but to point this out does not solve anything. It is simply to restate our basic thesis that Russia and the United States do not trust each other and that it is in the atmosphere of this long-standing distrust that their disarmament discussions proceed.

The Russian government attached great importance to what it would gain from participation in the war against Japan. President Roosevelt, in turn, placed a high evaluation on the Russian contribution to victory. There is good reason to think that this evaluation of the need for Russian participation was based in part on a high estimate of the number and quality of the remaining Japanese forces on the Asiatic mainland, an estimate which Stalin might have corrected if he had been entirely open and aboveboard in his dealings. The atomic bombings brought the war to an abrupt end. This limited severely the Soviet contribution to the victory. How deeply the Russians resented that has been abundantly demonstrated by the flood of propaganda asserting that it was the Russian entry into the war and not the bombs that were decisive for victory. Furthermore, the advance of the Russian armies was stopped sooner than the Russian government had anticipated. From the outset the Russians evidently believed that the American government took the fearful risk of launching atomic war, when by no stretch of the imagination could this be regarded as necessary for victory, precisely in order to be able, in addition to claiming chief credit for victory, to stop the advance of Russian forces and thereby to enhance American power in the Orient.

That they were correct in this surmise seems to be incontrovertibly established by Henry L. Stimson, Secretary of War at the time these events transpired.

In an article in *Harper's Magazine* for February, 1947, Mr. Stimson explains how the decision to use the atomic bombs came to be taken. He quotes almost in its entirety a memorandum which he submitted to President Truman on July 2, 1945. At the end of that memorandum, after stating in detail the case for using the bombs, he says: "If Russia is a part of the threat"—which Japan must meet if she refuses to heed the warning to surrender unconditionally—"the Russian attack, if actual, must not have progressed too far." There seems no escape from the conclusion that the Hiroshima and Nagasaki atrocities were in one important aspect a move in the power struggle between the United States and Russia.

The prevailing opinion in the United States at the time of writing is that all this is now water under the bridge and that if the United States has made some mistakes, she has demonstrated her willingness to make amends by the submission of the so-called Baruch plan to the United Nations. The plan provides for the eventual establishment of an International Atomic Development Authority, equipped with full powers of inspection and charged with promoting the setting up of plants for the peaceful uses of atomic energy in such a way as to be fair to all peoples. The Authority is not to be hampered in its work by the big-power veto. When the machinery is operating the United States will dispose of its stock pile of atomic bombs and its efforts in the future to make such weapons will be subject to the same inspection, detection and punishment as those of any other nation. The official and unofficial propaganda for this plan suggests that in all history no nation has ever offered to surrender such a military advantage as the one the United States has in the possession of the bomb. It is generally regarded in this country as a sensible, honest and generous proposal.

The Russians are not impressed—at least not favorably. For one thing, they object to the American proposal to deal with atomic weapons separately and to strive to set up elaborate controls for atomic energy first, rather than dealing with disarmament in all its phases, one of which would of course relate to atomic weapons, from the outset. Whatever their motivation may be, and I hold no brief for them in that respect, the Russians appear to be making a valid point here. If, for example, an elaborate and really thorough system of atomic inspection is set up, it seems obvious that inspectors would have access to all the important industrial processes in which a nation might be engaged. Otherwise, how be sure that atomic weapons are not being secretly prepared? Thus it would seem that secrecy with respect to any weapons would be abolished. If it is argued, on the other hand, that it would technically be quite feasible to segregate inspection of atomic weapons from other types of weapons—biological, for example—then it seems obvious that after the Baruch plan went into effect a nation might still be engaged in formidable armaments activities. But with war thus remaining in the picture, realistically minded people would be persuaded that governments would be under irresistible temptation to outwit inspection and, even if they did not succeed, once a war broke out all bets would be off and each government would go feverishly to work making atomic weapons, unless by then still more deadly ones were available, in which case the whole business of setting up the Atomic Development Authority would have been lost labor.

In this as in every other important international situation, however, the chief difficulty is not in this or that item in a program but in the fact that the mutual confidence which would make any agreement possible simply does not exist. We do not trust the Russians and they do not trust us.

When the United States today emphasizes the importance of eliminating the possibility of atomic war, the Russians wonder why we did not think of that before Hiroshima. In those days we did not trust them and we had a card hidden up our sleeve, an atomic bomb, no less. If we are now eager to get rid of that weapon and to make it impossible for any other nation to acquire it, the Russians probably wonder whether that is because we now have another card up our sleeve, such as the biological weapons our papers discourse about so freely.

If we now regard the weapon as so very dangerous, is it because we are afraid it will go off in our own hands, so to speak, some day? Because we have suddenly bethought ourselves that we are very vulnerable to atomic attack? If so, Mr. Gromyko suggests, let the United States stop making àtomic bombs and take apart those it has. That would be convincing evidence of how seriously we regarded the threat of atomic war and would also indicate that we trusted the Russians a little and were not determined to hold all the cards in our hand. With our mechanized army and huge navy and air force, we would still not be quite "defenseless." But Americans cannot believe that Mr. Gromyko is honest when he makes this proposal and think that his objections to the Baruch plan mean that the Russians are on the way to producing atomic bombs and that the Russians would presently be holding an atomic bomb over the defenseless head of the United States. It is by no means obvious that this American fear is groundless. It is pretty certain that the Russians will make every effort to avoid accepting anything like the Baruch plan until they have themselves developed atomic weapons, one reason being that without them they believe they have to play second fiddle to the United States in the power conflict and they are determined not to remain in that position. Furthermore, on any other basis, even if atomic weapons were abolished and the present differential with respect to other arms lessened, the Americans would still have a monopoly of the know-how for making bombs. I am sure the Russians would regard that as a threat hanging over their heads and are determined not to acquiesce in such a situation. It does no good to protest that in engaging in an armaments race the Russians are running the risk of becoming involved in an atomic war. The United States is doing exactly the same thing.

Another sore point with us is Russian expansion through her armed forces and through Communist infiltration and penetration. We fear this. Where will it end? Will Russia not take control over the whole world if she is not forcibly held in check? The Russians counter by insisting that the United States has a Monroe Doctrine for the Americas. The Atlantic is an American lake. What vessel can ply its waters unless the United States acquiesces? By insisting on a so-called United Nations "trusteeship" over the former Japanese mandated islands with sole administration and right to arm in American hands, we have made the Pacific into an American lake. Of United States foreign policy with respect to Greece and Turkey so conservative a publicist as Dr. Douglas Southall Freeman, the noted biographer of Robert E. Lee, said: "The new foreign policy undoubtedly commits the United States to be the anti-Communist policeman of the world and the guardian of every government" which we regard as "potentially in the American world." When the United States government regards Greece, Turkey and Korea as being "potentially in the American world," and refuses to permit Russia to promulgate and enforce a "Molotov Doctrine" with respect to such lands on her border, the Russians not unnaturally conclude that the United States intends to dominate the entire world and to keep Russia strictly hemmed in. The Russians do not like it. They are frightened by it. Americans who can envisage how frightened were the statesmen and people of their own infant republic, born of the Revolution of 1776, of having monarchy, tyranny and feudalism fastened upon them by European powers ought to have some understanding of how the statesmen and people of the infant Russian republic, born of the Revolution of 1917, are frightened by the threat of encirclement today.

In the final analysis the typical American, in office or out of it, rejects the analogy. When Monroe proclaimed his Doctrine, it was a case of a democracy standing for human dignity and freedom protecting itself against effete monarchies and ancient tyrannies. Today it is a case of American democracy—now grown very powerful and successful as it deserves—having to guard itself against a new tyranny, modern totalitarianism. It has just fended off world domination by the German form of totalitarianism. Whatever the price may be, it must keep the Russian form also in bounds.

I am not interested for the moment in disputing this viewpoint, though I think the case for it is greatly weakened by our frequent fail-

ure to practice the democracy we profess. However that may be, the
Russians believe the analogy is pertinent and valid. They think that
their way of life, their organization of economic and political life, is
superior to ours. It brings the oppressed multitudes of mankind the
new and true freedom. Britain's day, they point out, is done. America's
will also soon pass. The future is with Russia and the Russian way.

Much of the behavior of Russian representatives in the United Nations, with respect to such matters as the retention and exercise of
the big-power veto, must be interpreted, it seems to me, in the light of
this Russian conception of their mission and destiny. It is Russia's task
to organize the world in "the right way." They are consequently in no
hurry to have a world organization set up so long as it would be under
American hegemony—likely, among other things, to be used to maintain the present differential between the standard of living in the
United States and that in other countries. They think they can afford
to wait until they are in a position to organize the world in their way.

Americans who find this behavior stupid or malicious should bear
in mind that the United States is quite as responsible as Russia for
the original adoption of the veto device. American leaders wanted to
be sure that the United States would not be outvoted in and bound
by the United Nations in matters affecting its "vital interests." If some
of these leaders are now insistent on abolishing the veto in connection
with control of atomic weapons, the Russians do not take it for granted
that these men have now become fully converted to the idea of international organization at whatever cost to the sovereignty and vital interests of the United States. They think the change would not have
occurred if it were the United States rather than Russia which was
being consistently outvoted in the councils of the United Nations.

To our pronouncements about Russia forcing herself on other countries and about Bolshevik terrorism, the Russians reply in two ways.
In the first place, "You hem us in now as you and other nations did
after World War I, by force, with the help of Greek monarchists, Turk-
ish totalitarians, Spanish Fascists, the Vatican, and other such agencies.
Do you expect us to submit in abject and cowardly fashion, to betray
the Revolution, to desert the oppressed masses?"

In the second place, they say to us: "Your day is over; ours is at hand.
When you, Englishmen and Americans, were leading the van, you

were not brutal just for the sake of being brutal. We do not think you were or are that kind of people. But toward the Indians in America, let us say, or the Filipinos, or the people of India in the Orient, you were as brutal as you needed to be in order to prevail. Now Russians and Communists are not brutal for the fun of being brutal either and we resent being accused as such. But now that the burden of destiny rests on our shoulders we intend to be realists and as brutal as we think we need to be in order to discharge our mission. And we do not think that you, who have recently fought the most destructive war in all history and who launched atomic bombs on two Japanese cities when there was no clear military necessity for it, are in a position to read us moral lectures about ruthlessness. If you want to know why we are insolent and insulting, it is because you are, in our estimation, hypocritical, insolent and insulting."

Thus we come back to the problem which was posed at the beginning of this chapter, the problem of achieving world organization, collective security through an "international police force" and general disarmament. Our analysis has made it clear that there may indeed be a strong and widely diffused wish and hope for peace through world organization among the masses in all countries; but on the part of the ruling elements in the American and the Russian regimes there cannot be said to be an effective will to peace and world order and there is no substantial conviction that these goals are in our time capable of achievement. This is not to charge that these men "want war" and are in that sense warmongers, though the leaders on each side tend so to regard the leaders on the other side. It is simply that, given the assumptions with which these men operate and the forces, material and spiritual, which they conceive to be at their disposal, they cannot believe that the goals mentioned are politically realistic.

The task which confronts those who advocate world government and general disarmament under these conditions of profound mutual distrust can be stated in the following terms:

1. International machinery must be devised so powerful and so certain in its operations that great nation-states which are profoundly attached to their own way of life and abhor that of the other, which are in a high degree self-satisfied and self-righteous, which do not trust each other and do not intend to, may each believe that this interna-

tional instrumentality will keep the other in check so that it will not be exposed to any risk from that other's "aggression."

2. This international peace-enforcing organ must be set up while each of these nations pursues its own national interest, defends and seeks to extend the sway of its way of life, in fact, engages in a continuous power struggle with the other which constitutes war, hidden but none the less real. Each nation is consequently engaged in feverishly developing its military establishment, since without this each feels that it is defenseless until the new organ is completely set up. Moreover, how can either antagonist be sure that the international agency will work once it is set up? This contingency also must somehow be guarded against if possible, and some planners actually advance schemes so rigged up that each nation will still be able to "take care of itself," if need arises, and possess unilateral security after the presumably foolproof international security system has been established.

3. A way has to be devised by which these heavily armed and distrustful nations feel some day that it is safe to move out of the regime of competitive armaments into the new regime of collective security which, *ex hypothesi,* they have helped to build while at the same time keeping up their own defenses. At some magical moment a switch has to be thrown, the trains which have been driven with ever greater speed in an atomic armaments race must stop dead in their tracks and in the same motion change engineers and go speeding in the opposite direction toward world order and peace.

To state the problem of world order, disarmament, control of atomic energy, in these terms—and they are the only ones corresponding to present reality—is enough to demonstrate that the problem is not soluble in these terms at all. Two nations which are engaged in war are not at the same time engaged in building a world government and peaceful community. If during the recent war someone had suggested that the United States, on the one hand, and Germany and Japan, on the other, were, while seeking to annihilate each other, really working together to build a world peace organization, the absurdity of the suggestion would have been apparent to all. The mere fact that the present war between Russia and the United States is not in its shooting phase does not alter the fundamental absurdity of the suggestion as applied to them.

Before going on to draw the conclusion which we believe needs to be drawn from this analysis, one more comment on the contemporary political scene needs to be made. Since some time in 1946 the foreign policy of the American government has been based on the assumption that this nation is engaged in a power struggle with Russia and that the sound course is to be "firm" or "tough" with Russia, preventing further Russian expansion and backing up this policy with military force. The advocates of this policy claim that it provides the best hope for peace, though many of them freely admit that it is a slender one. Russia, it is argued, is at the present time in no condition to risk war on a large scale. In truculently pursuing an expansionist policy the men in the Kremlin are bluffing. They have to keep the Russian masses, including the returned soldiers who have seen that life is not so bad on the western side of the "iron curtain," in line by playing up the threat from without. At the same time they must maintain the dogma of the infallibility of Russia and its great leader Stalin, extend the Russian sphere of influence steadily, and so make the promises that life will before long be easy for the Russian masses seem plausible. However, the men in the Kremlin are realists. Let the United States once make it clear that they have gotten as far as they are going to be permitted to go, and they will be ready to come to a sensible understanding. Moreover, when the Russian people once realize that Stalin and Company have met their match, the dictatorship will cease to exercise complete control, democratic tendencies in Russia will have a chance to assert themselves and thus the "be firm" policy will promote democracy as well as peace.

The argument has a superficial plausibility but it seems to me that even a little reflection makes it clear that this program does not offer a solution for the dilemma which we have presented but is simply a restatement of it. It is not a way to avoid war but a phase of the war which is in process. I believe the chief promoters of the "be firm" program among American military and political leaders quite sincerely regard it as such, believing that eventually there will have to be a showdown with Russia. In so far as they give backing to the arguments advanced a moment ago, it is partly because as men with humanitarian impulses they would like to believe that there is a possibility to avoid all-out war, and partly because they do not think that American public opinion is as yet completely ready to accept the idea of the inevitability of atomic war and, therefore, political leaders have to lead the people by gradual steps to that conviction. In the meantime, these leaders make no attempt to conceal the fact that it is their policy to make the United States ready for war with Russia, just in case.

In general, history does not encourage the notion that when two great power entities like Rome and Carthage, having eliminated other contestants, face each other, all one of them needs to do is to show that it means to be "firm" to persuade the other to be "reasonable." They fight it out—even if it takes several Punic Wars. There are already men, and not just cheap alarmists, who envisage the possibility of several more world wars. And why not? There have already been two in a generation. It may well be that World War III, if it comes, will not be the last.

If we think specifically of the Russian case, it seems to me that the same conclusion is inescapable. There are those who appear to think that the policy of being firm with Russia is a brand-new idea, something very bright which no one thought of before and which of course solves everything! As a matter of fact, except for a brief interval of what might be called appeasement during World War II, the policy of Western nations toward Russia since the 1917 Revolution—not to go back any further—has been that of "firmness." And this remark could easily qualify for a prize for understatement. Let Americans consider where Russia was after the 1917 Revolution and in the years following and where the Russian regime is now in spite of all the invasions and interventions. Then let them ask what possible result another attempt to suppress that regime by force can have.

This is not to say that a show of force may not result in temporary suspension of the Communist advance or even in a retreat. Lenin did plenty of retreating. His disciple Stalin will not hesitate to follow his example if it becomes necessary. One of the grave dangers we now face is precisely that a show of American determination and force may result in temporary easing of tension and some sort of "peace" arrangement based on a temporary and precarious balancing of power against power. When was there a great war which was not followed by a similar development arousing false hopes in the hearts of people? After the abysmal weakness and suffering of 1917-24 the Russian regime is where it is today as co-victor in World War II and as moral leader of hundreds of millions of people in the Orient and even in the Western world. Stop that regime temporarily now by a show of force and it can only result in a determination to plot new ways to come back presently with all the greater vigor and vindictiveness. In the meantime the hold of the dictatorship on the Russian people will be strengthened. Its accusation that the United States is determined to thwart the Russian people and to dominate the world will, in the estimation of the Russian masses, be proved to the hilt. The United States will likewise move with fatal precision down the road to militarization, totalitarianism and war.

Thus, however we shift and turn, our backs are forced against the wall. The situation with which we are confronted is not an ordinary one. The threat is incalculable and frightful. The remedy, if there is one, will have to be extraordinary too. "Where there's been one organism," there have to be two—and suddenly—though that is of course impossible. "Old ways are suicidal"; a new way will have to be tried, though men are firmly convinced there is none.

When the political situation develops into such a stalemate as our age confronts, which cannot be resolved on a political basis and by political methods, it is proof that the crisis is deeper than politics. The real crisis is in the mind and spirit of man. The solution must be found on that level. It has to be a psychological and spiritual one. The way of life, the basic philosophy, of the age is responsible for the crisis. The question is, therefore, whether a different philosophy and way of life can be found. The house built on sand is collapsing. A rock on which to build a new house must be found. In religious language, man in his extremity must turn to God. God must forgive man, who confesses his helplessness and lays aside his wisdom and pride, and must save him from self-annihilation.

We have pointed out that in relation to the specific issue of eliminating atomic war, the very means the nations use to provide themselves with apparent or temporary "defense" and "security" constitute the great obstacle to the attainment of genuine or permanent collective security. They want international machinery so that the atomic armaments race may cease; but the atomic armaments race has to stop or the goal of world order recedes beyond human reach. Men want world government, a reign of law, so that they may be able to trust each other; but while they distrust each other they cannot co-operate to establish the reign of law. Government is needed in order that the community may function, but government—least of all world government—cannot be established by legal or constitutional fiat. Community creates government, and there is no world community.

Men and nations crave peace in order that the scourge of war may be abolished, but they are engaged in war and they have to stop fighting in order to build peace. Albert Einstein gave a perfect statement of the dilemma at a meeting of atomic scientists at his home in Princeton in November, 1946. "Making peace," he said, "is a psychological problem. But you have this dilemma: You want to make peace and you want to prepare for war. You cannot serve these two masters. You cannot prepare for peace and for war at the same time. It is psychologically impossible."

We cannot escape facing the question, therefore, whether it is possible for a nation to get war out of its system by a moral decision to renounce war. Not whether machinery can be devised by which another nation can be kept from waging war against us. That is what the United States and Russia are each trying to do and it results in the hopeless attempt to prepare for peace and for war at the same time. The question is, Can a nation renounce war and preparation for war as sinful and thus resolve "the crisis of confidence," which is the fundamental crisis of our world?

Clearly this raises basic questions as to the spiritual sickness of our age and as to the nature of man, of human society, of the universe itself. To a consideration of such matters we must, therefore, devote ourselves for a time. Later we shall return to the question as to what the sound psychological-spiritual approach to the political crisis is and what might be hoped for from the application of that approach.

Chapter III

The Individual Conscience Against the Atomic Bomb

The magazine *Time* on August 20, 1945, in the first issue following the dropping of atomic bombs on Hiroshima and Nagasaki, contained a remarkable statement for such a publication: "Each man is eternally and above all else responsible for his own soul, and, in the terrible words of the Psalmist, . . . no man may deliver his brother, nor make agreement unto God for him." An equally remarkable utterance appeared in the issue of *Life* on the same date: "Our sole safeguard against the very real danger of a reversion to barbarism is the kind of morality which compels the individual conscience, be the group right or wrong. The individual conscience against the atomic bomb? Yes. There is no other way." These sentences reveal how men presumably accustomed to think in secular terms also found that their backs had been forced against the wall by the advent of the atomic age. They felt compelled to think in ethical and religious terms about the nature and destiny of man and human society. The words they wrote in that solemn moment provide us with an admirable starting point for our own reflections on these themes.

We stand in the presence of an overmastering, awesome demonstration of material power, the atomic bomb. Dr. Harold C. Urey, one of the men who played a leading role in developing this instrument of destruction, writes in one of the popular magazines an article entitled *I'm a Frightened Man.* He speaks for all those who have some real comprehension of this instrument and its potentialities: "I write this to

frighten you. I'm a frightened man myself. All the scientists I know
are frightened—frightened for their lives." We stand over against the
atomic bomb which can blow a hundred million human beings to bits
in an instant. And to ward off this terror, over against this awesome
power we are to place—what? A human being equipped with that
most intangible, most elusive, most dubious, most antiquated weapon,
a conscience. The contest seems hopelessly unequal to the modern
mind. On the one hand, reality, power. Indubitable reality, tremendous power. On the other hand, an illusion, a figment of the imagination.

Where the situation is so desperate, however—Frankenstein's monster
veritably coming to life and terrorizing his creator—we cannot afford
to overlook any expedient, however unpromising it may seem at first
glance.

From one point of view man has always seemed utterly and tragically
pretentious and insignificant, a very thin-skinned, sensitive, awkward,
defenseless animal infesting an insignificant planet. "When I consider
Thy heavens, the work of Thy fingers, what is man that Thou art mind-
ful of him, or the son of man that Thou visitest him?" And yet, "Thou
hast made him but little lower than God."

Reflect first for a moment on the role of man's intellect, though, as
we shall see, it is not there that power, and our defense against the
terrors which beset us, is ultimately to be found, nor there that our
ultimate problem centers. The perfection of the bomb, the *New English Weekly* observed, meant "breaking the foundation of material
being itself, by resolving matter into energy." But it was the mind of
man which accomplished this. Even to the veriest layman the description of the processes by which elemental power was released, yet controlled, is fascinating and awesome. How much more to those who are
able to understand their intricacy and true nature.

There is, superficially regarded, a monstrous incongruity between
the power released and the mind—or brain if for the moment you prefer that term—which performed the miracle. The laughable aspect
of the contrast struck me recently when I heard an atomic scientist tell
the story of the bomb. He was not one of the top-flight men, yet a
person of some importance in the execution of the project. When he
was a boy he must have resembled the stock caricature of the infant

prodigy, or of Johnny Boston Beans. Even now he looked boyish, though he was a Ph.D. of ten years' standing. He was fair, slender, with a weak voice lacking in color or resonance. Striding back and forth in a mechanical way, like a professor before a class of freshmen, he expounded the less abstruse phases of his subject. He might have been talking about any little gadget. He was, as a matter of fact, talking about an event of cosmic significance. He was talking about the atomic bomb. He, Professor Boston Beans, had helped to make it. He could look with those rather listless eyes of his into the innermost secrets of the material universe. He could kill a hundred thousand men. Maybe he could blow up the earth.

Modern war is an illustration of the same incongruity. Men witness the detonation of the atomic bomb and say to themselves: "That is power; that is reality; that is what you must respect." So they look at war, at the battleships, the submarines, the planes; the guns, big and little, of every description; the vast piles of munitions blown against cities, forests, men, babies; the endless marching regiments; the men at close range hacking away at each other in titanic conflicts. And again it seems to them that here they witness power; they are face to face with what is indubitable and real. But once again, when you penetrate behind the façade you come upon this intangible, elusive thing.—mind or brain. It is the scientists and the technicians who make modern war possible. Let them withhold their thinking and planning for a few days, even a few hours, and all the armies in the world would stop dead in their tracks. Over against the whole enginery of modern war, as over against the atomic bomb, is Professor Boston Beans who created it and who alone can manage it.

There is in modern technology and war, furthermore, an inexorable tendency to carry the thing to its conclusion—logical and magnificent, or pitiable and absurd and mad, as you choose to regard it. We are on the eve of the push-button war, we are told. A few professors, none of whom, perhaps, could qualify as a combatant soldier, will sit in the midst of intricate machinery in underground laboratories and will level the proud cities and the little towns to dust. By the hardly perceptible pressure of their fingers on delicate instruments the little professors will make a shambles of the planet, so that in the minds of those who may survive all those who once claimed the name of warrior—

Sennacherib, Attila, Genghis Khan, the scourges of mankind, the butchers of history—will seem mere tyros in comparison.

It is characteristic of our age that men locate power in the irrational forces of nature, on the one hand, and in the machine, on the other hand. But obviously it is the scientist who incarnates power; it is in the brain or mind that power is to be found. It is the result of a distortion, a severe disturbance of focus, that modern men should believe in, never question, never think of questioning, the reality of the machine but not conceive of either the builder or the tender of the machine as equally and indubitably real. It is a symbol of what is wrong with us that chemistry and chemical materials seem real and tangible to us, but not the chemist; physics, matter, energy seem real (even when the scientists are in the act of reducing them to mathematical formulas before our eyes) but not the physicist. The atom is real, mighty, enduring, eternal, but Urey, Oppenheimer, Wilson, Fermi are creatures of the moment, intangible, illusory, "such stuff as dreams are made of."

Yet as we observe these contemporary developments and pursue our reflections upon them, we also become aware of the fact that, mighty as is the intellect of man, it does not solve our problem nor provide the needed defense against the catastrophe which threatens us. The mind of man, it is true, devised the atomic bomb, and reality and power inhere primarily in the creator and not in that which he created. But looked at from another and much more important angle the fact that man made and used the atomic bomb is the symbol and proof of his weakness, not his strength; his foolishness, not his wisdom; his captivity, not his freedom and power of self-determination; his infantilism, not his maturity; his dehumanization, not his uniqueness.

As some philosophers have emphasized, the intellect as such is a tool, an instrument. Perhaps it always tends to become like a machine, a mechanism. Certainly, in modern times and especially in its connection with the evolution of modern war and the weapons of warfare, it has tended toward mechanization and mechanical, impersonal behavior, disregarding moral standards, indifferent to the ends which it served. The spectacle of virtually all the top scientists of a nation combining; enlisting hundreds of lesser scientists and tens of thousands of workers who had none but the vaguest idea of what they were being enlisted for, but robotlike followed the lead of the big names; conniving at the expenditure of two billion dollars of the taxpayers' money without any notion on the part of the latter or even their representatives in Congress as to what the money was being spent for—all in order to manufacture a gadget with colossal capacity for destruction and then to turn it over without conditions to a politician and a general or two—illustrates this process of depersonalization and mechanization. The great minds have become a munitions factory, as it were.

Perhaps we are to go still farther. One reads descriptions of a robot-like instrument about eight feet high standing on the deck of a battleship capable of following a plane or a ship anywhere in the world and unerringly directing a missile against it. Perhaps our picture a moment ago of a few atomic scientists in underground laboratories is already old-fashioned. A few robots here and there, ultimate creations of the clever, proud mind of man—of our "best brains"—will carry out the job of exterminating the human species. There are poets who have dreamed of such things.

Life did not say: "Our sole safeguard against reversion to barbarism is the human mind. The mind of man against the atomic bomb? Yes. There is no other way." If it had said this, it would have said something unimportant or untrue, depending upon one's standpoint. It is "the individual conscience against the atomic bomb" which constitutes our sole safeguard.

We are confronted with material power raised to the *n*th degree. With it comes suddenly the realization that the vast, impersonal forces which in one sense we have created and to which in another sense we have ourselves been assimilated, have driven us to the edge of the abyss and are about to drive us over. What force are we now to counterpose to them? Whence is our salvation? And the answer is "the individual conscience." It is man whose mind penetrates the secret of the atom and releases its energies. It is also man, the individual human being, who is constantly confronted with the necessity, the inescapable command, to make a moral decision, to choose: Whether to use atomic energy for this purpose or that. Whether to make atomic bombs. Whether, having made them, to use them. Whether, having used them once, twice, to use them again. When you have a brain that can unveil the mysteries of the physical universe and can release its deeply hidden energies, then you are made suddenly aware again that you must comprehend the nature of the moral universe also, which moderns have tended to think of as so unreal, that you must be able to tap vast springs of moral energy. There must be a conscience to match the brain, a moral science to match atomic science, or catastrophe is certain.

Finding that statement on which we have been commenting in so unexpected a spot as an editorial in *Life* reminded me of the surprise I experienced a year or two ago in coming upon a passage in a letter written by Rosa Luxemburg, the fiery German antimilitarist and revolutionist and a founder of the Bolshevik International. The letter in question was written during World War I in a German prison in which she was confined for antiwar activities. The passage reads: "Everything would be much easier if I only didn't forget the basic commandment I have set myself for life: the main thing is to be good. Simply and plainly to be good, that is what binds and unbinds all things, it is better than all cleverness and self-righteousness. . . . I decided to be good, again, simply good at any price: that is better than 'being right' and booking every injury." She too, it would seem, confronted by an impersonal economic system which man had created and which had become his master and by the elemental forces which produced the class struggle and were unloosed by it, felt suddenly the need of another kind, another order, of power, of a moral science to set over against political science, and so turned to conscience, being good, simply, plainly and at any price, for deliverance for herself and the exploited peoples!

Ordinary experience teaches men this truth: that in the final analysis we have to rely on conscience in the human individual, on moral integrity. We do not mean this in a simplistic fashion. It does not mean that the material and social environment is not important. It does not mean that, in seeking to avert the threat of atomic warfare, we need not be concerned about effective world organization. But when all allowances have been made, our final reliance must be on moral integrity. "They constantly seek to escape from the darkness outside and within," wrote T. S. Eliot, "by dreaming of systems so perfect that no one will need to be good." But it's no good. The saying that there is honor among thieves is revealing. There has to be some honor, thieves have to be able to rely on each other, on some sense of responsibility in each other, or their activities would be impossible.

Their "societies" are so short-lived and precarious precisely because there is so little "honor" or moral integrity among them.

Men who are largely lacking in moral integrity or who scoff at moral standards and values often unconsciously betray their real though deeply hidden conviction by expressing "moral indignation" against others who get the better of them or treat them shabbily. What is the basis for moral indignation, if morality is synonymous with expediency and moral integrity is a disease or an affectation?

The inability to get away from the need of investing ourselves with moral dignity and our goals and strivings with moral sanction, the need therefore of standards of morality independent of the convention of a particular society or age and regarded as not the *ad hoc* creation of a given national state to suit its momentary interest, has probably not been more strikingly illustrated in recent serious literature than by my former associate in the Trotskyist movement in the United States, James Burnham, in his book *The Machiavellians*. In the conclusion to that book he speaks of a dilemma which will confront an "elite" which tries to rule "scientifically." The masses have to believe in the moral basis of their national life: therefore, "the political life of the masses and the cohesion of society demand the acceptance of myths." But the scientific elite cannot believe in these myths; they know too well how they themselves achieved and retain power. Nevertheless, they must profess to believe the myths, i.e., they must lie. But "lies are often not convincing when told with a divided heart. The tendency is for the deceivers to become self-deceived, to believe their own myths. When this happens they are no longer scientific!"

Having written this, Burnham, however, goes on to accuse "our leaders—not only the governing elites but those other sections of the elites, such as those grown out of the labor movement, which have been moving toward increased power," not only of being nonscientific and even antiscientific but of moral delinquency, and ascribes the calamities of our time to that fact! These leaders "admit no *responsibility* except to the fiction of the mass, which is only *the projection of their own unloosed will to power.* Proceeding in *this manner . . .* they have brought civilization to the *most shattering crisis of recorded history.*"[1]

[1] Italics are mine.

Not only that, but the concluding sentence of this section and of the book itself holds out hope for a better future, though not indeed for "the perfect society of our dreams," and rests that hope squarely on moral grounds. We may hope that this future "will *permit human beings at least that minimum of moral dignity which alone can* justify the strange accident of man's existence." [2]

Furthermore, all men have in some measure and at some times been conscious that there is power in moral integrity. Something that inspires awe takes place when a human being makes a moral decision and at no matter what cost to himself stands by it. Power flows through such a man. Men touch the hem of his garment and they are healed. Weaklings look into his eye and they, too, are strong.

The term "morality" is often synonymous with weakness because the so-called moral people are only conformists to the current mores. Their actions are not genuinely moral, the result of inexorable decision, at all. Goodness is often partial or sham goodness, and rightly scorned.

But men recognize the real thing when they see it—the thing Thoreau had in mind when he said: "It is not so important that many should be as good as you, as that there be some absolute goodness somewhere." He added, "For that will leaven the whole lump." And again: "Action from principle, the perception and the performance of right, changes things and relations; it is essentially revolutionary, and does not consist wholly with anything which was. It not only divides States and churches, it divides families; ay, it divides the individual, separating the diabolical in him from the divine."

It is well known that you can crucify the man of conscience, of complete moral integrity, but that when you do so you have not destroyed or diminished the power that was in him and flowed through him. Rather, you have performed an act even more stupendous than that of splitting the atom: you have unleashed power that will indeed "destroy this temple" but will also "in three days build it again"; that will end an age and a civilization and build another.

But here we have come to the very heart of our problem, of the crisis of modern man and contemporary civilization. War itself is only one phase of that problem, a symbol of that crisis. Before the atom was split, man was split and his world was atomized. The atomic bomb and the

2 Italics are mine.

threat of atomic warfare are the result and not the cause of these catastrophic events. Here we must pause, then, and explore as deeply and systematically as we can that "moral science," that science of man and society which must provide us safety from the atomic bomb and skill to use atomic science.

Man no longer believes in himself. Over against his own machines and the vast centers of politico-economic power which daily conscript him, he can no longer feel that he, himself, is real, that he counts and "belongs." To prevent an atomic war is indeed a question of survival for mankind. But inwardly men are not sure they want to survive. Certainly in many the will to survive is weak. They believe already that the atomic war will come—"and what can anyone do to prevent it?" It is not enough to prevent atomic war, important as that is. It will indeed hardly seem important to men unless they can believe in the possibility and reality of another kind of life than that which periodically and inevitably begets war. If men are planning new wars and defenses, a brilliant literary critic observed recently, "It is that they hate their lives. . . . Surely the problem is not to make things work a little better, but for people to want anything at all enough not to bomb it all to hell."

Now we know that in the moment when a man makes a moral decision, when freely he chooses that which is to him right rather than safe or advantageous or merely the path of least resistance, and when he acts upon his decision, he is not troubled with this sense of his own unreality or of the illusoriness or emptiness of life. Later when he reflects he may be troubled again. But in that moment of inward and outward action, of decision, he experiences himself as real. There are moments of intellectual insight or aesthetic experience also when man approaches this sensation that he is real and that life and the world are supremely good; but even these by themselves lack something of the depth and completeness of realization which man experiences in the moment when he achieves moral integrity, when he faces an absolute, a choice, and makes his decision for the right.

This, by the way, if I understand that remarkable book, is the chief or a chief theme of Hermann Broch's *The Death of Virgil*. Virgil, as his death approaches, wants to destroy the manuscript of his *Aeneid*. Augustus, the emperor and his patron, as well as his closest friends,

seek to dissuade him, charging that it would be a veritable act of sac-
rilege to destroy this work of beauty. But it is just because it is merely
an expression of beauty, of life observed from without, that Virgil
thinks his life has been in vain and the poem, which consists merely of
words about life and will never contribute to an understanding of the
real meaning of life, ought to be destroyed: "High above the law of
beauty, high above the law of the artist, which was only greedy for
corroboration, there was the law of reality, there was . . . the Eros in
the urge of existence, there was the law of the heart, and woe to the
world which had forgotten this last reality. . . . For creation is more
than form, creation is resolution, is parting the bad from the good,
oh only this election is truly immortal. . . ."

Life, creation, is "more than form, creation is resolution"—decision,
choice, the leap into purposeful action—"is parting the bad from the
good." When thus engaged man feels that he is living, is certain of his
own reality. But there is another element in this experience which is
important in connection with our problem. In this moment when man
is and feels himself to be most free, he is also, paradoxically, most
bound. In this moment when he is profoundly and blessedly aware of
his own reality and significance, he is, paradoxically, also sharply
aware of Reality beyond himself, in the presence of which he is utterly
insignificant. The forces of the material universe, though his body is
often at their mercy, he can nevertheless manipulate and control so
that they serve him. But here he encounters that which he cannot
manipulate or command. At the moment of moral decision, in the
realm of the spirit, he is face to face with Reality which commands *him*.
Moreover, he experiences this Reality as absolute, inexorable, inescapable, eternal. Such is the nature of the moral order. When man is
speculating about it, it may indeed seem to him unreal; but when he
is acting as a moral being, then the moral order has this quality of supreme reality, of absoluteness and inexorability. "So help me God, I can
do no other."

He may in his actions and in his speculations try to ignore the moral
order, may at times convince himself that he succeeds. But actually he
does not. If he disobeys its mandate, he and his societies suffer. "God
is not mocked." On the other hand, as we pointed out a moment ago,
when he commits himself in faith and obedience to the Reality which

makes its absolute demand upon him, it is as if an atom fission had taken place in his soul: mighty powers are released and flow through him. "It changes things and relations . . . and does not consist wholly with anything which was."

We used the term "God" just now of the Reality beyond himself of which man is aware in the moment of decision, when he achieves inner integrity. It comes easier to modern man, whose mind is focused almost entirely upon the outer rather than the inner, upon the surface rather than the depths, upon objects which can be looked at, measured and dissected rather than upon subjects which live and act and create, to use the neuter in speaking of this Reality. Let me assure the reader who reacts against the term "God" that I am concerned about the experience itself which we are seeking to understand and not primarily about the terms in which it is described. The experience of love is not the same as the description of the experience. Nevertheless, I am convinced that the transaction which takes place between man and the Other in the moment of moral crisis is essentially and intensely personal and not impersonal or mechanical and—recognizing the limitations of all language in dealing with ultimate realities—can be most fruitfully discussed in personal terms, as a transaction between spirit and Spirit.

It will not do, because it is not a factual statement of what takes place, to say that the moral order with which man finds himself confronted in the moment of moral decision and action, when he recovers the sense of his own reality, is a verbal phrase, an idea or ideal of his own imagining. With these he could do as he chooses; but the basic characteristic of the Other who confronts him in the moral experience is precisely that He cannot be ignored or manipulated. The Other is not the creation of man or of society. He sits in judgment upon them. They disobey and defy Him and they are shattered.

Again, real existence for man consists, as we have been pointing out, in "resolution," in parting the good from the bad, in creative action. These are attributes of spirit, of personality. The Other with whom man deals in the supreme, moral, transaction of his life—the moral universe of which man knows himself to be a part when he is no longer a fiction to himself and his life is no longer meaningless, because he is making moral decisions—cannot be of another and lower, subpersonal, order. In that case man would be superior, would be the creator and sustainer of the moral order. In that case also he would be the highest type of moral or spiritual being in existence, and there would be nothing for him to worship and adore. But nothing is more certain than that man is not the creator of the universe in which he finds himself in any of its aspects. He is a created being, contingent, dependent. His creator cannot be of a lower order of being than himself. Moral responsibility, or obligation, is something that obtains between persons and arises out of the realities of their natures and their relationships to each other. A rock, the desk on which I write, the sun in the heavens, the fish in the sea and the birds of the air have no moral responsibility to me, nor to each other, nor I to them. But parent and child, sister and brother, husband and wife, neighbors, fellow human beings—between and among these there is mutual responsibility and obligation. Likewise, properly speaking, man has no obligation to an abstract moral order, to the idea or phrase "moral order of the universe." It is because a supremely good Being confronts him in the universe, as truly as his mother, his wife, his child, that he cannot escape the obligation to the supremely good, the obligation to assume the appropriate relationship to such a Being, the obligation, as so exactly stated by Jesus, to be perfect as his Heavenly Father is perfect.

If the moral universe is not in the fullest sense real, if right and wrong are infantile delusions or merely ideas imposed by dominant sections in any society for the purpose of maintaining "order" in their own interest (the "bourgeois ethics" so heartily despised by both Fascist and Communist theoreticians); if man's aspirations are the fantastic posturings of an ape in dress clothes and his sins are "natural" and the reflections of the state of his liver or of something called his libido—then man feels the sense of his own reality slipping from him again. His existence has no meaning. His unity is shattered. He wanders as an orphan in a trackless desert. There is nothing to keep human society from flying apart, as it is so obviously doing in our own day. "If there is no God, then I am God," cried a character in Dostoievsky, and then there is nothing but despair. But in the moment of moral decision when he feels himself most real, he is also at once exalted and abased because he knows himself to be standing in the presence of One who is infinitely beyond himself though somehow also infinitely near, who is utterly and absolutely real and also utterly and absolutely adorable. The supreme Good which confronts, judges, sustains his imperfect good and beckons it onward in his highest and most profoundly joyous hours is not less but more real than he is; it is the source of his own idea of good and of his desire to pursue it, not the creation of his own mind, the mere breath of his own voice. Involuntarily he cries, "My Lord and my God," God who is Spirit, person, who lives and acts as moral Being, though in a supreme sense, so that the moment we seek to put experience into words, we must fall back on symbols which hint at but do not define or contain the reality and the mystery.

We may state the case from a slightly different angle in the hope that its bearing upon the present crisis of civilization may be as clear and unmistakable as possible. We need, as has so often been said in recent days, a science of society, of what holds society together, provides it with dynamic and releases its energies, in order that man may be able to control and use for good the vast mechanisms he has created and the well-nigh demonic physical energies which he has unleashed. Now in the final analysis the problem of society is the problem of the nature of man. The basic character of this proposition is largely hidden from modern man because of his too exclusive reliance on mechanisms and on the methods for studying and dealing with phenomena which are peculiar to the physical sciences. But it is a fact that human society is a unique thing and must be studied and dealt with by methods appropriate to it, and that an economic, political, social order is just human beings living together in certain relationships. The character of these relationships is of immense importance and it is at our peril that we neglect the task of devising just and productive political and economic systems. Men cannot live a democratic life in a world which is autocratically organized, nor a peaceful life in a world organized for war. But it is equally, and perhaps in a sense even more fundamentally, true that the character of the social order cannot be abstracted from the quality of the persons who compose it. People who are autocrats and lovers of power in their own hearts, or whose egos are possessive, defensive and hence stricken with fear, are not going to build a democratic world. They do not want freedom; they want to dictate or be dictated to. People who know no peace in their own spirits do not really want peace in the outward order and their fitful and distracted efforts to achieve it will be constantly thwarted.

If, then, man is essentially an animal, society will always essentially be—no matter how the fact is temporarily camouflaged—a wolf pack, with the strongest, cleverest, most brutal of the wolves as the dictator; business and government will in that case always be a more or less open struggle as to "who gets what when"; and the future will in that case be with the totalitarians since they are building upon the realities of human nature and refusing to be deceived by idealistic illusions.

It is only if human beings are indeed creations of spirit, beings of moral dignity and worth, capable of discerning between good and evil and of choosing the good voluntarily, that a democratic society can be achieved or approximated on earth. Edmund Burke stated the problem thus: "It is inevitable that a restraint be placed on human will and appetite somewhere, and the less there is within, the more there must be without; it is contrary to the eternal nature of things that men of intemperate minds should be free."

But men are not beings of moral dignity and worth in themselves, apart from their relationship to a Reality beyond themselves. Man is not self-sufficient. He is the product or creation of something, Someone. His conception of himself, and the deeds which result from it, will therefore always depend upon his conscious or unconscious conception of the universe, the nature of the Being from whom his own life derives. The son is made in the image of the father who begot him. Man's relation to God is decisive.

Disaster consequently overtakes men and civilization when they lose a living contact with God. This is an inexorable spiritual law which has been demonstrated in many historical periods. The fact that the difficulty often stems largely from the character of the professed believers in God and the churches, and from inadequate and distorted conceptions of God, does not change the essential fact. When men no longer bow the knee to God or believe in the existence of a moral universe, the result is obviously not that they become upstanding, free men who no longer bow the knee to anything or anybody. It may seem to be so for a brief period when individuals or a civilization live on the spiritual capital of the past, but when that has been used up, as the power of the medieval and Reformation tradition is exhausted, for example, in our own day, then men bow the knee before such idols as Hitler, Mussolini, Stalin. Everywhere they seek refuge, a recovery of the sense of belonging to something beyond themselves, by surrender of their individuality, freedom and responsibility to absolutist states and monolithic parties. Those more noble and sensitive spirits who cannot bring themselves to do that sink into disillusionment if not cynicism. For they above all cannot be deceived, nor can they succeed in deceiving themselves. If the moral universe is not real, if there is no God and I am therefore God, they know that life is a fraud and a diabolical one. Of them Josephine Johnson wrote some years ago in a bit of free verse: "This is the trouble with us all, that we see under the shell and we see under the inner shell, and we see under what lies under what lies under—and we cannot look at each other without laughing"—or weeping hysterically as the case may be. They see through everything and everybody and are unable to see anything in anything or anybody any more. God, the universe, having been dissolved, man too is dissolved.

Ignazio Silone, who was once prominent in the Communist party in Italy and as a Socialist is still actively concerned with economic and political issues, has described the seat of our malady, individual and social, in the sensitive prose of his novel *Bread and Wine*: "There are malcontents and there are perpetrators of violence, but Men are lacking. . . . To use an old expression, it is a matter of conversion. It is a matter of becoming a new man. Perhaps it is sufficient to say that it is a matter of becoming a man, in the real sense of the word. We are so far from manhood now that he who starts comparing his present plight with what he might be cannot fail to be disturbed. He discovers he is mutilated, disfigured, deformed, degraded. At heart every revolution puts this elementary question afresh: What, it asks, is man? What is this human life?"

And the hero of that novel arrives also at what the remedy for such a malady must be: "All that remained alive and indestructible of Christianity in me was revived: a Christianity that neither abdicates in the face of Mammon, nor proposes concordats with Pontius Pilate, nor offers easy careers to the ambitious, but rather leads to prison, seeing that crucifixion is no longer practised."

The moral life, the life of "conscience," i.e., truly human life in

which man recovers his sense of selfhood, is, then, essentially a relationship between Spirit and spirit, between God and man "made in
his image." It is religious life. From this standpoint, it is rightly said
that our salvation as individuals and as nations depends upon moral
conversion and spiritual rebirth. One must not confuse this with the
"religious revivals" of which we hear so much in certain circles. Nor
must the reader think that I am writing of matters ecclesiastical or
theological in the dogmatic sense. And as I urged a few moments ago,
let him not be deterred by the words we are employing from trying
to understand the experience and the reality which we are endeavoring
to describe. That we should understand the nature and laws of the
spiritual universe is immeasurably important in this age when there
has been such an immense enlargement of our knowledge of the
physical universe.

As to the essence of the malady and the remedy there can, as we
have said, be no dispute. We cannot recover our faith in democracy or
the will to strive for a just and peaceful world unless we recover our
sense of the reality of our own selves and of the rationality of the
process of history which now seems to us like a fluid, rushing cataract
on which we toss about impotently. And we cannot recover our faith
in man and in the meaning of his historical experience unless we recover our faith in God, creator of man "in his own image" and Lord
of history.

In the nature of the case, these things cannot be demonstrated like
a mathematical formula or a scientific law. Nor, and this also in the
nature of the case, can the demonstration be forced upon us. We
cannot, indeed, escape the consequences of breaking the moral law
and disobeying or disregarding the will of God. But the moral act
must be a voluntary one. God, as someone has said, "is unconditionally
on the side of freedom." The things we are discussing have to do not
with matters which can be observed from without and thus adequately
understood, or with man as an observer, but with man as participant
in life, man in the creative moment of moral decision and action.
Truth in this realm is apprehended and understood as we act upon it,
behave as responsible persons, not as things. Man knows God his
Father when he lives and acts as a son of such a Father.

We come back, then, to the centrality of the individual conscience.

Organizations, institutions, movements, masses, "the people," cannot make moral decisions, behave as children of God. The reordering of our lives and of society, the establishment of control over atomic energy, must begin within the individual spirit. Just as man must, so to speak, penetrate the microcosm of the atom, and the appropriate and necessary processes must there be set in motion in order that the energies of the microcosm may be tapped, so must we penetrate the microcosm of the individual spirit, and the appropriate and necessary processes must there be set in motion in order that the power of God may be at the disposal of those "of a little faith" and thus the chaos of the social order may be abolished, the rending of civilization may be stopped and man's historic destiny to subdue the earth and not be subdued by it may be fulfilled.

"The individual conscience against the atomic bomb? Yes. There is no other way." But conscience, unless it be a mere word, an abstraction, means you and you and me, never they. The healing and recovery of civilization, the taming of the atomic bomb and all that it implies must begin with and in you and me. Unless it takes place there, it will not take place. "The bell tolls for thee." "No man may deliver his brother, nor make agreement unto God for him." "Lord, and what shall this man do? What is that to thee? Follow thou me."

The sense of the obligation to act as an individual, regardless of what anyone else does; the sense of the meaningfulness, aye, the revolutionary, explosive character of individual conscientious action; the obligation of not "going along," of refusing to be regimented and conscripted, of not waiting to withdraw, to step out of line, until a hundred, a million others do so; the obligation not to wait until there is a new government or economic order and a righteous state, and the efficacy of doing just that—these must be recovered. Ours is a world which regiments men. It will stop doing that when a man comes forth who refuses to be regimented. There a power to match atomic energy and to reverse the present fatal course of civilization will emerge. It is the atomic scientist alone before conscience and God here in this room —not the colleague in the next room, or the many hundreds in the Federation of Atomic Scientists. It is the teacher here in this classroom alone before conscience and God in the presence of these children— not the teacher in the next room, or the National Education Associa-

tion. It is the minister here in this pulpit standing before these people
—not the man in the pulpit across the street, or the general assembly
or conference of his church. It is this soldier aiming a flame-thrower at
his yellow-skinned brother over there—this soldier, alone with conscience and with God who made him and is the sole source of his life,
not his pals, not his commander, not the Army, not "our peace-loving
Government, our great and glorious country."

The moment a man thus acts as a responsible moral being and not
as a cog in a machine or as the member of any gang, no matter how
respectable, all doubts about the reality of his own existence vanish,
as we know. Power flows into and through him, for the barrier between
him and the eternal source of spiritual power has been broken. Whenever groups of men thus act from conscience and not expediency, obeying God rather than men, a new day dawns, a new order comes to
birth. Macaulay's immortal description of the Puritans in the "Essay
on Milton" comes to mind: "The Puritans were men whose minds had
derived a peculiar character from their daily contemplation of superior
beings and eternal interests. . . . They had their smiles and their
tears, their raptures and their sorrows, but not for the things of this
world. . . . They went through the world . . . mingling with
human beings, but having neither part nor lot in human infirmities,
insensible to fatigue, to pleasure and to pain, not to be pierced by any
weapon, not to be withstood by any barrier."

"The individual conscience against the atomic bomb? Yes. There
is no other way."

Chapter IV

Love Against the Atomic Bomb

Because of our starting point in this discussion we have chiefly spoken of the moral order, of God, as infinite justice and righteousness, as One who imposes on man an absolute and inexorable obligation to do right at whatever cost, One who will allow him no substitute, before whose august tribunal we stand each moment and to all eternity. This does indeed describe one phase of our status as human beings. But not the whole and not the most important aspect of our relationship to God. Behind and within and all around His judgment is an infinite mercy. His justice will not let us off because His love will not let us go.

In the moment of moral decision and action we discover that we are true beings, true selves (not mere egos), beings of moral dignity and worth. We are persons, not things, and the whole material universe is not commensurate with the value of a person, a single human soul. We did not make ourselves, bestow this dignity upon ourselves. God knows how persistently we seek to deny and escape it. Yet we cannot. It is so. There it is.

This is of course calling attention to the fact which the language of religion expresses in the statement on which we have already commented that God made man in His own image, and in that other statement, to which we must now turn, that God is Father, God is Love. With man He shares His own being. He has bestowed upon us infinite gifts out of infinite love. "Brethren, now are we the sons of God and it is not yet made manifest what we shall be." There is still no better way to express the essential truth of man's nature and of his position.

The fact that we cannot escape from conscience, from the demand to make moral decisions, means, then, that God has not disowned us, has refused to banish us out of the moral universe in which alone we can exist. But this also means that when we "come to ourselves," to use Jesus' phrase in the Parable of the Prodigal Son, when we undertake to act responsibly again, self-righteousness and sitting in judgment upon our fellow men become impossible, out of the question entirely.

For how does a man in the moment when he seeks to be truly good, when he no longer runs away from the absolute demand of conscience and God, see himself? As a sinner, surely. As one who has tried to deny his own being. As one who, in so far as his will and his powers permitted, sought to shatter the moral universe and make human life impossible. He sees himself moreover as one whose dereliction and sin have in the last analysis been committed against boundless and unmerited love which sought to bestow the highest dignity in the universe upon him. Therefore, he must cry out: "Against Thee, Thee only have I sinned." There can be no attempt any longer to put himself in the right. The only attitude which becomes him is, as all the prophets proclaimed, the attitude of "self-noughting" and repentance.

Yet in the same moment he knows himself as the recipient of forgiveness. For he who wanted as a moral being to destroy himself, he who should have been blotted out, still lives, still hears the command of God to be what he was meant to be, to act as a being of moral dignity and worth. And in the degree that he believes and obeys the summons this sudden accession of power of which we have spoken before flows into and through him. The hard inner core of his ego, his rebellion, his rigidity, his defensiveness, his self-righteousness, has been split and, painful though the experience be, out of that cataclysm of the soul power is produced.

All this is of the utmost importance in dealing with war in all of its manifestations both within man and in the outward order. Let us pause for a moment to consider how.

Each person feels the need of being able to respect himself, to think well of himself. The psychoanalysts have unquestionably rendered a great service in pointing out the rationalizations in which people indulge in order to maintain their self-respect, in tearing the mask of pretension off the human countenance and the human soul. But often they leave the job less than half done because they tend to conceive of ethical standards also as rationalizations. They do not realize that the reason the subterfuges in which men indulge produce inner tension and breakup of personality is that men are spiritual beings meant to live in a moral order. Pretending to be good, "justifying" oneself, is destructive, not because goodness is meaningless or illusory, but precisely because men were meant to be—not to pretend to be—good.

Thus, in every being who retains any semblance of sanity, this imperious need to respect himself exists. But it is difficult, indeed impossible, to respect the man you see when you look yourself straight in the eye in the mirror or regard yourself in the light of God's righteousness. Thus men manage the necessary business of thinking well of themselves by comparing themselves with other people: "When I look at him, I'm not such a bad fellow. Something went wrong, but it was not my fault. Somebody ought to do something about this, but not I."

Jesus' symbol of the almost hopelessly bad man was the Pharisee who as a matter of fact was not merely eminently respectable but in many respects a good and a religious man. "Nice people" in particular will always miss the real point of Jesus' characterization of the Pharisee and will always be looking too far afield for him unless they begin with a very favorable view of the Pharisee, such as they are likely to entertain about themselves, for example. What then was at fault in the Pharisee? He was the kind of man who could stand before God and pray: "God, I thank thee that I am not as other men are."

The cardinal error and sin is this error and sin of separating oneself from others with whom as a matter of fact we are in every way identified. Biologically we are of one blood. Culturally we are products of the same influences. "They" are bone of "our" bone, flesh of "our" flesh, spirit of "our" spirit. We see ourselves reflected in them: if we were in their place we would behave as they do. We are one family, one community. Above all, we are children of one divine Father. Setting oneself apart from anyone is the key mistake, the most hideous sin.

For I am not better than you; "we" are not except in some quite negligible sense better than "they." The moment, therefore, we add to our other sins the sin of thinking that we are better we have fallen as low as it is possible to fall. Swimming in the sea of life we have thought to save ourselves by separating ourselves from the others, and thereby have put a millstone about our necks. Therefore, to Jesus the publican, a Jew Quisling who had sold out to the Roman conqueror and was squeezing taxes out of his own people for the imperial treasury, was nearer the Kingdom than the Pharisee. So were the harlots. For they were not making claims for themselves any more. They had stopped setting other people over there in a lower category. The publican prayed: "God, be merciful to me, a sinner." Of course a publican who prayed: "God, I thank thee that I am not as other men, or even this Pharisee," would himself have been a Pharisee!

There was a Frenchman who lived in the latter part of the last century and until 1914 who, I am sure, grasped this truth and apprehended it emotionally, also with an extraordinary intensity and clarity. His name was Charles Péguy. He was the son of poor parents in Orléans. Very early he became a Socialist and even as a schoolboy collected money for the relief of strikers. He drifted away from the Roman Catholic church and for a time adopted a secular outlook. But presently he became aware of a fundamental malady which afflicted both exploiters and exploited, those who were for the status quo and those who thought they were for overthrowing it:

"All these people think 'ready-made' thoughts, feel 'ready-made' emotions, utter 'ready-made' catchwords, pursue 'ready-made' party aims, and cherish a 'ready-made' party truth. How can anything new come into existence under these conditions, that genuine and original novelty which is the product solely of an inspired spirit, of mysticism, and not of politics?"

Thus he became convinced that "Socialism must inevitably prove a dangerous delusion when it is not a product of the Christian spirit. . . . He, the Socialist heretic, must save Socialism as a spiritual movement." He became a convert, according to his own testimony, to Catholicism, though he intensely disliked the word "convert." But this created for him a terrible dilemma. As one of his biographers states, "He believed the entire content of the catechism, and since he believed it, he must also believe in hell." But that meant believing in the eternal damnation of some. "Was he to enter the boat of the Sacraments and reach safety and abandon the others to sink or swim?" He refused to do so, refused, therefore, to become a practicing member of the Church, which in the circumstances meant accepting damnation for himself. As his biographer, Karl Pfleger, says: "Life had no object, had not the least significance, if there were no community." As Péguy himself put it, much more concretely and poignantly: "We are one with the eternally damned. We cannot admit that there are human beings who must be thrust away from the entrance of any community."

That is a modern version of the Parable of the Pharisee and the Publican.

Let us now probe a little more deeply into Jesus' profound psychological teaching. Until a person has achieved integration and rebirth, unless indeed he experiences it in each moment of existence, in each contact with others, he is constantly enacting the role of the Pharisee. I see myself as standing here and the other person is over there, quite separated, not the "other" whom I am to love as I love myself, to forgive as I have been forgiven. And I justify myself. I experience thus a glow of satisfaction. That is to say, in my imagination I put myself up here and the other person down there. But it is clear, is it not? that this is already a kind of warfare: I am pushing him down, committing an assault upon his spirit and slandering it. This sort of thing goes on all the time in the most respectable circles, in the Ladies' Aid societies, and the official boards of churches, and in the peace and pacifist societies, and throughout the discussions of the apparently superior sophisticates—"invulnerable, impossible, immune"—to whom a contemporary poet shouts:

> Go take yourselves apart, but let me be
> The fault you find with everyman.[1]

And the other person knows of course that all the time, behind a mask of smiles and respectability or indifference, I am in my imagination making war upon him. So his defenses are up, his ego takes up

[1] "The Intellectual," from *V-Letter and Other Poems* by Karl Shapiro (New York: Reynal & Hitchcock, Inc., 1944) p. 53. Used with permission.

arms, he sets me apart and compares himself with me that he may save his wounded self-respect: "You think you are somebody; but I'll show you." Thus even when the surface of life is calm, in those conditions we call normal, perpetual tension exists, an intense warfare goes on.

Jesus pointed this out. "Ye have heard that it hath been said, Thou shalt not kill; but I say unto you that whosoever shall say to his brother [in his heart, in his imagination], Thou fool, shall be in danger of the hell of fire." Like all such sayings of Jesus this is not a threat but the statement of a fact, a law of the spiritual world. All the tension, the bitterness, the conflicts of life originate there in the perpetual assaults which human beings who set themselves above others in order to maintain a good opinion of themselves perpetrate. "Unaccountably," it seems, hell breaks loose, but the right word is "inevitably." In the language of a modern philosopher, Maritain, "External events and forms of things depend on the invisible patterns which our free wills delineate within us. . . . The drama of human history is like a visible projection of that which proceeds within ourselves."

On the other hand, have we not all experienced dozens of times what a complete change comes into any situation the moment there is someone in it who is no longer trying to justify himself, to think of himself as morally superior to the others, who does not indulge in the pleasant pastime of calling upon the others to repent and mend their ways, but himself repents? With that act of changing one's whole focus, removing oneself as a morally superior being out of the situation, seeing oneself utterly undone and evil in God's sight, every true moral decision within man and every achievement in reconciliation in human relationships begins.

It was either an extremely happy accident or a profound insight which led the writer of that editorial in *Life* on August 20, 1945, to link "conscience" and "humility" as aspects of the nature of man on which we must rely to deliver us from the perils now besetting us. "The thing for us to fear today is not the atom, but the nature of man, lest he lose either his conscience or his humility before the inherent mystery of things." The intellect by itself is amoral, conscienceless. It is given also to arrogance toward men and nature. It looks upon them coldly from without, dissects them, takes them apart experiences its ecstasy in controlling and manipulating them. Here are the seeds of strife. Here is no power to reconcile. Unless both conscience and humility—which are indeed, as we have shown, complementary and inseparable aspects of truly human, morally responsible life—enter in, the process becomes diabolical and the outcome is diabolical.

To say that God is Father and that He has made men in His own image, that He shares His moral and spiritual being with them, is, as all the high religions have taught in one fashion or other, to say that men, being children of God, are all brethren, members of one spiritual family, so intimately bound together that the neighbor is "the other self" so that if one sees his neighbor truly, as he is, one will love this neighbor as oneself. The moral life is a life of relationships among persons. The purpose of God, the ultimate secret and center of the universe, the true and only end of life, the peace and salvation of man, is in community, fellowship, love.

All the great teachers whom men most revere have in their various tongues proclaimed this truth. Each of us has experienced it in those moments of which a brilliant young French writer, Simone Weil, speaks in a remarkable critical essay, "The Iliad—or The Poem of Force," which appeared in the November, 1945, issue of the magazine *Politics.* "A monotonous desolation would result," she writes, "were it not for those few luminous moments, scattered here and there throughout the poem, those brief, celestial moments in which man possesses his soul. The soul that awakes then . . . awakes pure and whole; it contains no ambiguities, nothing complicated or turbid; it has no room for anything but courage and love. . . . It is in a moment of love that men discover their souls—and there is hardly any form of pure love known to humanity of which the Iliad does not treat," including, she points out "the purest triumph of love . . . the friendship that floods the hearts of mortal enemies."

She quotes then the passage in which first "Priam fell to admiring Achilles," his archenemy, and then in turn "was admired by Achilles who watched his handsome face" until presently *"they were satisfied with contemplation of each other."* [2]

Surely that is one of the greatest lines in all the literature of the centuries. Men seldom stop really to look at each other. They do not

2 Italics are mine.

contemplate and truly see one another. Therefore, each is unreal, a thing, to the other person and to himself. Life, too, is unreal and stale and swings back and forth between bored exhaustion and furious combat in the hope that madness may provide relief from boredom. "Finite beings," Josiah Royce said long ago in a statement of the same truth as that contained in Homer's great line, "are always such as they are by virtue of an inattention which at present blinds them to their actual relations to God and to one another."

When we do "attend" to ourselves, to one another, then we know that love is our destiny, our task and our joy. When I love, then I fully realize my own selfhood, I am most real to myself. We have already, of course, pointed out that it is in the moment of moral decision and action that man experiences himself as real and life as meaningful. To say that it is in the act of loving and serving another that one is supremely and joyously aware of one's selfhood is not a contradiction of this earlier statement but rather flows out of it. Since human beings are spirits of infinite value and are members of one spiritual family, the highest and the only perfect moral decision is to love. We are not yet according human dignity to another until we see in him a spirit of infinite worth and as such love him in some real sense. It is because the oneness of the human family and the worth of each member of it is so absolutely basic that every experience of love in its various forms brings its ecstasy, for in it the one who loves consummates life's purpose. It is also because of this that the greatest ecstasy of all comes to those saints, whether conspicuous or obscure, whether obviously "religious" or not, who have ceased to defend or indulge their own egos and who love all men in God.

Hermann Broch in *The Death of Virgil,* from which we have already had occasion to quote, makes a remarkably profound statement of the psychological situation which we are here contemplating: "Law? There was only one law, the law of the heart! Reality? There was only one reality, the reality of love. . . . He who partakes of this blessing perceives reality; *he is no longer a mere lodger in the realm of personal consciousness in which he is caught.*" [3] How often, how constantly indeed, those who engage in introspection at all have this sensation that the self is a mere lodger, a stranger—even an outcast or

[3] Italics are mine.

prisoner—"in the realm of personal consciousness" or perhaps a bubble floating on "the stream of consciousness." It is always so until a person somehow breaks through the barrier of mere "personal consciousness," ceases to be an observer of things and of life from without, until he ventures—"we live by faith not by sight"—lives and acts. In the creative leap of decision and action, above all in the decision to love, to penetrate somehow into the spirit of another, man "comes to himself" at last, can believe in his own reality and worth. Similarly when I see and therefore love him, then the other person also loses his illusoriness for me, becomes real to me. To quote Broch again:

oh homecoming, homecoming into the divine, homecoming into the human! mortal to us, indeed, our fellow-man whose fate we have not taken upon ourselves, on whom we have bestowed no help, the unloved human being, whom we have not included in our own life and whom we have thereby rendered unable to embrace us inclusively in his own being, oh he seems undivine to us, we seem undivine to him, so enhanced in chance that we hardly know if he, who appears before us as living, who passes by us, who staggers by us and turns the next corner, whether he, creature of fate like any other, like ourselves, has not long since died or perhaps has not even yet been born.

The love of which we are speaking is not sentimental and "sweet." It is indeed the source of all pure joy and ecstasy but it is also and primarily a demand upon us, an absolute and to sinful and weak and self-indulgent man a terrible demand. Life bestows its greatest gift upon us, "God manifests his own love toward us," by confronting us with a moral order and by making us partakers in it, citizens and members of it. On the one hand, this means that we are not, either as individuals or as social entities, permitted to escape the consequences of our willful or accidental or even unconscious violations of the laws of justice and brotherhood. Thus love is judgment. On the other hand, we are never released from complete moral responsibility. After each dereliction and in spite of the deterioration which it causes in our own souls, the same standard confronts us still, the same demand that we do justice and love mercy, that we be perfect as God is perfect. As we have said, this is the demonstration of God's love for us. He will not suffer us to be cast adrift, to be banished from the moral universe, to fail of achieving life's objective. As the parables put it, He cannot abide that a single sheep be lost or perish. But the human being who is astray does not necessarily want to be found; and the experience of being found is in its first phase the most awful that can befall him. "It is a fearful thing to fall into the hands of the living God." As that other prophet said, "Who can abide the day of his coming? and who shall stand when he appeareth? for he is like a refiner's fire."

Similarly, love as it manifests itself in us is not sentimentality. Who, for example, has not wished above all that he might escape the accusing and the hurt eye of one who loved him? Again, to love means to see a human being, every human being, as a spirit of infinite worth who must be dealt with as such. Thence the refusal of the prophets and saints to overlook or condone hypocrisy, exploitation, callousness and injustice, to compromise with these things in themselves, to let others rest at ease while they ignore, perhaps even benefit from, these evils. They see human beings for what they are and truly love them. They know, therefore, what really takes place when a human soul is disadvantaged and hurt. It is for this reason that the true prophets and saints, no matter how "nonpolitical" they may often be, are always felt to be subversive of the dominant institutions of a culture. They are revolutionists over against them because they know what the institutions and the bureaucracies do to human beings, both to those who run them and to those who are run over by them. They apply to every institution the test of fellowship or community. Out of their insight and anguish is wrung the cry which has so often dismayed the privileged, the arrogant and the complacent: "There shall not be left here one stone upon another which shall not be torn down." And that other cry: "It were better that a mill-stone were bound to your neck and that you were cast into the midst of the sea, than that you should cause one of these little ones to stumble." They, because they understand what life is aiming at and how great the task, are the very ones who will not tolerate the so-called "reconciliations," the specious, easy "good will," the false "unities," the superficial reforms and the hasty, violent pseudo revolutions, which are based on a superficial understanding of the realities in a situation, on an evasion of issues, a blurring of differences. They know that true reconciliation, in whatever realm, must be based on a resolute facing of the truth and a rejection of easy compromises, and that love, the only source of peace among men, always comes first of all with a sword, which as Thoreau, echoing Jesus, observed, "not only divides states and churches, it divides families; ay, it divides the individual separating the diabolical in him from the divine."

Thence also the paradox which makes the simple, human love of man and maid, parent and child, brother and sister, friend and friend, so all-important and yet potentially so dangerous. As the Apostle points out, we cannot love God whom we have not seen unless we love the brother whom we have seen. And how shall we love the brothers whom we do not see at all, or seldom, save as we love the brothers whom we do see, those persons to whom we are close enough so that we do indeed at moments "see" them, them and not some image that they put on or we put over their faces, and so that we do indeed become united with them, spirit embracing spirit? We are limited creatures and love cannot deal with abstractions. Therefore, we apprehend God always in His incarnations and we learn and experience intensity of involvement, which is of the essence of love, in concrete instances. It is also in daily serving those whom we thus love, and only in this way, that we become truly sensitive to human need at a more than superficial level and learn to deal with wider circles of contact and social problems on another basis than the impersonal and mechanical which characterizes so much social work. But this suggests at once that the intenser loves we experience in the family or elsewhere cease to be love when they make us less eager and less skillful, instead of more, to love other beings, all other men, and to seek their good. These loves must be of such a character that they can daily, hourly be offered as a pure sacrifice to God. Otherwise it is literally better to "hate father, mother, wife, child," or our own country, i.e., to recognize that we are indeed hating, corrupting, injuring the very ones we think we love most and our own selves, when we come to think of love as the thing which shuts in rather than opens up, as that which makes us center upon ourselves rather than upon God and all His children.

On the other hand, I do not believe that the command to love all men, even our enemies, even the most unlovely, means simply that we are to have, quite unemotionally, what is sometimes called a constructive attitude toward them, that we are to refrain from injuring them. Rather, in the degree that is possible, there must enter into every relationship something of that emotional intensity, that free flowing of spirit toward spirit, which gives depth and rapture to our most intimate relationships. Where this does not take place, in its measure we are dealing with a fellow human not as truly a human being but as a thing, an object; dealing not with a living soul but with an image of a person. To one whom we do not in a real sense love we are not yet according human dignity; and that is the great, original sin and the most potent source of evil in the world.

The human race being what it is, men long, often much more deeply than they are aware, for fellowship. Furthermore, there is more of it in the world than they usually realize. It is well to dwell on this for a moment because we are very likely in this age of vast mechanisms and big noises and atomic bombs to lose sight completely of what is genuinely important and what it is that holds human society together. Gandhi once made a seemingly elementary but very profound observation: "If the story of the universe had commenced with wars, not a man would have been found alive today. : . . The fact that there are so many men still alive in the world shows that it is based not on force of arms but on the force of truth or love."

We had occasion some time back to observe that the mighty armies and the armadas of sea and air would fall apart if the mind of the scientist and technician were withdrawn. Paradoxically and tragically enough, the wars can go on because there is always so much at work in the world of that spirit which is the exact opposite of them. Even during war that spirit is at work and when the tumult and the shouting dies, as it always does, the work which is inspired by that spirit is resumed. Through all the centuries of man's existence on earth it has held the human family, the foundation of social existence, together, and not with a sword or a gun. The patient and so beautiful labor of men and women, year after year, century after century, as they plow the land and sow the seed and reap the harvest; as they grind the wheat and bake the bread and spin the thread and weave the cloth; as they build their houses and schools and the temples in which they commune with God—all this is born of that spirit of love, that central force which draws men ever together, which makes it so hard to keep them from fraternizing when they are not supposed to. This is the most pervasive and potent and permanent fact of life and history. In the degree that it is lacking anywhere, things fall to pieces.

Even American business, in so far as it is truly "efficient," has to build on it! Some years ago a learned study was made by experts connected with the Harvard School of Business Administration. Several books were at one time and another written about it, perhaps the most important *Leadership in a Free Society,* by T. N. Whitehead, which is in parts remarkably pertinent to the subject we are discussing in this book.

An experiment in making production more efficient had been begun by a great manufacturing corporation. The workers involved had to a considerable extent been drawn into participation. When the usual things were done to improve lighting, temperature and seating, to introduce rest periods and other such devices, production went up as had been expected. But when poorer facilities were introduced to check the findings, the expected lowering of production did not result. It was discovered that the real basis for increased efficiency was that the workers had been drawn into real participation, had been treated as sentient human beings. Further confirmation was provided when interviewers were appointed to whom the workers might report their grievances. The interviewers had been instructed, however, to let the workers talk about anything they wanted to. What they talked about were their personal and family problems. Father confessors were what they had really needed. In an urban, big-industry situation they had been starved for human contact and so they were inefficient. In his own language the professor states:

Much of the difficulty in leading groups of industrial workers springs in the first place from a social poverty in their working-relations. . . . There can be no question of maintaining an employee force as isolated individuals. . . . Change to be acceptable to a group must come from within, and must appear as the visible need of its own activities. Change imposed from without is a disaster, comparable to an earthquake breaking in. . . . It presents itself not as a sensible adaptation to a visible situation, but as a blow from management wrapped up in a tissue of unanswerable logic. The better the logic the more irritating the blow.

In that last sentence we have in nine words the reason for the failure of all the good ideas, the correct solutions, the magnificent programs, the "goodness," the "sacrifices," which are rooted in self-righteousness, which see human beings as things to be manipulated from without instead of as persons who can only act from within and who must be loved—with whom, that is to say, one must associate as essential equals whose self-realization is precisely as important as one's own.

One or two other observations are necessary in order to carry this very inadequate outline of the implications of the personalist, pacifist philosophy to its conclusion. For one thing, no human being is excluded from the circle. No one can declare himself out, can escape the moral order and responsible participation in it. But neither can anyone else declare him out and treat him as if he were not a human being to be respected and loved. In the family all "belong." So in the human family. The individual as individual does not choose his brothers and sisters in either case. But they are there and he is there; he is his brother's keeper and his brothers are his keepers. That is in the everlasting nature of things.

The reasons given for refusing to love another, treating him as a thing and not a person, are never sufficient. Rightly understood, they are indeed reasons why he should be more truly and wisely loved. If a man is unworthy and does not rightly play his part, has the family, the society, in which he was brought up no responsibility for this? How then can it escape from helping him to bear that burden and eventually to cast it off? We fail to solve problems, personal and social, and then we must have a scapegoat. That is illustrated in the elementary fact so often observed that the thing we most often criticize in others is our own failing. We do not want to see it in ourselves, so we see it or imagine it in the other person. A society does not know how to put its unemployed to work at peaceful occupations, so it makes itself believe that the Jews are to blame. A society based on greed, competition and strife makes scapegoats in its prisons of those who insist on introducing unconventional variations upon the accepted social pattern. Probably in some degree, and often in a high degree, hate of another is self-hate which we refuse to face honestly; punishment of another is self-punishment from which we shrink. The law, "Thou shalt love thy neighbor as thyself," has the inevitable though seldom realized consequence that if you will not love him as yourself, you will hate him as you hate yourself.

This is not to say that other men are not hateful and aggressive, sometimes outrageously so. But again, as the psychologists have demonstrated, that aggression is the result of love denied or frustrated, very likely in infancy and childhood. Those who hate are those who were unwanted, i.e., hated. Those who hurt are those who were hurt. Those who hurt terribly and irrationally are those who were irrationally and terribly hurt. They do not thereby escape moral responsibility. That we have emphasized more than once. But neither do we escape moral responsibility for them. They are still brothers and sisters, members of the family. They may be considered ill and treated as such, provided we who undertake to treat them are aware of our own illness and are paying the price of mental and spiritual health. But to hate and hurt those who are what they are because they have been hated and hurt will not solve anything. It will intensify the evil.

Force in the ordinary sense of the term, violence, is on this account ruled out of transactions in the realm of moral, i.e., human, life. To do violence to others is to treat them as objects, things, to be manipulated from without, perhaps even to be chopped in pieces or shot to bits, instead of as persons who can only be moved from within, i.e., in the last analysis by love. Furthermore, the one who uses violence also becomes a thing and ceases to behave as a sensitive, responsible person dealing with his brother, his equal.

This immensely important consideration I have never seen more convincingly and poignantly stated than by Simone Weil in that essay on the Iliad upon which we have already drawn. Force, she says, may be defined as "that X that turns anybody who is subjected to it into a thing. Exercised to the limit, it turns man into a thing in the most literal sense: it makes a corpse out of him. Somebody was here, and the next minute there is nobody here at all." Then she points out that the threat of force, the presence of force in a situation, has the same effect: "The force that does not kill, i.e. that does not kill just yet." It has "the ability to turn a human being into a thing while he is still alive. He is alive; he has a soul; and yet—he is a thing. An extraordinary entity this —a thing that has a soul. . . . It was not made to live inside a thing."

But "force is as pitiless to the man who possesses it, or thinks he does, as it is to its victims; the second it crushes, the first it intoxicates. The truth is, nobody really possesses it." Those who have force, therefore, inevitably "exceed the measure of the force that is actually at their disposal . . . suddenly things cease to obey them. . . . Such is the nature of force. . . . To the same degree, though in different fashions, those who use it and those who endure it are turned to stone. . . . Battles are fought and decided by men . . . who have dropped either to the level of inert matter, which is pure passivity, or to the level of blind force, which is pure momentum." Miss Weil calls attention to the fact that Homer reached the same conclusion as Jesus after him: "Ares is just, and kills those who kill."

Thence the deceptiveness of that seemingly plausible escape from reality which at every new crisis tempts men: "Very well, we did the wrong thing with this individual or this nation, a year, five, ten years ago; and if then we had done otherwise, this evil would not have arisen. But now, now—now when we are confronted with the fruits of our sin, our failure to be just and to love—what can we do but beat this monster down by violence and war, monstrous as these are?" But as Miss Weil points out and as those who have eyes to see have witnessed twice in one generation, war and violence have their own logic. By treating men as things and then carrying that treatment to its utmost conclusion, we do not make men out of them again, nor do we ourselves become men. Somehow the vicious circle must simply be broken into, and the risks of that course must be accepted.

Chapter V

The Man on the Cross Against the Atomic Bomb

What, then, is the ultimate risk involved in refusing to resort to violence, to try to cast out Satan by Satan, to do evil that good may come? This brings us to the final consideration which we must face, the profoundest mystery of human life and the moral universe.

In the play *Jakobowski and the Colonel,* Jakobowski, the refugee, says to a Nazi engaged in tormenting certain victims: "There is one advantage the hunted has over the hunter—that he never becomes the hunter." The inference is that the victim has an overpowering, an infinite advantage over his tormentor. He is the fortunate one of the two. He is blessed. He is to be envied.

This is the implication of what we have been saying about the moral order, and conscience, and the nature of man and the universe. The moral order either does not exist at all, or it is the supreme good, the ultimate value, for the sake of which men will gladly "count all things but loss." All human beings are creations of spirit and equal before God, or else none is. We are all of us parts of a spiritual unity, bound together so that what happens to any, happens to me, or there is no unity. The maintenance of that unity by love in every moment, to every person, is either the ultimate good or it is sheer illusion.

When a man suffers cold, hunger, thirst, injustice, imprisonment, slavery, humiliation, it is a terrible thing. But it is literally as nothing compared to what has happened to him when he has done a wrong, when he has treated another human being as a thing instead of a person, when he has injured another or been lacking in love and fellow-

ship toward him, when he has failed even to the extent of withholding
a cup of cold water. Men can suffer and still be beings of moral dignity
and worth. They can suffer, and the moral universe, the fellowship of
spirits, still holds together. But when a man violates conscience and
inflicts injury on another, then the moral universe is shattered; a soul
is shattered. In the spiritual realm an atomic explosion has occurred.
It is what a moral being does to himself, within, that constitutes the
incomparable evil. It is this tragedy which has occurred in the spiritual
—the most real—realm that leads to the evil and suffering that happen
to other men and in the outward order. Therefore, also, the evildoer is
the one most to be pitied, most in need of help. Upon him catastrophe
has descended. He has banished himself, though he may not be aware
of it and may even glory in his shame, from the circle of life and
fellowship, and is lost.

Most men pay at least lip service to this idea that the hunted has
the moral advantage—hence the only meaningful advantage—over the
hunter, the victim over his tormentor. But it is a difficult idea for men
to grasp and hold securely. They need to "repent," change their whole
focus on life, in order to see it clearly and hold on to it with the mind
and so practice it. Most of the time most of us are bothered a great
deal more even about little annoyances than about our sins, are much
more afraid of those that kill the body but cannot kill the soul than we
are of "him who is able to destroy both soul and body in hell." That is,
of course, why our moral force is usually so weak. We then go on to
conclude that moral or spiritual force is inherently weak as against
Hitler or the atomic bomb, for example. But perhaps we are all along
aware, somewhere deep within us, that this is a rationalization of our
unwillingness to face ourselves and our true situation.

It is, nevertheless, eternally and unquestionably true that the hunted
has the advantage over the hunter. It is better to suffer than to inflict
suffering, to be deceived than to deceive, to be killed than to kill, to
have atomic bombs dropped on you than to drop them on others.

This is why the greatest religious teachers and saints have virtually
all in one way or another arrived at and preached the doctrine of nonviolence or nonresistance. It is surely remarkable that there is such
unanimity among them on this point. Yet a moment's reflection makes
it clear that it could not possibly have been otherwise.

If the supreme evil and tragedy is indeed not in the realm of the suffering that is endured by men but in the soul of the man who inflicts suffering on another, is in treating another human being as a thing and not as a person and a brother, then the temptation which must at every cost be avoided is the temptation to meet evil with evil, violence with violence.

This is the most insidious and terrible temptation which besets the "good man." He is not inclined to turn hunter and aggressor. He may even submit willingly and cheerfully to injustice and suffering inflicted upon himself. But when it is the innocent Jews who are persecuted, the "defenseless" little nations which are attacked, the cause of democracy and human decency which is threatened, must and may a man then "stand by and do nothing?" Granted that, if he resorts to war or other forms of organized violence in the effort to curb aggressive evil and to save its helpless and innocent victims, he must in turn practice evil and violence, is this not a lesser evil and loss than if no positive effort is made to curb the aggressors? And is not the pacifist who refuses to take up the sword even against Hitler in part responsible for the material and spiritual suffering of Hitler's victims and hence an evildoer in the same way as those who, reluctantly, drop bombs on German cities in order that Nazi domination may be broken?

It is proper and necessary to point out that, whether we assess motives or results, in so far as it is possible to calculate the latter, where complicated issues and conflicts on a global scale are under consideration, the case of those who resort to violence is open to serious criticism.

For example, the pacifist is not the only one who at times and at least to outward appearance stands by and does nothing about injustice and suffering. If, that is to say, going to war about them is the only way to do something. In a world where there are always multitudes who are oppressed and mistreated in the most outrageous fashion, men often feel helpless to take any action that seems at all effective. They are after all not omniscient and omnipotent and are not morally responsible for the ordering of the entire world. Those who have no faith at all recognize that much has to be left to chance. Those who believe in the reality of a moral order and in God know that God is the ruler of the universe, that He has indeed given man a limited and sufficiently awful responsibility, but that beyond that limit men do well to remember that "the everlasting God, the Lord, the creator of the ends of the earth, fainteth not, neither is weary" and that in the day when "even the youths faint and are weary, and the young men utterly fall, they that wait for the Lord shall renew their strength." When the pacifist says that in certain circumstances he is seemingly helpless, can only "stand by and do nothing," he is in principle doing the same thing that his nonpacifist brother also does in many instances.

In other words, men choose the occasions when evil is so outrageous that they "must" resort to war to stop it; and the motives and occasions which lead to such decisions require more careful scrutiny than is usually given them. As a young minister in 1916, I was taught a lesson in this connection which had a great influence on my subsequent thinking. The Protestant ministers in the section of a suburban city in Massachusetts where I lived were much disturbed by the "Belgian atrocities" which were then allegedly being perpetrated by the Germans. (I leave out of account here the fact that these allegations were later proved largely baseless and in some instances deliberately manufactured by Allied propaganda.) It was agreed that the community should bear its witness against these outrages. Since some of us were pacifists who were opposed to going to war over them whereas others believed that the United States should enter the conflict, it was also agreed that our protest should be so worded that both groups could unite wholeheartedly in the demonstration. I was sent to the rector of the Roman Catholic parish in our community to ask him to participate with his people. He and they were Irish. I told him my story, to which he listened politely. Then he said: "Mr. Muste, have you and your colleagues ever heard of the Irish atrocities?" It was about the time of the "Easter Massacre" in Dublin! I told him, of course, that we had. He then said: "Well, they have been going on for several centuries; and as soon as you and your friends have joined us in a few protest meetings against the Irish atrocities, we shall join you in a meeting to protest the Belgian atrocities."

Our excitement about the Belgian atrocities was not as purely and clearly motivated as I had assumed. It was tied up with ancestral and emotional associations and, to a much greater extent than even the pacifists in the group were aware, with the side we were on in the war. The practice, often unconscious, of a double standard of morality which affects both our ethical and our political analysis constitutes in my opinion one of the basic evils of our age. As Americans and Russians, whites and blacks, Orientals and Occidentals, Catholics and Protestant, left-wingers and right-wingers, we constantly condone or justify in ourselves and those who are on our side what we subject to the severest condemnation when practiced by others. At the moment of writing, it is generally admitted that the Russians are subjecting Germans in territories taken over by Russia and Poland to the most ruthless treatment as they are driven out of their homes. Not only do those who pleaded most vociferously that we must go to war to stop Nazi atrocities not suggest that we go to war against Russia. Many of them become highly excited when the outrages perpetrated by the Russians are so much as mentioned and brand as fascists and warmongers those who do speak of them.

It is especially noteworthy in this connection that for the most part those who demand that we go to war as a nation for a "cause" or to stop suffering inflicted on unfortunates abroad are not equally stirred about the injustices to Negroes or laborers at home and that practically without exception they unequivocally condemn resort to violence on the part of these victims and on behalf of the cause of social or economic emancipation. Here they are sure there is "a better way," and insisting that this better way than violence be found is not condemned as merely standing by and doing nothing. They are sure that resort to violence would be the greater evil in this case. As Randolph Bourne said of certain elements in 1918: "Numbers of intelligent people who had never been stirred by the horrors of capitalistic peace at home were shaken out of their slumber by the horror of wars in Belgium. Never having felt responsibility for labor wars and oppressed masses and excluded races at home, they had a large fund of idle emotional capital to invest in the oppressed nationalities and ravaged villages of Europe." Incidentally, the war expends the "emotional capital" of most participants, and we witness, therefore, after cessation of hostilities, the indifference and self-indulgence which mark such periods, including the one in which we now live. Surely this is another consideration which should lead us to reflect on who they are who "stand by and do nothing" and what it is that produces this attitude in individuals and nations.

Furthermore, it is a sheer illusion that nations go to war when they can no longer stand by and watch injustice or the sufferings of the victims of persecution. The moment when war breaks out is not chosen by those who feel moral indignation. Nations which stand by when democratic Czechoslovakia is raped go to war when reactionary and anti-Semitic Poland is attacked; and having contended that this was necessary in order to put a stop to unilateral action in respect to Poland, they ratify and legalize similar unilateral action in Poland and elsewhere in easter Europe when it is taken by an ally in the war. Moral indignation and the morally indignant are used as tools by those who go to war for amoral or immoral purposes and serve to place a cloak of respectability over the latter. After the war the morally indignant have to stand by for the most part and do nothing while the consequences of the war work themselves out and then they are likely to become pacifists of a sort again!

We have dealt in an earlier chapter with the question whether intervention by the method of war and violence is effective in stopping war and violence and achieving the results which its idealistic defenders strive and hope for, and we shall not attempt here to adduce further proof of the self-defeating character of this method. With reference to the specific ethical problem under consideration at the moment, we may make this further observation. What the pacifist does in certain situations in which others resort to violence is often in our opinion more effective than nonpacifists may be willing to admit. We grant, however, that there are times when he may be likened to a man who stands by helpless when his own or his neighbor's house goes up in flames because there is no water or other means of extinguishing the fire to be had. If his neighbors at that juncture discover a lot of gasoline and begin throwing it on the fire, we think he is rational and behaving as a responsible moral being when he chooses to stand by and let the fire burn itself out rather than join in adding fuel to the flames.

We have also pointed out previously how the United States, in resorting to war in order to put a stop to Nazi and Japanese militarist atrocities, itself descended to the lowest depths of atrocious conduct and left itself and the rest of the world with no moral or other defenses against the illimitable atrocities of the atomic war of the future. That is the logic of resort to atrocious means even with the best intentions. Since writing those earlier observations we have come upon a striking confirmation of them from an unusually authoritative source in an article in the February, 1946, issue of the *Atlantic Monthly* entitled "One War Is Enough." The author, Edgar L. Jones, saw forty months of war duty, much of it in the front lines, as an ambulance man and later witnessed the fighting in the Pacific as a special correspondent for the *Atlantic Monthly*. He says: "What kind of war do civilians suppose we fought anyway? We shot prisoners in cold blood, wiped out hospitals, strafed life-boats, killed or mistreated enemy civilians, finished off the enemy wounded, tossed the dying into a hole with the dead, and in the Pacific boiled the flesh off enemy skulls to make table ornaments for sweethearts, or carved their bones into letter openers. We topped off our saturation bombing and burning of enemy civilians by dropping atomic bombs on two nearly defenceless cities, thereby setting an all-time record for instantaneous mass slaughter."

Since war in the future will necessarily be atomic or "super-atomic" war and more diabolical than anything we have yet seen, it might seem that our argument could rest here, since it may well appear inconceivable that any moral justification can be found for such irrational and indiscriminate slaughter. But, alas, this is not the case. Unless we abolish war altogether, those who do not undergo a spiritual revolution will, after a period of protesting that atomic war "simply must not be," find a moral justification, or more accurately excuse, for engaging in it—always, of course, on the right side, "our" side. Those on the other side will be devils incarnate. Furthermore, there are other forms of violence than international war. And we are now at the very heart of the moral issue we started to explore and must grapple with it.

When men and nations resort once more to violence in order to overcome or limit violence, all the rationalizations and miscalculations of which we have spoken will enter into their thinking and their decisions. Our nonpacifist friends are under moral obligation to take this into account; and this applies particularly to nonpacifist Christians who must disregard or "interpret" so much in the New Testament—so much that is, furthermore, at the very heart of the Gospels and Epistles

—when they take up the sword which the Lord told Peter to "put up into its place." But the behavior of our nonpacifist brethren cannot be altogether accounted for as the result of thinking which can be safely dismissed as coming under the head of rationalization and miscalculation. They take up the sword because they feel that they cannot stand by and see the weak and innocent struck down and that, if they were to do so, they would lose their moral integrity and violate the command of their Master as it comes to them. If they have to face the risks which their course involves, pacifists have also to attempt a final reckoning with the possibility that they are accomplices in the suffering, material and spiritual, of the weak and innocent, that they fail to advance the Kingdom of God on earth in the only practical and possible way that is open to men in a given situation. In other words, can pacifists guarantee success if individuals and nations try their way?

All the greatest religious teachers and saints, as we have pointed out, are in some form expounders of nonviolence or nonresistance as the methodology of love in both personal and social relationships. They are also—and as we shall see presently, necessarily—expounders of the law of suffering and crucifixion. They are people who confess, and in a sense glory in, weakness and failure.

There is a kind of pacifist who thinks that if only men will meet evil-doers, the Hitlers, for example, with kindness and gentleness and a smile, we shall quickly convert them, atrocities will soon stop and all will be well. We do not live in such an idyllic world. Those who go to war take terrible risks, risks which in my opinion cannot be justified on any basis. But those who will not meet violence with violence also take risks. For the good of their souls they must realize this and must not hesitate to admit it to others. It may be that the innocent, or at least the relatively innocent, will perish. Multitudes may be subjected to suffering. But the religious pacifist in the final awful showdown takes his stand on his interpretation of the essential nature of the moral life, his evaluation of what is essentially and supremely evil. The hunted has an incalculable advantage over the hunter. Never, whatever the provocation may be, must one add to the essential evil in the world by himself hunting, hurting, killing another human being. We cannot, except in a very small degree, control the world and determine the course of history. The amount of suffering on earth is also in only a limited degree subject to our determination. But there is one thing that is absolutely within the control of each of us, namely, his own moral decisions and acts. I can refuse to add positively to the hurting and the violence in the world. I can in face of all that comes strive to love, to reconcile, to heal. I can act on the maxim that it would be terrible for the American people to be wiped out by atomic bombs but far, far more terrible for the American people to wipe out another people by atomic bombs—even though America's refusal to do the latter might subject it to the risk of suffering the former.

It seems to me beyond a shadow of doubt that Jesus faced this dilemma that love and nonviolence may fail, fail utterly and horribly. I cannot but believe that it was his wrestling with that awful problem that wrung the bloody sweat from his brow in Gethsemane and from his lips the cry: "Father, if it be possible, let *this* cup pass from me." What cup? He had been certain that God had called him to liberate his people. He had been certain also of the way he must use, the way of nonviolence and love, love even for the enemy, a way so contrary to the thought and expectation of most of his people. Yet it was God's way: "*Thou* art my son in whom I am well-pleased," not these other Messiahs, nor Caesar. And since it was God's way surely it must succeed. But now it was clear that there would be failure. His people would not heed his call. Rome would go on its way of dictatorship, and of terror for all who would not yield to that dictatorship. Calamity would overtake his people: "There shall not be left here one stone upon another." His disciples would betray and desert him. They would be exposed to danger. He would be killed. The cause would fail. Even now it need not be. There were "ten legions of angels." Even now he could turn the tables on his enemies. But that would mean turning upon his hunters and in the name of the hunted, of righteousness, of God and His Kingdom, becoming a hunter. This he could not do without violating his deepest conviction, denying himself, denying the Father who had been revealed to him in the deepest hours of his life since boyhood, the God who did not requite evil for evil, who made His sun to shine on the evil and the good, who would have sons, not subjects and servants. Whatever might betide, in the face of utter failure and the imminent triumph of the satanic powers, he would not relinquish that conviction, deny this God of love. He would stand by—helpless, despised—and let the blows fall on him and on the cause. He would die and fail. "Father, if it is be possible, let this cup pass from me. Nevertheless, not my will but thine be done."

We suggested a moment ago that the expounders and practitioners of nonviolence are "necessarily" also expounders and practitioners of the law of weakness, suffering and crucifixion. There are at least two basic reasons for this, both of them repeatedly set forth in the New Testament and especially by Jesus himself.

In the first place, in a world of moral beings made to live in a community of those who know that each must find his good in the welfare of the others, but in whose midst disruption has entered, where men have sought to deny the truth of their being by turning to hinder and hurt others, the supreme need is a love that insists the community must not be broken, that insists no one must be permitted to banish himself from it. Under these circumstances, the love which embraces only the worthy and the lovely is obviously a poor, inadequate thing. It is not worthy of the name of love at all. All the great religious teachers have said that, too, in their various tongues. If ye love them that love you, do good to your benefactors, what reward have ye? Do not even those you esteem least do that? The love of God for man is always love for the unworthy and undeserving. Forgiveness is primary and essential in it. "While we were yet sinners, Christ died for us."

It is these sinners who have suffered the greatest calamity in causing their brothers to suffer. If there can be said to be degrees in love at all, it is these who have sinned rather than those who have been sinned against who must be pitied and loved the most. They, in the language of religious symbolism, are in danger of eternal damnation. They must be cleansed, restored to the family of God.

The fact that in a universe governed by moral law a sinner suffers the inexorable consequences of ignoring or defying reality does not solve the problem. He may be driven to greater excesses or to despair. Alternatively he may strive by prudential behavior to avoid unpleasant consequences. Since freedom is of the essence of the moral life and the universe is built to permit the exercise of such freedom, a man may in considerable measure "get by" with such prudential behavior, by being discreet when the police are watching him. But in none of these

ways can a truly human society, a family, a community of love, be built
or restored.

The sinner must freely, from within, choose to renounce his sin and
he must be assured that forgiveness is available, that there is a community of love to which he can be restored. This can happen only if
there is exerted a love that cannot be provoked or transformed into
indifference or hate by evil, a love great enough to hold on to and
draw back the unlovely, those who in no sense merit love.

Since the use of violence is excluded, since the evildoer encounters
no "resistance" in the conventional sense of the term but is given
freedom to choose the evil and to visit its consequences not only upon
himself but upon others, the God of love, the Father in heaven, inevitably appears weak, rather foolish and not altogether fair. See the
Parable of the Prodigal Son and the Sermon on the Mount. God
makes His sun to shine and His rain to fall on the just and the unjust
alike. Prudential morality and religion are not the same thing at all.

If God will not make the evildoer to suffer, the evildoer will mock
God and make Him suffer. If God keeps on loving in the face of
rejection and evil and sin, He must suffer. The concept of God as weak
and foolish and enduring contempt and suffering, of God as represented not by power but precisely by the renunciation of power, is in
one way so difficult to accept, seems indeed so sacrilegious, that men
constantly try to find formulations which may enable them to avoid a
complete acceptance of it. God Himself does not suffer, they try to
make out, but He "so loved the world that he gave his only begotten
son." But then they have to turn around at once and say that if you
want to know God you must know and believe in "Jesus Christ and
him crucified. . . . God was in Christ." For Christians certainly there
is no escape: God is the Father and His children carve the Cross on
His heart.

This brings us to the second reason why the practitioner of nonviolence is "necessarily" the victim of crucifixion and the exponent of
failure. He has to be true to the inner nature of the love and nonviolence to which he has committed himself, he must follow out its
logic to the end, even though that spells defeat, even though it nails
him, "forsaken of God," to the Cross.

Those who, however reluctantly, resort to violence are also bound by the inner nature of the weapon they employ. Material or physical force finds its ultimate expression in the power to kill, to destroy the adversary. If you resort to violence, then you have to be prepared, if it is required for the accomplishment of the end in view, to kill. Otherwise you are bluffing, and your bluff will be called. War, as we have seen, has its own logic. It becomes ever more destructive and indiscriminate. But that does not deter men, except those who renounce war unequivocally, from engaging in it. The next war or its successor will probably bring Western civilization to an end, and with it the American republic. It may quite possibly mean the annihilation of the human race. The American government is, nevertheless, devoting itself wholeheartedly to preparation for this war. There will also be churches to bless it in the name of Christ, if not explicitly, then by way of giving their members to understand that it is right and necessary to engage in atomic war—but "penitently."

If the ultimate expression of violence is killing the opponent, the "aggressor," the ultimate expression of nonviolence or soul force is quite as obviously the willingness and ability to die at the hands and on behalf of the evildoer. The pacifist must be ready to pay that price. If he is not willing to go that far, he is bluffing, and his bluff will be called. Until men are willing to pay for the way of peace something like what they pay for war, they do not truly want peace and they certainly will not get it.

The suffering need not be sought. Indeed it must not be. Martyrdom for the sake of martyrdom is suicide by exhibitionism, not redemptive crucifixion. But we may not seek to evade suffering. It must be voluntarily accepted. The son must trust the Father, though He forsakes and slays him. He must do the Father's will, though that means drinking the cup of defeat and failure. Love must seek no return. Its ultimate vindication, the seal that it is indeed divine love, will be that, no matter what the suffering imposed upon it by evildoers, it will not resort to violence and hate in turn. It must be willing to accept death on behalf of evildoers and in the hour of death love them and pray for their forgiveness. That price may in fact be exacted.

When such love is manifested, then the paradox at the heart of the universe is revealed and the miracle which transforms men and history takes place. Out of weakness comes strength; out of defeat comes victory. Out of death springs life. When love is confronted by evil in its most irrational and inexcusable form—evil that would crucify even Jesus—and triumphs because it will not alter its nature, because it insists on loving still and forgiving, because it asks no boon at all from God, no "well-deserved" victory, then God himself in His inmost being stands revealed. Then God has entered into history and its course has been forever changed. Here is released the power which in the political and social realm is the counterpart of the fission of the atom and the release of atomic energy in its realm. If the Christian religion means anything, it means this. If the experience of mankind has taught anything, it teaches this.

It is not—be it noted once more so that there may be no mistake—that God can be inveigled into making a bargain: love, refrain from violence, pretend to be willing to sacrifice, and peace and comfort and well-being will be yours. Nothing is guaranteed. The element of risk and cost cannot be removed from the life of men or nations. The nation which goes to war has no guarantee of victory. The strong man fully armed guarding his court may suddenly be confronted by one stronger than he who overcomes him and takes from him his whole armor wherein he trusted and divides the spoils. God will not make a bargain with the nonviolent either. Pacifism cannot guarantee a cheap and painless solution. Life is dynamic and unpredictable. We have to make the leap of faith. We have to risk failure and stark defeat. The Cross is central.

Yet the other side of the paradox is also there. God is not a hard taskmaster or a vindictive sovereign. The universe is a universe of law. They that take the sword shall perish by the sword. And on the other hand, "The work of righteousness shall be peace; and the effect of righteousness, quietness and confidence forever." The ordinances of God are true and righteous altogether, and in keeping them there is great reward. Love is the law of life, not of death. If the price of death be exacted of those who follow the way of love and nonviolence as it is exacted of those who take the sword, the former have still chosen by far the better part, for in crucifixion there is redemptive power; suicide whether of men or of nations is sterile.

Thus, in the end, "The individual conscience against the atomic

bomb? Yes. There is no other way" becomes, "A dead man on a cross
against the atomic bomb? Yes. There is no other way." The atomic
bomb is the symbol of the power to destroy and kill raised to demonic
proportions. What shall be set over against it? What shall overcome
it? A still greater power to destroy and kill? Obviously, there is nought
but still more awful destruction in that. In this extremity, is it not at
last clear that our sole alternative is the love that absolutely refuses to
destroy, will not be tempted to violence and is able and willing to die
in order that the diabolical chain of evil linked to evil may be broken?

The awe-inspiring and destructive explosion of the atom is the symbol and the result of the far more terrible disruption which has taken
place within the human being and within the family of man. It may
serve as a warning and a prophecy of the far more catastrophic moral
and social disruption which may yet take place. It may serve to remind
us, also, of how mighty and how different must be the force which over
against these disruptive elements will hold the society of mankind and
the universe together. It may serve to convince us that now, when man
has laid his brain and hand upon the secrets of the physical universe
and thus has unleashed the forces which may wipe out mankind and
perhaps even shatter its earthly home, we must at last devote ourselves
with all the energy we have to searching out the nature of the moral
and spiritual universe and that we must, with the passion, single-
mindedness and humility of the scientist and with the patience and
ingenuity of the technologist, learn to lay hold upon those forces
which can stay the disruptive elements confronting us and can hold
the society of mankind and the universe together.

Obviously our age has not yet penetrated to that burning inner core
of the spiritual universe where reside those silent and almighty energies
which can control the atom and the suns and use them for good and
not for evil. We still meddle, fussily and distractedly by turns, with
time-worn devices, shabby political tricks, the old false or partial solutions that have not availed to ward off disaster. We know that the
energies we now have in ourselves and in our national and other social
groups are utterly insufficient. We dare not go on thus, repeating the
past.

At its central core, the universe is love. As love is the source of creation and joy in the human spirit and in all human life, so is it the source of the infinite creativeness and of all beauty in the universe. As it is love that gives to the human soul whatever unity and direction it has, as it is fellowship by which all the societies of men are bound together, so is the whole universe bound together by love.

This is the truth about the spiritual realm. God is; and God is Father, is love. In love He created us. We cannot escape from our own nature any more than a man can jump out of his own skin; therefore we cannot escape the demands of conscience and of love. Therefore, also, we cannot escape the consequences of our denial of love, our refusal to be good. Nor can we destroy God. Hence we cannot change the essential character of the universe or defeat His purpose. But on the other hand, God will not force Himself upon us. Love will win its kingdom "by entreaty and not with contention." God is He whom we can despise and insult. We can waste our substance which He has given us in riotous living. He will wait. He will love. He will suffer crucifixion. He will not compel. He will still be the God "who forgiveth all thine iniquities; who healeth all thy diseases." That is why you live. That is why in spite of all disruptive forces mankind lives. That is the tremendous force which holds the atoms and the suns together.

In the nature of the case, this cannot be proved by intellectual demonstration. That conscience is a response to a moral order you can prove only by making moral decisions and acting conscientiously. If God is indeed love, then you can apprehend Him only by loving Him and His creatures. If He is the power which binds all life into unity, you find Him only if you abide in that unity and do not seek to live in any sense for yourself.

Thus responsibility falls again on the individual, on the person endowed with moral responsibility. "The bell tolls for thee." The fate of mankind rests upon each of us, far more than upon any organization or institution.

As we have pointed out, we have to make the venture of faith. Evil will not overcome evil; violence will not destroy violence. Only by good, by love, can evil be overcome and the world redeemed. We are given no guarantees in advance if we love. We may have to see evil unconquered. We may be simply crucified. Love will not falter or alter because of that. It is simply its nature to love, to give, not to demand, not to bargain.

Yet, paradoxically, in the degree that we give ourselves unreservedly to God and to the love of our fellows because of Him, we know indubitably that we have laid hold on infinite power as well as love. Nothing will defeat us. If we are killed in the service of love, we know that all the more power will be released.

We have spoken of the Puritans and of how a new day dawns and a new order comes into being when men apprehend new moral truth and serve it with complete integrity and devotion. But that is nothing compared to the change which takes place in human life when men come to know God as love and loving Him love their fellows. There was a little company of Christians in the days when the Roman emperor ruled over "the inhabited world." They were unarmed. They "resisted not evil." They adored as Lord one Jesus of Nazareth who had died on a cross. One of their leaders was a man named Paul. He had but recently been one of their fiercest persecutors. Recently he had stood by "consenting" when a young Christian named Stephen was stoned. Stephen had died "crying with a loud voice, Lord, lay not this sin to their charge." Paul when he himself joined the little company expressed their strongest conviction in the words, "Love beareth all things, believeth all things, hopeth all things, endureth all things. Love never faileth."

Their outlook on life and the future he expressed in the same document in these words: "We preach Christ crucified, unto Jews a stumbling-block and unto Gentiles foolishness; but unto them that are called both Jews and Greeks, Christ the power of God and the wisdom of God."

What the Jews saw in that day was the mighty Roman Empire which had conquered and humiliated them. That to them represented power, reality. And over against that when they listened to the Christian preachers they saw only a dead man on a cross, completely discredited at the early age of thirty-three, rejected by the rulers of his people because he would not stop exposing their hypocrisies and rejected by the masses because he would not deliver them in the only way that to them seemed practical. He might indeed have been a great national hero, perhaps even Messiah: "Let him now come down from the Cross and we will believe on him." But he would not save himself and his cause by "practical" measures. And that to the Jews was a stumbling block. What the Greeks saw was also this Roman Empire and its culture, so much of which Rome owed to their own tradition; and that was wisdom. Over against that they, too, saw a dead man on a cross: that to the Greeks was foolishness.

What the Jews and the Greeks and the Romans heard in those days were the disputations in the great universities, and the clank of the money on the exchanges, and the laughter in the palaces and the night clubs, and above all—above all—the steady tramp of the Roman soldiers on every road of that world. That surely was real; that was power. Over against that they did not hear Jesus at all, because of course he was dead. They did not hear his disciples, a discredited little sect of Jewish fanatics.

But what Paul and the early Christians saw was nothing of that sort at all. They saw the great empire tottering and falling. It was built on rotten foundations, not according to the specifications of their Lord. It could not possibly endure. And on the other hand, they saw that crucified Lord "high and lifted up, seated at the right hand of power." He was Lord, not Caesar in Rome yonder. What they heard was not the disputations in the universities, the clank of money on the exchanges, the laughter in the palaces, even the tramp of the Roman soldiery. All that, for them, was already silent in the dust of history. What they did hear were the angelic hosts and the ages to come shouting: "Crown him with many crowns, the Lamb upon his throne." And they were right. They understood the nature of power and they discerned the future.

It seems foolish today that what we have to place against the atomic bomb is conscience and love. But we have to get away from the wisdom and realism which have brought us where we are, very far away from them and very quickly. We have to look in the opposite direction, at that which in its own order is perhaps as invisible to the naked eye, seemingly as devoid of power, as the atom. In the presence of the forces which have been released from the atom and all the material power that is displayed in our time, we must try to understand the profound truth of Paul's observation that God—who seemingly can be so easily overlooked—"chose the foolish things of the world that he might put to shame them that are wise; and God chose the weak things that he might put to shame them that are strong; . . . yea, and the things that are not that he might bring to nought the things that are."

We must try to understand the profound wisdom of the early Church, which discerned "the *Lamb* in the midst of the *throne*." The Lamb, symbol of meekness, of gentleness, of seeming utter helplessness in the face of evil, of suffering love, which is at the heart of all real power and the secret of every final victory.

Chapter VI

Moral Man and Immoral Society

There is, if I understand the situation, no considerable or weighty body of opinion—certainly not in Christian circles—which denies that the individual in his relations with other individuals ought to live according to the law of love which we have been examining. It is generally agreed that it is such love, imperfect though it may be, and not a club or a gun, which holds a good home, the basis of all stable society, together. But there is a persistent questioning as to whether this law can and should be applied also in the larger social relationships. Is the nation, for example, also commanded to love? Does the idea make any sense in this connection? Is the law of the nation's survival also set forth in the saying that he who would find his life must lose it? Before we are ready to grapple with the question as to whether the United States is in any sense called upon to fill the role of a "savior-nation," and what that would mean in terms of national policy, we need to make some theoretical and general comments on this problem of "moral man and immoral society."

In the first place, the notion that there is or can be one law for the individual and another for society, one for the Israelite and another for Israel, seems to me to find no support whatever in the Jewish-Christian Scriptures. It is entirely out of harmony with the prophetic world view, which rules out also a dualism between political and religious behavior. The prophets address the nation or the community quite as much as the individual. The nation has sinned, the nation is called to repentance. The nation must become the Suffering Servant of Jehovah by whose stripes other nations are healed and brought back to the One God. Jesus stands squarely in this tradition.

I dealt at some length with this interpretation of prophetic faith in an earlier work, *Non-Violence in an Aggressive World,* and I venture to urge the reader who is interested in the matter to read the relevant sections in that book and especially the chapter entitled "The Cross in History." Suffice it here to refer to two significant recent statements of the same interpretation, the first by an internationally known Jewish writer, Waldo Frank, and the second by a well-known nonpacifist Christian publicist, Dr. Dwight Bradley. In the *Contemporary Jewish Record,* February, 1944, Mr. Frank briefly summarizes a position, essentially a pacifist one, which is more extensively set forth in his book, *The Jew in Our Day.* The article referred to is entitled "The Jew in Our Day: Preface to a Program." Mr. Frank refers to the Hitlerian charge that the Jews have been guilty of a great conspiracy and accepts the indictment: "The lines of this great conspiracy are drawn in the Old Testament. By the seed of Abraham all men are to attain unto the knowledge of God and of their brotherhood. The prophets had no other theme. Within it Jesus preached."

This means that "in every crisis of modern life, under his Covenant with God, to serve truth, love mercy and do justice, the Jew must be ready to die, the Jew must know enough to die: even to die in his son and in his seed—in order that Israel may live. No natural law has been more ruthlessly, more objectively tested by experience. Organic knowledge is action. Man cannot organically know the good and do evil. What he does is the physiology of his knowledge. This—this alone, explains Israel's survival."

Mr. Frank then goes on to stress the point that we are dealing here with social, communal laws and with the conditions of national survival: "Individual wisdom lived in many ancient lands: India, Egypt, China, Greece. The supreme original contribution of the Hebrews was to communize wisdom, first to their own, then to all the peoples. Within this social consciousness of the Jews matured the first *whole* person." He uses a very pregnant and illuminating phrase in describing the nature of the prophetic social consciousness and the goal for human life and history which this implies. This social consciousness is "the *will* to naturalize the earth for the human spirit." The human spirit is not essentially bound to earth and compelled to adapt itself to its laws. Rather is the earth to be "naturalized," adapted to and made the abode for the human spirit. In other words, it is of the essence of prophetic religion that the will of God—not something else or less—should be done on earth, His Kingdom of righteousness and brotherhood made actual in men, but also by and among them, on this earth naturalized for the human spirit.

Parenthetically, far too little attention has been paid in recent years among Christians, and probably for that matter among the Jews themselves, to the strong strains of pacifism in great Jewish teachers building on the vision of the Second Isaiah. This is notably true of that incomparable succession of rabbis—Hillel, Yohanan ben Zakkai and Akiba—who flourished roughly in the first century and a half of the Christian era. The reader is urged to study their teachings and careers in such a book as President Louis Finkelstein's (Jewish Theological Seminary of America) life of *Akiba: Scholar, Saint and Martyr.*

Dr. Bradley's statement occurs in an essay on "Pacifism and Civilization" in the summer of 1941 issue of *Christendom*: "Christianity has been pacifistic from the beginning. Its roots lie in the soil of Judaism which, according to its basic tradition, is committed to non-violence (meekness) as a way of life. . . . The major Hebrew prophets, in contrast with the court preachers and priestly sycophants, kept themselves unpopular because of their insistence that the destiny and duty of Israel was to be an ethical nation whose example and teaching should some day reform and redeem the whole world. . . . It was upon this ancient and well-founded tradition that Christianity took its stand. Jesus personally accepted the role of Suffering Servant which the major prophets had originally assigned to Israel as a whole. . . . By the constant intermingling of pacifistic Christianity with the life of political man in all its institutional forms, that which can rightly be called a Christian civilization is created and re-created. On the other hand, if Christianity is bereft of its pacifism it becomes ethically meaningless and therefore socially valueless."

The familiar argument that Jesus himself recognized two spheres, Caesar's and God's, which has done so much to confuse and corrupt Christian thought and practice ever since the days of Constantine, is neatly and conclusively disposed of in a recent work by the brilliant

English novelist and publicist, Howard Spring. In his autobiographical *And Another Thing* he asks: "Is it certain that there are things of Caesar and things of God, with a comfortable smoke-screen of ·commercial convention and 'business morality' in between? Isn't it a fact that we shall have no rest, no peace till the affairs of Caesar are done in the name and spirit of God?" He speaks of a young parson who had been reprimanded for dragging politics into religion but sees "an unapologetic God dragging religion into politics." [1]

We may state the case in another way without direct reference to the teachings of prophetic religion. The idea that the personal and the social, the life of the human being and the life of his communities, can be separated is without foundation in reason or in the facts of life and history. To say that the nature of the human being is such and such is also to declare that the nature of the society, the nation, in which he lives must be thus and so. The human being, we have said, is a person. He is a being of moral dignity and worth, and subject to the moral law. In the final analysis he is a child of God, the essence of whose being is love. The command to obey the moral law is, therefore, ultimately the command to love; and the deepest need of man's nature is, on the one hand, to obey that command and, on the other, to be sustained by the love of his fellows and of God. But all this is nothing if it is not a description of a free and creative society, of community or fellowship. Man being what he is can only strive to build such a society. It follows also that only in the degree that any given society or nation conforms to this pattern is it able to endure and function, to retain the allegiance and to serve the needs of its members. In the degree that it fails to conform to this pattern and embodies instead tyranny, inequality, hatred, egotism, a society or nation falls to pieces.

We cannot speak correctly of a person behaving in one way as an individual and in a fundamentally different way as a member of society; or in one way in one society—the church, for example—and another way in another society—the nation, let us say. Behavior is simply the functioning of a person in society, in the community of his fellows. The attempt to split a person up into several beings subject

1 Harper & Brothers, publishers. Copyright, 1946, by Howard Spring, pp. 156, 157.

to a variety of moral laws can only result in schizophrenia and in moral disintegration.

In these various attempts to separate the personal and the social, the society or nation is really thought of as an abstraction supposed to exist apart from human beings. But there is no such thing. Economic and political systems, churches and states, are human beings living together in certain relationships. The church or the nation in so far as it can be said to "behave" at all, must behave according to the laws of a moral universe, in conformity with the will of God, or suffer the consequences of its defiance of reality, its attempt to live in a world of its own imagination and self-centered will.

This truth has recently been stated in more exact and academic terms by Professor John Wild of Harvard University in his study of *Plato's Theory of Man.* Paraphrasing Plato's thought he says:

What we mean by 'democracy' today is movement in the direction *away from* tyranny and private opinion—*towards* some society actually integrated, as our present-day 'democracy' only pretends to be, by a common reference to the stable, and therefore superhuman, source of all genuine science and wisdom. If such a society is impossible, then what we mean by 'democracy,' that is, escape from tyranny, is also impossible. If that which is really good does not rule, then man must be subjugated by a class or a mob or an individual. From the tyranny of human opinion and force in its myriad manifestations there is one and only one alternative—theocracy.[2]

As the nature of the person determines the nature of any true society, so the nature of the society or pseudo society which men may build is reflected in the actions and the character of its members. If a nation acts on the animal principle that "self-preservation is the first law of life," that the nation must by any means and at every cost fight for its survival, it is idle to expect that the citizens or subjects will for their part renounce that principle, live for a goal beyond themselves and for its sake gladly sacrifice their lives. The acts which the nation performs in its brute struggle for survival and domination are all performed by the leaders and the people of the nation; it is inevitable that these actions should affect their dispositions and characters. It is of course true, as the history of all totalitarian regimes demonstrates, that the need of

[2] Italics are Professor Wild's.

human beings for community and fellowship—need for something beyond themselves to live and die for—is so great and basic that, in their anxiety to escape from a regime of atomistic individualism and anarchy in which it is "every man for himself and the devil take the hindmost," men will submit to and even embrace a regime which calls upon them to lose themselves in "the folk" and the state. But they do this in moments of utter frustration and despair. Furthermore, even a totalitarian regime is compelled to pay lip service to the moral law and, even while asserting that the state must at all costs survive and expand and be true only to "the law of its own being," to claim some higher sanction and worth which other, lesser, breeds "ought" to recognize.

This does not, however, enable the people under such a regime—the Germans under the Nazis, for example—to escape the dire psychological effects of their participation in the selfish, militaristic and brutal actions of the regime. They become morally insensitive, tough, increasingly concerned about mere survival, self-centered—unless of course they break with the regime. The result is that in the higher circles of such a regime mutual confidence and genuine devotion to the dictator disappear and that it can maintain its sway over the masses, who conform increasingly to its own principle of naked egotism and brute force, only by an ever increasing use of bribery and terrorism. Disintegration, collapse and death ensue. The law that he who would find his life shall lose it operates in this realm also and cannot be evaded. The power state presently has no power because its citizens no longer respect anything except power. The nation which has survival for its object perishes because its people as individuals lose interest in anything but survival.

Much of our current thinking about international problems is vitiated by the prevailing conception as to what holds society together, what is the source and nature of authority. We think of authority as being primarily and well-nigh exclusively dependent upon instruments of coercion, and of society or the nation as being held together by these. Authority is regarded, as someone has recently put it, as "a beneficent by-product of the hangman's rope, the torturer's rack, the soldier's bayonet, the policeman's club."

This notion of what holds a nation together internally is, I surmise, greatly influenced by the actual character of the nation-state in its relation to other nation-states. Looked at from this vantage point, the thing that impresses the beholder is naked power and belligerency—nation arrayed against nation—and the tremendous instrumentalities of naked power and war, battleships, bombers, submarines, generals, admirals, soldiers and sailors in war paint, atomic bombs and the implements of biological warfare. These surely are the instruments of authority and here we may see its source and inmost nature. From this it seems natural to conclude that the nation is also held together within itself by clubs and guns.

Conversely, this idea that the policeman's club holds the nation together has a tremendous influence on current thinking about international organization. It is assumed that there needs to be first of all a great center of well-armed international authority, "an international police." Before the war collective security was to be achieved by having the good nations band together and act as policemen with so much armed force at their command that they could easily lick the gangster nations if by any chance the latter were not immediately and completely overawed by this display of authority, i.e., force. The limitations of that idea are now fairly generally admitted. There must be, it is agreed, a "genuine" international authority; but it is still commonly thought of as a body equipped with preponderant military force, sole custodian perhaps of the atomic bomb, to enforce the peace on nations which are thought of as not really desiring peace and as constantly on the point of breaking it.

It seems to me very doubtful whether in the realm of political thought there is a more devastatingly harmful approach than this and that there is no hope for peace in our time unless we can focus on the problem in an entirely different way.

A moment's reflection should make it clear that an army and a police force, war and the exercise of police power, cannot be equated. There may be a sense in which it is not possible to draw a clear line between the various gradations in the use of force from its slightest manifestation up to the wiping out of human life on earth in an atomic war. The scientists assure us there are no clear lines either between organic and inorganic matter or between the various forms of animal life from the amoeba to the elephant. In the world of reality there are real dis-

tinctions all the same, which we take into account and do well to take
into account. As such political scientists as Hamilton, Madison and
others of the Founding Fathers pointed out long ago, when we get
away from any notion of making political entities—states—keep the
peace by the armed force of a central organization and get down to the
exercise of police force on individuals, if at all, we shall be in a position
to establish international authority, or federal world government, but
not before.

Furthermore, a little reflection on the part of any moderately intelligent person will make it apparent that to think of the policeman or
the F.B.I. as the force which holds the United States of America or
American society together is, to put it in the most conservative terms,
to exaggerate the role of these officials. Every American knows how
few the police are compared to the population and how ridiculous they
make themselves when they try to enforce an unpopular law.

What holds a society together, then, as we have already seen, is that
it conforms to human and social reality, i.e., to the moral law. Both in
a material and in a spiritual sense it offers men that "community" or
free association which makes life meaningful and satisfying to them.
It is the degree of justice which is embodied in any organization which
measures its stability.

To quote Mr. Joseph M. Lalley on the point, "Far from being
primarily dependent upon the instruments of coercion, real authority
has its origin in a super-rational process of assent. . . . It is the creation of the collective imagination and of a general faith." To say that
what holds the American nation together is the "American Dream"
is to come infinitely closer to the truth than to say that it is police
headquarters, the county jail and the federal penitentiary. The basis of
the authority vested in the state is not so different from the authority
vested in the scientist, the administrator, the virtuous man, the head
of the family or the saint, as is commonly supposed. In each case
fidelity to an order of reality, a law of the universe, is basic. The more
force and violence there are in a society the less community there is
and the more certainly the society in question is either on an extremely
primitive level or on the way to breaking up.

It is often argued by those who recognize that coercion and violence
are not the decisive factors in a civilized society that it was nevertheless

necessary to use violence against the Indians, the savages, the backward peoples, the desperadoes on the frontier, before order was established in the first place. It is inferred that international order will in the first instance have to be established by violence. The argument is in my opinion the product of the same kind of historical and sociological analysis as has led to the writing of history books in terms of wars and generals, as if these represented the truly important developments and forces. It is significant, and ought to make us suspicious, that the argument is ordinarily advanced by those who are interested in justifying some current exhibition of violence on the national or international stage.

It is patent that the kind of internecine conflicts referred to have been as common in human history as wars. But that is far from saying that they were either unavoidable or essential or salutary. We can hardly be expected at this late date to accept the wars of "civilized" nations against "savages" and "barbarians" as means resorted to with regret for the purpose of establishing order. The fact is that they created chaos. Often there was obviously no need for the violence even from the conventional nonpacifist point of view. The Quakers in Colonial times, by the way, demonstrated that it is possible for the nonviolent to live in safety even under such conditions. These conflicts may be described as struggles between one kind of "order" and another, both, perhaps, and certainly the "higher" one, of an exploitative character. But this sheds no light on the question how a true community may be established and what the source of cohesion and authority is in such a society.

As for the frontier struggles in American history, their violent aspects have certainly been exaggerated by those concerned with the exciting and the picturesque. It would be interesting to see the statistics if they are available of the actual number of casualties in such struggles. Far too little attention has been given to the fact that where such struggles took on serious proportions they were basically class conflicts between herdsmen and farmers, farmers and merchants, or bankers, and so on. The violence was not clearly the indispensable prelude to and instrument for the establishment of order: it was the means for determining who was to be top dog in the "order" that obtained or was in process of being established.

As for revolutions, the role of violence in bringing them about has also been exaggerated. Furthermore, a revolution which resorts to violence ends by establishing a pseudo order still based on violence and betraying many of the aims of the revolution. This theme I have also explored at some length in my *Non-Violence in an Aggressive World* and I refer the reader to the chapters on "Pacifism as Revolutionary Strategy" in that book.

In any case—and it is of the utmost importance to note this carefully because of its bearing on the problem of achieving an international order with which our generation is confronted—whenever "order" is achieved a prominent and essential factor in the situation is that the individuals and groups involved in the society in question lay down their arms. Disarmament is an essential component of social order. Where the "citizens," whether they be individuals or social or political groups, go around with guns on their hips there is no society and no security. "Blessed are the meek for they shall inherit the earth."

At this point we shall perhaps be reminded that even if all that has been said be granted, the fact remains that civilized societies have laws, legislatures, executive and judicial organs, police, courts and prisons. Surely, we shall be asked, these are not negligible factors in social life and in providing security for the people? Would not anarchy and chaos ensue in a few days if the agencies of law enforcement ceased to function? Would not the citizen be mad to lay down his sword until an agency equipped with supreme power is created to keep his fellows from plundering and exterminating him?

Now if this is a proposal to slip in again the Hobbesian notion that human beings are selfish, brutal and vile, embodiments of naked power, each by his "nature" driven to a brute struggle for survival and domination against each, and so all threatened with extinction until they somehow decided to create Leviathan, the state, a vast reservoir of power, to which each surrendered his power and "rights" and which in turn forced the brutes into line and kept them there—then our reply is that we flatly reject this notion. This is the police state over again. Leviathan's police are also human beings, so there have to be police to watch and terrorize the police and then more police. . . . This ends in a madhouse or the grave. It is not a human society. We have to hold firmly to what we have already learned—that human society, including political organisms, has its source in God and is possible because human beings are children of God, standing in need of and endowed with capacity for fellowship.

If the reference to the organs of government means that there is need of authority and that "humanity could no more exist without some degree of authority than without food or without water or without warmth," that we grant is an important truth. Our contention throughout has not been about authority versus no authority but about the source and nature of authority. We are not arguing that no principle and instruments of social cohesion are necessary but as to what the principle and the instruments are. To state the matter in another way, the problem is whether power is subordinate to authority or authority is subordinate to power.

Since a society can be integrated, to quote Professor Wild again, only "by a common reference to the stable, and therefore superhuman, source of all genuine science and wisdom," since "if that which is really good does not rule, then man must be subjugated by a class or a mob or an individual," all authority derives from the nature of the moral universe, i.e., from God. Its power over men is moral and spiritual; in the final analysis they have to give their free assent to it. Government rests on the consent, not the subjugation, of the governed.

The organs of any human authority are, therefore, subject to the moral law. Otherwise the subject has no appeal as against the dictator: the dictator has the power, what more does he need if power creates authority?

By the same token, all organs of human authority are limited. In any good society or democratic order there will be all kinds of associations each with its authority and instruments for exercising it. Authority and power will be diffused. The notion that the government or the state has a unique, absolute authority which no other human agent has is radically false and a supremely dangerous heresy. One of the reasons why it has been and is so difficult to stop the inroads of totalitarianism is that the people of the so-called democratic countries have themselves so generally shared this pernicious heresy about the state.

Reinhold Niebuhr in an article in the *Nation* of March 16, 1946, makes another observation which flows from our concept of authority and the nature of society. He will, by the way, not be suspected of pacifism. Niebuhr in criticizing certain types of proposals for world organization rejects the theory that "men and nations create communities by the fiat of government and law. That all human communities had a long history of organic cohesion before they ever began explicitly and consciously to alter or extend it is ignored. . . . If our Constitution created a 'more perfect union,' the union which the Constitution perfected had already been established." Communities create governments, law, courts, police—rather than the other way around.

Now states or governments have power and agencies of enforcement —policemen—which other associations or centers of authority do not have. Even here it seems necessary to point out that there is probably not so much difference or so qualitative a difference between governments and other associations as is commonly supposed. Churches, for example, have not been without sanctions, nor are they now even in countries where churches cannot call on the state to enforce their decisions. For multitudes the social circle to which they belong may enforce sanctions much more dire than the government of the day. Nevertheless, government has material, physical power at its command. Is the exercise of that power consistent with the theory of man and society we have been expounding and compatible with the love-ethic of the New Testament, the way of nonviolence?

It has been made sufficiently clear that the pacifist will be inclined always to question the exercise of physical power by one man on another. However, I do not believe that the answer to the question just posed need be a categorical negative.

The very theory we have been expounding rules out the idea that human beings are isolated atoms which do not impinge upon each other. The mere fact that one exists means that he impresses himself on others and limits their possible choices. When parents or educators decide to pursue a hands-off policy with respect to children, they create a certain type of environment for the children to grow up in and exclude them thereby from another, and all without the children being in a position to do anything about it. The "nonresistant" who refuses to take part in war cannot in my opinion claim that he is not resisting and is not engaging in a "political" action which in some sense "coerces" his fellows. "What would happen if there were a lot of you?" the nonpacifist with perfect propriety inquires. Major General Hershey, head of the Selective Service Department, once speculated in my hearing on how many "termites"—conscientious objectors and Communists were mentioned in the context—a government could afford to tolerate and at what point it would have to begin "to exterminate them to keep the house from falling down!" There is, incidentally, no guarantee that we shall not, however unwillingly, inflict suffering on others no matter how nonviolent our course may be.

We do not believe, either, that any absolute line can be drawn between the application of physical force, on the one hand, and what might be called psychological pressure on the other; and that the one can be adjudged *ipso facto* bad and the other good.

The test to which the exercise of police power is, according to our thesis, to be subjected is whether it is moral in purpose and in effect. This implies several conditions. In the first place, the police must represent the will of the community and not of a section or faction of it. When the citizen meets the policeman he must as it were recognize himself and recognize the embodiment of the law to which he has given his consent. In the second place the well-being of the alleged offender as also a person and a member of the community must be a consideration in anything that is done. In the third place, the application of power, force, must be kept to a minimum.

Professor Wild, in the note already referred to, makes an observation which is pertinent here: "The very words 'sovereign,' 'leader' and even 'executive,' which are characteristic of modern usage, carry with them a false implication of blind action for its own sake, the root conception of fascist political thought. Power is always the power for something; execution requires *something* to execute. *Pure* sovereign power, or executive leadership, far from constituting the normal state, is really a characteristic form of social insubordination or intemperance."

When we say that the use of force must be kept to a minimum in order to conform to the laws of social life or the moral universe, we are naturally faced with the question where to draw the line. And this is one of those problems one often encounters in life outside the study, to which there is no answer in the sense of a mathematical or logical formula. The answer has to be given in actual practice and not in theory. In the final showdown we live by faith and not by sight.

One way to check ourselves is by observation of our motivation when we resort to any form of force. If the desire is to help all who are involved in the situation, including the offender—to help, to forgive, to redeem—the action itself may be permissible and good. When hate, fear, the desire to punish, humiliate, avenge, enter in, the impure inner state will give rise to bad action. For the rest, we have to see the case upon the insight which is basic to pacifist thought, namely, that "power corrupts and absolute power corrupts absolutely" and that violence which is "naked" power is evil and destructive in its very essence and must therefore be renounced. Put up your sword in its place, therefore.

Now all human experience teaches us that the temptation to increase the amount of power applied and the occasions when it is used, the temptation to use "naked" power, violence, is ever present and extremely insidious. At the bottom of the condition which seems to justify resort to violence is some shortcoming in or denial of community, an injustice, an unredressed wrong. The resort to violence against those who seek to redress that wrong diverts attention from the real issue. The grievance instead of being removed is, therefore, intensified. Then more violence has to be used, and so on until disaster comes. This is why the argument that "violence and war can never accomplish any positive good but they can stop outlaws and give us a chance—though perhaps a slim one—to build a peaceful world or a just social order" always proves to be a trap. Violence begets violence and not something else.

Thus violence is used against labor in a society where there are great disparities in income. But throughout the Western world in recent decades the result has simply been that class conflict is intensified. Presently the nation is split into opposing camps and, whichever camp wins, totalitarianism and violence are enthroned and democracy lies violated and dead.

This is a point which should be noted by those theologians and expounders of social and Christian ethics who say that pacifists, when they condemn the use of instruments of coercion and force, are in danger by their extreme reaction against tyranny of plunging society into anarchy. The concern for "law and order" has all too often been used for sinister purposes. Present-day civilization stands in far more danger of totalitarianism than of anarchy. There is too little revolt against authority and conscription. The real anarchists in the contemporary world are the nation-state, both in their conduct toward each other and in their treatment of their citizens, or, more accurately, subjects.

To cite another instance in support of our point, in a society where "every man for himself" is the dominant ethic and a good many make easy money out of highly speculative enterprises, gangsters and racketeers grow up in slum areas. Violence may avail to "clean up"—deceptive phrase—a particular set of gangsters. We do not find, however, that we can then reduce our police forces, close up at least some of our prisons and mental hospitals, and live quietly and securely in this "civilized" community.

When we apply the same general approach to the treatment of "criminals" when they have been apprehended, the result is such as Dr. Lindner, psychiatrist formerly attached to the federal penitentiary at Lewisburg, Pennsylvania, and now on the staff of Johns Hopkins University, describes in his book, *Rebel Without a Cause*. To get the full force of Dr. Lindner's evaluation the reader should bear in mind that the practice in the federal institutions is far in advance, according to the standards of the more enlightened penology, of that in city, county and state jails. "In spite of the self-flattery in which criminologists, penologists and the assorted professional and warder complement of the modern prison indulge, we are not today treating criminals; and, what is worse, in only a few isolated instances are we even learning anything about them. In all its bald essence, what we are actually doing today is removing a wrong-doer from the community; and while he is in the place of detention we are submitting him unmercifully to the unrequiting ministrations of an expensive officialdom. But beyond the half-hearted employment of a 'shot-gun' technique which fires its charge in all directions at once, we do nothing fundamental about crime or the criminal."

We thus near the conclusion of our argument and answer the question raised at the beginning of this chapter in the affirmative. That is to say, the social group, and more particularly the nation, is subject to the moral law. It exists and can only exist in a moral universe.

Furthermore, the command to obey the moral law is finally the command to love and necessitates the renunciation of violence. The nation, like the individual, will lose its life if it is simply bent on finding and perpetuating it. It can find itself only by losing or at least being willing to lose it in the fulfillment of a universal, i.e., a divine mission.

The case was stated in metaphysical and theological terms some time ago by Professor Paul Tillich in his *Interpretation of History*. It is impossible to deal with the problem without taking account of his profound and penetrating contribution, which is in a sense the more impressive because he is not a pacifist. He speaks of might as "existence as such" and of power as "social existence as such." Accordingly, "the lack of might is the disintegration of social existence." Nevertheless "might" and "power" do not constitute their own justification even in the world as it is. He points out that even a materialistic philosophy such as Marxism falls back upon ethical considerations: "Even in Marxism the proletariat, as bearer of the coming fulfillment of human existence, ... has an objective *quality of holiness, a 'vocation' on the strength of which* it can wage the battle of power. . . . *The holiness of power is the critical norm* to which it is always subject." [3]

But this necessarily involves the inclusion also of the element which we have been describing as love and self-renunciation: "In every power is an element of renunciation of power, and the power lives on this element." Plainly, this is the ancient prophetic and New Testament law of survival by sacrifice.

Professor Tillich goes on to point to the Church as obviously and supremely subject to this law. A true church is a group "unified by the free decision to have power only in the paradoxical form of the renunciation of power." But can this line of thinking also be applied to the nation, in practical, political affairs?

"We must ask whether a people or a group which originally is not the church could renounce power by a common decision [choose the way of renunciation of all war and domination] and thus become the church." What is the answer to that crucial question? "This possibility is not to be rejected fundamentally." So Professor Tillich concludes his thought by pointing out, as we have sought in this essay to

---

[3] Italics are mine.

do, that our task and decision are ethical and spiritual rather than in the sphere of politics and economics, in so far as these are conceived of as independent of ethics. The decision to renounce power "must not come into existence with the help of state power." That is to say, the way of love cannot be imposed on men, true community cannot be achieved by violence. "A people can become the church only if in an unexpected historical moment it is seized as a whole by the transcendental idea and for its sake renounces power. Such an event would be one of the great turning-points in human history; it would perhaps create 'mankind.'"

We have now to deal with the application of these principles by the United States in the present critical moment in history—a moment in which we must indeed "create mankind" or face the end of civilized existence, possibly even the extinction of the race. Before undertaking to deal with this practical issue in the next chapter, it is, however, necessary in order to round out our presentation to comment briefly on three items in the field of general principles with which the present chapter has sought to deal.

In the first place, our exposition implies an answer to the assertion fairly often encountered in theological circles—curiously enough in both naïve fundamentalist and highly sophisticated quarters—that Christians or the "regenerate" are called upon to practice the ethic of love and sacrifice, but not the "unregenerate." It is true that sinful men actually carry out the will of God only in the measure that they avail themselves of His grace and that they need repentance and the rebirth which is consequent on repentance. But that does not mean that there is more than one set of laws or principles of behavior for human beings. The moral law is the statement of the structure of the moral universe in which persons live. Both as a fact and as a demand or divine command it confronts all men and allows no escape. Any attempt to introduce dualism into this sphere leads to moral and political confusion, and either to spiritual pride or to moral laxness and complacency in individuals.

Secondly, the question, what is involved in conformity with the law of love in any concrete situation, is an infinitely complex and difficult one. It has to be resolved continuously in the process of imaginative, creative living. It is an "existential," not abstract or theoretical, matter.

Any impression that may have been conveyed that the pacifist has an easy and simple solution is heartily and unreservedly rejected. Moreover, we are all sinful men and we fall short of doing the gracious will of God which is our life and our peace. Thus humility becomes us all and in each moment of existence. But again this cannot mean that God's will is not single, that it is one law for one man and another for his neighbor. Moreover, the Niebuhrians are in my opinion on unsound psychological ground and thoroughly in error in assuming, as they appear to do, that it is the pacifist seeking to obey the love-ethic who alone and in a peculiar sense is confronted with a painful dilemma in the moment of decision and action, a dilemma which is somehow avoided or resolved when "justice" or "proximate justice" rather than love is put forward as the standard of action. On the one hand, it is not really possible to draw such a sharp line between justice and love. There is no basis for justice in a naturalist or materialist philosophy. The requirement to "do justice" rests on the same foundation as that "to show mercy" and to "walk humbly with thy God." It is because human beings are persons, ends in themselves, that they are entitled to just treatment and obligated to give it in turn. Love can and does include justice—"to each what is his right"—because in the family, for example, love requires that children share according to their respective needs in the available food or in the attention of their parents to their educational needs. Many handy rules based on experience as to what is "just" are required, especially in the larger social groupings, and are not in any necessary conflict with the law of love. But equally the basis for justice, namely, that human beings are persons and not things or animals, is also the basis for love; and as we have repeatedly pointed out, the command to obey the moral law is—and it is surely impossible for the Christian to deny this—the command to "love the Lord thy God with all thy heart . . . and thy neighbor as thyself."

On the other hand, the determination as to what is "just" or "proximately just" in a concrete situation presents the same complexities and difficulties as the determination of what "love" requires. The differences of opinion and action in this context among nonpacifists in the churches or in general society are certainly proof enough of this contention. In exchange then for a largely illusory advantage those who turn to "justice" as a means of escape from the complexities of the love-ethic run the risk of lapsing into moral relativism and removing that very "tension" born in the soul by the "impossible" demand of the Gospel which on their own showing is of the essence of Christian thought and life.

The line of thought which we are here criticizing is commonly advanced by those who feel that an act of violence, such as a war, must be justified and who in general lay great emphasis on the power struggle: from this struggle or in connection with it somehow a "relative justice" is to emerge. But these considerations, as our whole argument has made clear, serve precisely to put us on guard against rather than predispose us to accept this line of thought. Violence and the struggle for power are indubitable facts, but it is the contention of this book that they are the great taproot of evil and must be radically dealt with, not accepted by Christian teachers as normative for Christian thought and practice.

In the third place, pacifists are often accused of holding a superficial, optimistic, nineteenth-century-liberal view of the nature of man, which minimizes sin and its power in the hearts of men and in history and which consequently also underestimates the cost of moral and social advance. Undoubtedly the charge has on occasion been justified. We have already given some indication of our own view of the matter in what we have said about the Cross as the price of victory over sin and of progress.

We may add that in a sense the real meaning of this book is that the situation is much worse than we ordinarily think it is and its purpose is to bring conviction of sin to ourselves, i.e., the respectable and complacent. When we support "law and order," the vast enginery of punishment and suppression with which the so-called civilized community is equipped, and when we tolerate and condone and support war, we are unconsciously, if not consciously, assuming that all this is necessary because there are people who are not like ourselves. If, that is, other people were honest and industrious and peaceable, as we of course are, then we could do without police and prisons, not to mention war. The instruments of suppression and violence are necessary in order to protect us, the innocent and law-abiding, against the lawless and aggressive elements in our own land and abroad. But surely we must some time stop to wonder whether this picture, in which we stand in the center thanking God that we are not as other men are, is an accurate one.

If we did stop to look more closely, we would realize that it is we who have great possessions and privileges which others lack and which we are very reluctant to share. We would see that a large part of society's enginery of force and violence is there to protect these possessions and privileges of the self-righteous and complacent—and that the insecurity and fear in our hearts have their origin precisely in the things we cherish and the instruments we have built up to provide us security. Under the moral law we are not entitled to these possessions. The fact that we hold on to them by violence, i.e., by the agencies of "law and order," aggravates the situation in the eyes of God and further embitters our fellow men.

Seen in this light we are the sources of the tension in society; we are armed and belligerent; we are the aggressors. In subtle ways we hate and despise our fellows and thus hate and bitterness are aroused in them. We think that it is the guns, physical and spiritual, in the hands of others which create insecurity and against which defenses must be provided. We do not realize that it is the guns in our own hearts and hands which threaten us and that Jesus was sane—not mad—when he taught that men would be better off and safer in a society where they gave away their coats and put up their swords.

If this approach saves us, on the one hand, from a certain brand of optimism, it saves us equally from a certain type of pessimism about man and the world. It is probably safe to assume that those who profess the blackest pessimism about human nature and the possibility of changing it, and so on, are not usually thinking of human nature as exemplified in themselves. Paradoxically, therefore, when men see themselves in a true light and therefore know at last what it means to despair, they can at last also begin to hope and act again. For in the moment when one knows himself as a sinner before God, he also knows that he is forgiven and reborn, and that all things have become possible again. After all, to say that men are sinners is to say that they are prodigal sons who have a Father who is Lord of the universe and of history.

Chapter VII

My Country: 'Tis of Thee

If ever in its long history mankind has stood in need of a nation capable of leading it to a radically new adaptation to an unprecedented situation, it is now. If ever, in the providence of God, there was need of a nation willing to assume the burden of being a "spiritual Israel," seized as a whole by the transcendant idea and for its sake willing to renounce power, it is now.

In one sense, every nation is equally subject to the moral order and the divine demand. Yet there are perhaps reasons, already stated or implied in the pages of this book, why a special responsibility rests upon the United States. To whom much has been given, of him much shall be required. And how big that "much" is in the case of the United States!

In any case, I am an American writing primarily for Americans. We have a direct responsibility for the policy of our own government and some possibility of exercising a direct influence in the making of that policy. The influence we can hope to exercise upon Russian thought and the course of the Russian government, save through the policy and behavior of our own government, is negligible.

There is, furthermore, the injunction to take out first the beam out of our own eye and to stop indulging in the pleasant pastime of repenting of other people's sins. We have spoken of the psychological and spiritual stalemate which underlies the political stalemate. The Russians think we ought to repent; we think the Russians should. So long as these attitudes obtain, there will be no repentance and we shall

all perish. Repentance is unilateral business. No respectable prophet ever said to man or nation, "You should repent, if so and so does." In passing, no prophet with proper credentials ever said: "Repent tomorrow, after one more good binge."

What would it mean, then, for the United States in the present crisis to assume the role of a nation seeking to apply the law of good will, love and self-sacrifice?

We suggest that it would involve three main courses of action. First, the United States would renounce warmaking as a national policy for any purposes and under any circumstances. War is violence in its most irrational, outrageous and futile form, and a nation seeking to follow a Christian or pacifist course simply could not any longer have anything to do with it. As evidence that the United States was through with warmaking it would disband its armed forces, scrap its guns and bombers, stop making atomic bombs and the weapons of germ warfare and destroy such atomic and biological weapons as it already has on hand. In other words, it would disarm unilaterally— at once—regardless of what other nations might be willing to do.

Secondly, the nation would launch navies and air forces on great missions of mercy to starving, sick and homeless peoples everywhere. It would spend the billions it would save by scrapping its war establishment, and perhaps a good many more billions, on rehabilitating the sick and broken-down economies of the world. We devoted three or four hundred billions to the work of destruction during several years of war. We are now proceeding on the assumption that what was knocked down at such terrific cost can be rebuilt with a couple of billion in relief and loans grudgingly given. Any high school child could tell us that it does not make sense. Incidentally, let us recall that while we were "giving away" hundreds of billions of dollars' worth of goods by shooting them at other people, the masses of our own people were better off than in peacetime: our "generosity" enabled our economic system to "work"! It is elementary that a program devoted honestly to restoring the economies of war-stricken lands would also give work to our people; only in addition it would give us customers again who could afford to buy from us instead of impoverished multitudes or corpses.

Thirdly, the United States would propose to participate in building the necessary world organizations both in the cultural, the economic and the political field, including probably some kind of, federal world government along some such lines as those of our own federal union. One of the important functions of such an organization would be the control and development of atomic energy for peaceful purposes. I surmise that this objective ought to receive more attention than it is getting either in popular organs of communication or in professional and intellectual circles. One of the ways in which the imagination of the American people and others might be captured and they might thus be won to doing something fundamental and revolutionary in the present crisis would be to hold constantly before them the vision of what the world might be like if men would stop fighting each other and enter into the heritage which God has prepared for them.

Obviously the key to these proposals, and their most controversial element, is that the United States should disarm. It is for this reason —and not because the proposals for rehabilitation and world organization are not immensely important—that we shall devote our attention primarily to the disarmament question.

Let us first, however, pause to observe that, although the proposals we have just made seem to many startling and even utterly fantastic, they do as a matter of fact closely parallel the conditions which historically have had to be met wherever a larger political grouping has been achieved in a relatively peaceful manner and has produced beneficent results.

There have been golden moments in the history of mankind when among states previously separated actual community and a sense of community have arisen on which the legal and political structure of a nation or federation or commonwealth could be reared. And these were not preceded by the sort of long-drawn struggle ending in the elimination of all but one contestant that made Rome supreme in the ancient Mediterranean world. Our own federal union is probably the outstanding example.

One indispensable condition to the formation of such a union is that the units entering into it must be disarmed or ready to disarm and renounce the power to make war independently. That power must rest henceforth in the union itself. As yet no community has been able to develop a political state as one of its organs where the units maintain their own armaments and retain the right in some eventuality to wage war against each other or against a power outside the proposed union. Undoubtedly the conviction that only by uniting would the units be able to cope with external foes has played an important role historically in bringing their peoples to the point of accepting and welcoming disarmament of the constituent units. Today we have the far more difficult task of achieving world organization with no fear of an external foe to unite us, unless it be the mythical Martians.

Another essential condition is that artificial economic barriers such as tariffs should be removed. There could have been no union if the American colonies had not become an economic unit, and the fact that presently over the expanse of the continent a great free trading area was established had much to do with the success of the union.

Third, spiritual unity around a common ideal is essential—a faith, in other words. The shared conviction that "a new nation, conceived in liberty and dedicated to the proposition that all men are created equal" had to be built, did as much as anything else to make a community out of the people of the thirteen colonies, thus enabling them to build a nation.

Of course, the task of devising the economic, political and legal structures which are necessary for an ordered and peaceful world in the twentieth century is much greater and more complex than that which confronted the Founding Fathers of our own country. But the building of machinery for the organization and channeling of great forces is a congenial enterprise for modern man. Our difficulty does not come from that quarter.

It is rather, as we have repeatedly had to face, that a sense of world community is lacking. There is no mutual trust.

We need not dwell at length again upon the point that, if men only exercised a little sense, fear of the effects of atomic war and other prudential, common-sense considerations might lead a nation just to have done with war. Fear may in certain circumstances and up to a point have salutary effects, as when fear of epidemics leads people to build a pure water supply system. As someone has said, when a man is pursued by a bull, he can run faster than he ever thought possible. But beyond a certain point fear leads either to the senseless lashing about of the panic-stricken, or to paralysis. On the one hand, men try today to persuade themselves that the atomic bomb is not so bad: It is not "the ultimate weapon," certain experts solemnly assure us; if it is a really big city it might take several bombs to wipe it out. So men go about their eating and drinking, marrying and giving in marriage. On the other hand, they say to themselves: "This thing is so bad that it is now more than ever necessary to keep ahead in the race. We must do everything possible to ensure that we suffer a little less and the others a whole lot more." Fear cannot solve our problem, since mutual fear is our problem: how to break that electric circuit running between Russia and the United States which becomes daily more heavily charged as the fear in each stimulates fear in the other?

Nor will common-sense, prudential considerations suffice any more. They lead nations to think of their "interests," of their "defenses," of their historic "missions." Under these conditions, they talk of peace but there is no peace. Nations which do not trust each other and which are self-righteous and unrepentant want to achieve security and well-being while they remain self-righteous and unrepentant. They want to build peace while they continue to make war on each other.

Similarly we cannot any longer rest our hope for resolving "the crisis of confidence" on the more moderate political measures which some, either because they are pro-Russian or for other reasons, are prepared to advocate. Certainly the United States ought seriously to propose universal disarmament. Russian demands for control of the Dardanelles ought to be met by a proposal to establish genuine international control, not only over the Dardanelles but also over such other strategically important areas as Suez and Panama. I believe that the proposal which has a number of times been advanced by leading atomic scientists, that, pending serious efforts to achieve disarmament or drastic reduction of armaments, the United States should suspend the further manufacture of atomic bombs and take apart those it has, is an excellent one.

But, alas, none of these proposals has even reached the point of being seriously considered in Congress or by the executive arm of the government. A nation whose people and leaders are pretty complacent and unrepentant is not going to make such proposals. It is convinced that the difficulty lies with the Russians. A very considerable psychological reorientation and spiritual conversion would have to take place before even moderate steps in the right direction could be hoped for. Besides, where the problem is one of a thoroughly bad mental state the solution lies in a genuine, not in superficial and partial, correction of that state. An individual or a nation is the captive of its fears or it is not. Only if it is not can a new political course, which may indeed then have to unfold step by step, be charted and actually attempted. As things stand, neither Russia nor the United States will make a gesture to restore genuine confidence, some such gesture as the suspension of the production of atomic weapons by the United States. Bargains may conceivably be made which in the opinion of the parties will leave each in the same relative power position, but that solves nothing. It does not constitute a move toward peace but simply a move in the ongoing hidden war. For the rest, the United States dare not make a move which might actually weaken its relative power position: How can it be sure that the Russians will not take advantage of it? How indeed be sure that at that very moment the Russians may not perfect a weapon which will radically alter the balance and render the United States utterly "defenseless"? If, on the other hand, the United States—or Russia—makes a move which is only an apparent and not a real concession, the realists on the other side will, of course, recognize it for what it is and be accordingly unimpressed. Finally, there is the question: Suppose a nation, the United States, for example, recognizing how desperate is the need of preventing another war and, therefore, of resolving "the crisis of confidence," made some genuine concessions, risked its power position. Suppose these measures failed to "work," that Russia just "took advantage" of them. Would the United States then—too late perhaps—conclude that it had made a grave error and get back into the armaments race or would it persist in the path of reconciliation by self-sacrifice? Plainly, a nation which is not prepared to make the latter decision would be under the suspicion that it was in the final analysis bluffing and that would be decisive in determining its effect on another nation and on the total situation. Furthermore, a nation which was not prepared to make the decision indicated would be psychologically incapable of embarking on a course of reconciliation.

Thus we are again driven back to the conclusion that truly revolutionary political action is required and that this must arise out of a moral and spiritual revolution. The fact which we have finally to face, and which sinful men and nations are, alas, so reluctant to face, is that selfishness and fear do not lead to sensible action and to the preservation and enhancement of life. They lead instead to the grave. The fact is that nations as well as men are subject to the moral law. Their life and peace are in the doing of the will of God, which is love.

War is horrible, we say; therefore it must be abolished. We are thinking of the effect upon us if someone else wages war against us. Forty million people, says Professor Oppenheimer, might be killed in one night in a series of atomic bomb raids on congested United States centers. But we shall never get the matter straight and we shall not, I am convinced, actually get rid of war, until we see war not from the receiving but from the sending end. We must see what we are who have waged war, who dropped the atomic bombs on Hiroshima and Nagasaki, who make atomic bombs and the instruments of germ warfare, weapons which play their part in the hidden war, the power struggle, now going on, weapons which now strike terror into the hearts of men in all lands and which as all history teaches will presently be used in open warfare. We have to see who we are who are preparing to kill forty million people in one night to perpetuate our so-called national existence, to maintain our riches.

When we do turn our eyes inward upon ourselves we shall see that the basic issue is not how we can prevent others from waging war against us, but that we should be purged of the guilt of war and selfishness, should be purged of the guilt of the obliteration bombing and the guilt of Hiroshima and Nagasaki. When we see ourselves, we shall smite our breasts and cry, "God, be merciful unto us sinners."

We shall not need to be told then that there is only one cure for the malady which afflicts us as well as other peoples. That cure is repentance. And repentance always means unilateral action, though that may well stimulate multilateral action by means of example and contagion. No one can repent of the other man's or nation's sin. And when one repents he does not wait to see whether someone else stops sinning before deciding that he must quit. We shall, therefore, as a nation renounce the sin of warmaking, and that will mean disarming whether anyone else does or not, divesting ourselves of the means to wage war. What use has the converted sinner for the paraphernalia of crime?

In this realm of morals and religion, there can be no shilly-shallying. We cannot have it both ways. We utterly and unequivocally give up war as a policy because it is sin, or we shall not give it up at all. We may appropriately introduce here another quotation from that remarkable book by Howard Spring, *And Another Thing*:

> One thing about this kingdom is that you must take it or leave it. Within it, the rule holds absolutely that you cannot serve God and Mammon. If it were decided, for example, that those inventions of the devil called "V-weapons" should be for ever abandoned, that would be a service of God if the motive behind the abandonment were love of mankind. I have pointed out before, and I believe it to be true, that the validity of action is in motive; and if our motive in suggesting the "outlawing" of V-weapons is simply to save our own skins, knowing as we do that the development of these weapons will soon make the destruction of English towns a mere matter of mathematics, then our motive will not be strong enough to achieve what we desire. If the motive is love of mankind, then not V-weapons alone but all destructive weapons—war itself—will be renounced.[1]

Nothing but such a religious rebirth can save the world now. If the people of this nation were to experience it then they would adopt the course outlined at the beginning of this chapter. They would see the need for general disarmament and would propose it to other nations. But their own disarmament would not be dependent upon what others did. They would disarm anyway and as rapidly as possible because they would not want the blood of participation in another war on their hands under any circumstances. They might argue in the light of our previous discussion that they would actually and literally be safer and better off for having tossed their own infernal machines into the ocean. But that would not be the driving force of their action. That driving force would be spiritual, the purpose no longer to worship Moloch and throw their own and other people's sons into his flaming arms, but to worship the everlasting God, the Lord, the creator of the ends of the earth, whose name is love.

Impelled by that motive the people of this country would embark

[1] P. 235.

upon a great venture in relief and rehabilitation—building at home and helping to build abroad an economic order embodying justice and charity. They would join hands with other peoples in fashioning the machinery and the institutions needed by a world community.

Men are, as we have said, reluctant to face and accept this solution. They want—even the intelligent and well-intentioned ones—something more moderate, more sensible, more practical, more down-to-earth; something which doesn't cost so much; some device which will smooth everything out, not require taking any chances, any venture of faith. After World War I, after World War II. And above all, no repentance, no wrestling with the problem of corporate sin. But there is no longer any such way out. It is World War III or repentance and acceptance of God, and His command, and His love. God and history have us cornered now.

The course we have sketched is the course a Christian, a pacifist, nation would follow. What would happen if it did?

If such a savior-nation appeared—rather we should say, if the United States became such a nation, because on this plane action has to be unilateral: no nation can ask another to accept such a role—then it is most likely that other nations would acclaim us and would follow our example. Is it likely that other nations would attack and devour a nation which alone among the nations might conceivably have been able to conquer them all and which now came armed with food, clothing, medicine, machines, skills, instead of with atomic bombs and germ weapons? Is it likely they would hate the nation which had broken the tension, so largely caused by its own hideous weapons, that had held the world in its awful grip? Did you hate your mother who came to you in the dark when you were shrieking in the torment of a nightmare and took you in her arms and comforted you?

Surely people who think that if a nation such as ours were to give up the way of violence other nations would go right ahead and bomb and kill anyway are assuming that the law of cause and effect has been suspended. I assume that it operates. War comes because two nations pursue certain policies. It is the inevitable result of these policies. Then one nation radically changes its course. Will the other not be affected by that? The cause is fundamentally changed: will the results, the effect, remain the same? I do not think so. The trouble with the world is not that men do not reap what they sow but rather that, having sown the wind, they all too surely do reap the whirlwind. We shall not reap another kind of harvest until we sow another kind of seed. But if we do sow another kind of seed, though it be in tears, we shall presently reap in joy another kind of harvest.

Look at the situation for a moment from the standpoint of the likely effects of the adoption of such a program as we have outlined on the Russians. They are in an extremely painful economic condition. Reports at the moment of writing indicate that in some parts of the country actual famine conditions obtain. There is need of food and of large-scale aid to speed up rehabilitation of agriculture and industry. Offers of aid given grudgingly and as a sop while the United States insists on maintaining its dominant positions are rejected. Uncle Sam with bread in one hand and an atomic bomb in the other is under suspicion. If it is to be war, say the Russians, why should we let our enemies into our borders, even though they come bearing gifts? But economic aid, under the conditions we have proposed, would be hard to reject. A regime which did so would have serious trouble with its people.

On the other hand, people who are being fed, who are enabled to rebuild their economic life, whose standard of living is rising and who are getting the things they crave do not want war and are not good subjects for war propaganda. They might be, even under such conditions, in a world where hidden war was in progress and they lived in fear of an enemy who might attack them if they failed to take the initiative in attacking him. But in a world where their only formidable enemy was voluntarily abandoning war as a policy and where a war-weary people had so much to gain from developing atomic energy for peaceful purposes, it is very hard for me to believe that Russians any more than other people would be seized with the urge to make war just for devilishness, so to speak.

At this point the objection is always raised that behind the "iron curtain" the Russians would not be permitted to know the truth. There would be much more force to this objection if the truth withheld from the Russians had to do with such peaceful, reconciling activities on the part of the United States as those we are recommending. When Stalinist propaganda today tells the Russian people about American expansionism, the presence of American war vessels in the Mediterranean, our stock pile of atomic bombs, our support of antidemocratic regimes, it is unfortunately telling the truth to a large extent. Certainly we have to give Soviet propaganda something else to talk about before we are on sure ground in charging that they will lie about it or not talk about it at all.

Here is a Russian peasant who has been without food and now he eats; he has had no tractor and now he has one. Stalinist propaganda is a fearsome thing but I doubt whether it would succeed, even if it tried, in convincing the peasant that he was still not eating and still minus a tractor. Nor do I think the effort, if it were made, to hide the source of the aid from Russian workers and peasants would succeed for long. After all, millions of Russians have now been outside Russia and Russians generally are aware that tractors do not grow on rosebushes in Russia itself or in Poland, Bulgaria or Greece.

A word should be said at this point about a question based on a distinction between the Russian people and their rulers, which troubles many people. "Granted," they say, "that the Russian people are the same as other folks and may be expected to respond normally to fair and generous treatment, is it not true that the men in the Kremlin are totalitarians with vast power and may be expected not to relinquish that power without a bitter fight?" One possible answer to that question is that they do indeed have a vast apparatus of power and wield it ruthlessly, but that they have often demonstrated that they are realists. Being realists, they do not take our present inadequate and largely phony "peace" proposals seriously. By the same token, if they were faced with proposals which really made peace and the peaceful development of their own country possible, they would respond in kind. Thus democratic life might revive or be born in Russia. Critical as I have been of Stalinist leaders over many years, I do not believe that this possibility can be dismissed as simply silly.

But let us assume for the sake of argument that things do not work out that way and that the present leadership in Russia has to be removed before democratic life becomes possible. How, then, is that leadership to be removed? By force from without? Few indeed who have the slightest competence to speak will deny that this is the road to World War III. It is the policy of being "tough" with Russia, the maintenance of the threat from without, which bolsters up the dictator-ship. If the dictator or dictators have to be forced out, the Russian people will have to do it. They will do it only under the conditions of economic well-being and relaxing of international tension on which we have been insisting. If these conditions did obtain, it requires—I submit—a great stretch of the imagination to assume that the Russian people would continue to support a regime like the present one if it sought to remain in power.

Again, as we have stressed repeatedly, fear possesses the Russian regime and the people. Somehow the spell of fear must be broken. It will be broken if Russia's only formidable enemy comes to it in friend-ship and unarmed. Do people from whom the dread burden of fear has been lifted continue to behave as if it were still there? Do we not have abundant evidence that unsuspected creative possibilities are released under such conditions?

Between Russians and Americans, to look at the problem from one other angle, there is a conflict of politico-economic systems, of ideol-ogies and religions. The contest is obviously an artificial one so long as each nation tries to back up and advance its faith by armed might. Take the latter factor out of the situation and then each system can demonstrate its ability to meet human needs. But for those who are concerned about the democratic and particularly the Christian way of life, this is a matter of life and death. Turn back to the account in the Introduction of the discussion between the French Communists and the Christian pacifists studying the New Testament and the Sermon on the Mount together in a concentration camp under the Vichy regime. Jesus' way of love, reconciliation and self-sacrifice is the better way, the true religion, but—said the Communists—"it is not practical now; after the Revolution, it will be." The weakness of so-called Christian people, churches and nations today is that they hold the same view: "At some later time, when the United States and its friends are firmly in the saddle and there is no longer anything to fear from a Russia kept within safe bounds, the way of the Cross will be practical, but not now."

So long as this remains our position, we are licked. For we are try-ing to meet the Russians' reality, their real and intense commitment to an inadequate and in important respects false religion, with a sham, with profession of a faith in which we do not believe. There is no power in that. Even if we win in a military conflict on these terms, spiritually we shall be licked. We shall become victims of the militarism and totalitarianism which we set out to overcome and remove.

But if Stalin and the Russian people were to be confronted with the truly revolutionary spectacle of a Christian nation actually practicing the faith it professed, taking the way of the Cross—of good will, reconciliation and self-sacrifice—in this unutterably tragic hour, I cannot but believe they would be impressed. I think they would know they were in the presence of power—real power—power against which neither Russia nor the gates of hell could prevail. Does the reader doubt that? When professing Christians say they doubt it, is it because they really do, deep down in their hearts, or because they are not ready to meet the demands which their faith makes upon them, including that of being willing to be deemed foolish by men in order that as little children they may accept and live by the wisdom of God?

There is one more practical question to be dealt with briefly before we bring this chapter to a close with the consideration of the ultimate challenge that a nation may have to be willing to lay down its life that mankind may live. This practical question is: "Didn't the United States try pacifism, didn't we disarm after World War I—and what did we get out of it?"

Sometimes those who raise this point have in mind the fact that in a vague way people in the United States "don't want war." Neither, however, do the Russians or French or Germans or any other people. This general sentiment has no important bearing on whether peace is to be broken or, in so far as it does have a bearing, characterizes all modern peoples.

Sometimes people are thinking of the fact that many thousands of young men in countries like Great Britain and the United States signed the "Oxford oath" or its equivalent against taking part in any future war. But a very large number of these youth were never pacifists in the sense that they unequivocally rejected all war and organized violence. A good many, for example, held that a war under the aegis of "collective security," as a "police" measure, would be justified. A good many were Communists or under Communist influence and while rejecting "imperialist wars" were willing and indeed eager to fight in a class war or on behalf of the Soviet Union. A good many others had not thought things through carefully, were antiwar rather than committed to a pacifist way of life in all relationships, and did not join organizations like the Fellowship of Reconciliation, in which a pacifist life might find support and nurture. When, therefore, the heightening crisis subjected them to pressure, they found that they were not prepared to maintain their stand. They turned out to be "pacifists between wars." There were not enough genuine pacifists to have a marked influence on national policy. That is clearly demonstrated when we scrutinize the assumption that the official policy and behavior of the United States was actually pacifist between wars.

To cite a typical case, the then Secretary of State Byrnes in an important address on St. Patrick's Day, 1946, stated:

"Between 1918 and 1941 there grew up in this country an important body of pacifist sentiment. The dominant theme of this movement was that the way to end war was not to prepare for war. . . .

"If the United States were to scrap all its armaments and completely demobilize its Army and Navy, it was said, the force of its example would compel the rest of the world to follow suit. The peaceful instinct which underlay this point of view is an admirable one. The trouble with the idea is that it does not work.

"Without consciously deciding to do so, we actually tried it."

I believe Mr. Byrnes tries to be an honest man, and unfortunately a good many people think as he does about America's course from 1918 to 1941. Nevertheless, the statement that the United States tried pacifism and disarmament in those years is a colossal falsehood!

Peacetime expenditures *by the United States for war purposes were much larger after World War I than before, not smaller*. In 1913 the United States spent $244,600,000 for armaments; in 1931, in the middle of our "pacifist" aberration, it spent $727,700,000 for the same purpose. We did scuttle a few battleships, subsequent to the so-called Disarmament Conference in Washington in 1922, but only after disarming Germany and insisting on naval parity with Great Britain and superiority over all other nations on the basis of the 5-5-3-1½ ratio. With Mr. Roosevelt's accession to office in 1933 our military expenditures began to increase at once, so that as early as 1936 the taxpayer was being assessed nearly $3,000,000 a day for future wars under an annual Army-Navy appropriation of nearly a billion, and $5,700,000 for past wars, while he paid a miserly total of $270,000 per day for the Office of Education, the Children's Bureau, old-age pensions, the employment service and maternal and child health. The United States never disarmed. It never tried pacifism. It always intended in a show-down to resort to war to defend its "interests" and to maintain the balance of power in favor of itself and its actual or potential allies or satellites.

It may with some semblance of plausibility be argued that the United States, for example, did not rearm rapidly enough in the later thirties. But that does not mean that we decided too late to give up our pacifism as a nation. It would be much more to the point if those who are interested in such matters would recall that in the years leading up to the war Russia was selling manganese, the French tanks, Britain and America airplane motors to the Nazi regime. When in 1938 protests were being made at Washington over the arms we were shipping to Germany for transshipment to Franco, the State Department replied on May 12 of that year that while our postwar treaty with Germany pro-hibited the Germans from importing arms, it did not prohibit America from exporting arms to Germany! Relevant also would be the question whether it was lack of armament or lack of vigilance that was re-sponsible for the disaster at Pearl Harbor, which served for so many Americans as a justification for the war against the "sneaky Japs," atomic bombings and all!

At the most the arguments about pre-World War II preparedness come to this: that for some reason and by certain standards a nation which had always relied on military weapons as a last resort and which all the time had an industrial and military potential much greater than that of any other nation made a miscalculation when it came to translating its military potential into actuality. But there is no basis for the assumption that, in the kind of chaotic and selfish situation which prevailed, war could have been avoided by such speed-ing up. The Army Week slogan: "A Strong America Is a Peaceful America" is always countered by the slogan: "A Strong Germany (Russia) Is a Peaceful Germany (Russia)." This is just another nâme for an armaments race, for insecurity, not security. All that the con-tention which we are discussing really means is that if you are going

to depend on the war method you cannot be halfhearted about it—
any more than a nation will get anywhere by a halfhearted attempt to
follow a peaceful or a pacifist course—and that if you are going to make
war anyway, there may be an advantage in jumping in sooner rather
than later. There may even be an advantage in striking before an
opponent thinks you are ready. On this basis those who contend that
now is the time to lick Russia and to force disarmament by our military
might on the rest of the world are also right. "It will save many lives"
and so on, as the Nazis argued when they blitzed Rotterdam and
Coventry. All this has obviously nothing to do with pacifism.

We are, then, in an unprecedented political and spiritual emergency
proposing that the United States adopt a radically new, as yet untried,
course, namely, outright pacifism. And we repeat that it is likely that
other nations would welcome this example and follow it. The United
States would show that it was willing to "lose its life" as a nation-state,
was prepared to relax its hold on its special privileges, to set its own
house of democracy in order—and that, on the highest authority, is
the way to life and peace. He who loses his life shall find it.

But this very reference to Jesus and his teachings reminds us that
we do have to face the question: "Suppose the plan does not work
immediately, that other nations do not follow the example of the
United States, what then?"

It is of great importance for religious pacifists at this juncture to
realize that they will have to answer this question in any case. If they
advocate world government and disarmament by international agreement, the question is bound to be asked, "What do you propose if
other nations do not accept the proposal?" If they are consistent, they
have to answer that the United States should disarm anyway. The
notion that tactically something is gained by just not alluding to this
contingency, but simply insisting that the United States must make
the offer of mutual disarmament, is in my opinion an illusion. The
statesmen know very well that this question has to be faced and the
masses sense it too. And if the pacifist does stand by his proposal that
in any case the United States must abandon warmaking, he must
then be prepared to decide whether he would still advocate adherence
to a pacifist course by the United States if another nation were then
to remain hostile and were to threaten or actually make war.

True religion never suggests that there is a cheap and painless way to remove a long-enduring and deep-seated evil. Least of all does Judaeo-Christian prophetism minimize the cost. The figures of the Suffering Servant of Jehovah and of the Cross point to the central element in its teaching. To those who accept this teaching—to a nation which accepts it—the answer to our question is clear and unhesitating: it is the sin of making war which the nation must renounce, whatever the cost. If the fearful choice has to be made, it is better to have atomic bombs dropped on us than to drop them on others.

For the fainthearted and in order to strengthen our own conviction, three points may, however, be made. In the first place, let the doubters reflect on the risks we have already taken by using the war method and how utterly that method has failed. Let them reflect upon what the scientists have told us about the certain risks involved in atomic warfare, no matter how well equipped we may be. In the face of all this, is there not something to be said on very elementary and common-sense grounds for risking something in trying another method? Suppose there were a one-per-cent chance that it would succeed in ending war? What else are we waiting for before finally and unreservedly accepting the proposition that war besides being evil simply does not "work" or "pay"?

In the second place, there is a vast difference between the way of nonviolence and cowardly or apathetic surrender. The soldier is decorated by his country not so much because he killed but because he was willing to die for his cause: even when the fight was hopeless, his companions lying stricken about him, his own death certain, he fought on; he gave his life. Nonviolent resisters are people who, though they will not kill, have schooled themselves to die rather than collaborate with dictators and quislings, rather than co-operate with evil and tyranny. What happens within the souls of such people, as numerous cases of Quakers and Mennonites and members of the Fellowship of Reconciliation demonstrated in Germany itself and in occupied countries, is very different from what takes place in the souls of those who lack energy or courage and therefore submit to an evil regime and try to make the best of it. There were also many examples of people who had been very hot for war turning into collaborationists of various kinds when their own armies surrendered. Having depended upon force and believed in it in the first instance, they accommodated themselves to the greater force.

The nonviolent have their own ways of opposing evil. People who will not dig coal, run trains, operate factories at the command of foreign generals, on behalf of an evil regime, and who at the same time show that they feel good will toward the agents of that regime, will not kill them, insist on fraternizing with them and urging them to give up their dirty work while all the time refusing to collaborate— such people can constitute a problem for tyrants. Everybody can think of examples. Throughout history many people and groups have practiced nonviolence without being aware of it. Those who are interested can find data in such a book as Richard Gregg's *Power of Non-Violence*. Reflect for a moment on the brains and the money devoted to military strategy and tactics and implements and then consider what might happen if a nation were to devote something like the same brains and money to working out nonviolent means of defense. Granted there might be casualties, we have yet to hear of a war with no casualties and there is reason to think that we are rapidly heading into a war or wars in which there will be nothing but casualties. Is it anything but inertia, being hypnotized as it were by our old, habitual reactions, that keeps us from trying nonviolence?

The third, and perhaps most important, consideration may be stated thus: If Western civilization has reached the point of disintegration where a nation which followed the redemptive course we have described was subjected to attack and perhaps crucifixion, it would mean that in any event only four choices are now open to this nation and its people.

1. The first possibility is that the United States would be destroyed along with other nations in the general holocaust of an atomic war.

2. A second possibility is that the United States, with the guilt of first launching atomic warfare on its hands, would be defeated by Russia or some other nation in the coming war. Thus it would lose both in a material and in a spiritual sense. We have seen in an earlier chapter that this outcome is quite within the range of possibility.

3. A third possible outcome is that the United States would emerge as the so-called victor in such a war. How much it would gain or

rather save in a material sense under this supposition is highly problematical. The cost of such a war would certainly be colossal. Millions
of American lives would probably be destroyed. Whether the nation
could ever really recover in an economic sense is questionable. But let
us assume for the sake of the argument a fairly favorable outcome in
this respect. It would still remain that spiritually the nation would
suffer incalculable loss and utter defeat. It would have the guilt on
its hands of having first launched atomic war in 1945. The United
States of the American Dream would finally disappear and the nation
would "harden into bitter empire." The rest of the world would lie
prostrate and mangled at its feet. Having visited this havoc on mankind
in order to secure its own survival and dominance, this nation would
be hated and despised as no other nation in all history has been. It
would have the task, which no other empire has succeeded in achieving, of trying to rule the world. Does any sane person believe that it
would succeed? What shall a man, or a nation, gain if it wins the
whole world and loses it own soul? What shall be said of a nation which
loses its soul and the whole world as well?

4. The fourth and final choice is the one we are discussing, namely,
that the nation, having assumed a redemptive mission, having by accepting suffering washed the stain of Hiroshima and Nagasaki from
its soul, would be defeated, would suffer terribly, would perhaps lose
its existence as a nation-state. We must not yield to any disposition to
minimize the horrors this might involve. But on no ground that I can
think of is it clear that this outcome would be substantially worse than
the others. Whatever course the nation now takes, its national existence
is at stake. The only live option remaining has to do with the cause
for which we stake that existence. And surely no one who believes in
the Judaeo-Christian world-view can doubt for a moment that such a
savior-nation would be honored and loved more than any other in
all history by the generations to come—as men have always loved the
prophets and pioneers and martyrs, though in their lifetime they crucified them, and have understood well enough that the ultimate victory
rested with the sons of God.

The sickness of our age is such that there is no longer any cure for
it except that which might be wrought by a nation prepared to give
its life in order that the nations might be healed and return to God.

There is, of course, no nation which is not subject to the moral law, including the command to love. But if there be a nation on which a special responsibility rests, it is surely the United States. In any event, moral responsibility calls, as we have seen, for unilateral action. What we who live in this land have to do is to see to it that this nation heeds the call of God and of distressed humanity.

More passionately than words can express, I hope that this nation, my country, may by the grace of God rise to the awful and glorious responsibility of this hour. As I write, it is almost exactly fifty-five years since as a child of six I came with my parents and my brother and sisters from the Netherlands to this land. We came in the steerage as did so many millions in those prehistoric days before World War I. It was a long and rough winter voyage. When we got to this side of the Atlantic, my mother was ill; and so we were kept for a month in a hospital on an island in New York Harbor until she recovered.

The attendants at the hospital did not understand our Dutch, nor we their English, or American. But we got along famously with them and especially with one named John. If I ever meet him in paradise, I am sure my spirit will recognize his, even if he does not recall that slender, pale and tremendously excited Dutch boy with whom he once played.

When he found out that my first name was Abraham, he started to call me Abraham Lincoln and did so during the entire four weeks we were detained. We children did not know whether Abraham Lincoln was the name of a person, city, state, gadget or what have you. But it was of course natural that one of the first things we did when we got among relatives in Michigan with whom we could converse was to inquire who or what Abraham Lincoln was. And so it came about that very early in my life I began to read everything by Lincoln or about him I could lay hands on.

Early I learned to say, "Our fathers founded upon this continent a new nation, conceived in liberty and dedicated to the proposition that all men are created equal." Early I learned to say, "Fondly do we hope, fervently do we pray, that this mighty scourge of war may speedily pass away. . . . We must not be enemies. . . . The mystic chords of memory . . . will yet swell the chorus . . . when again touched, as surely they will be, by the better angels of our nature.

. . . With malice toward none; with charity for all . . . to do all which may achieve and cherish a just and lasting peace among ourselves, and with all nations."

That is how I learned about the American Dream. That is the American Dream.

Many times as a boy and a youth, dreaming that dream, I have paraphrased the words of the ancient Hebrew poet in exile and said: "If I forget thee, O America, let my right hand forget her cunning; let my tongue cleave to the roof of my mouth."

Yes, of course, I have learned, partly with the help of policemen's sticks and in my country's jails, that my boyhood conception of the reality which is America was naïve and idealized.

But the Dream was not altogether a dream. And even now, beyond any other under the sun, this is a "sweet land of liberty" and in all material aspects we are incomparably more fortunate than any other people.

But now we have come to the final crisis; we have one more chance. We have to take the Dream of equality, of freedom, of brotherhood, of peace, seriously now. Have to be deadly serious about it. And we have to share it with all the world, One World as it is with no boundaries and no defenses left. Otherwise the Dream will be shattered and the great republic will perish or "harden into bitter empire" and then perish, accursed forever.

That man, that we plain Americans, should conquer atomic energy —that is, conquer ourselves—surely that is too much to hope. But we dare no longer hope for less. And there are moments when it seems that the atomic bomb has created a new psychology, that in thousands, millions of Americans there is the feeling which justifies Raymond B. Fosdick of the Rockefeller Foundation—not usually regarded as a source of starry-eyed credulity and fantasy-weaving—in saying:

Although in 5,000 years of recorded human history we have never succeeded in stopping war, we promise ourselves we shall stop it now—in this generation. In spite of the fact that weapons once invented—from cavalry and gunpowder down to TNT and flame-throwers—have always been employed in subsequent struggles, we highly resolve that atomic bombs shall not be used again. . . . Confronted by the promise of death to our civilization, we insist upon life. In the face of a crisis more ominous than anything the race has ever met, we reaffirm our ability to master it. We have few analogies from the past to encourage us, and in a real sense the cards are stacked against us. But we will not give up hope. We believe we can abolish war because without that belief we shall succumb to a senseless horror and blow ourselves and our civilization into drifting dust.

Let the sons and daughters of the pioneers then listen to Whitman's song as the call to pioneer on the most perilous and magical frontier of all comes to them in the era of the Atomic Bomb:

And thou, America!
For the Scheme's culmination—its Thought and its Reality,
For these (not for thyself) Thou hast arrived. . . .

The measur'd faiths of other lands—the grandeurs of the past,
Are not for Thee—but grandeurs of Thine own. . . .
Love like the light silently wrapping all!
Nature's amelioration blessing all!
The blossoms, fruits of ages—orchards divine and certain;
Forms, objects, growths, humanities, to spiritual Images ripening.

Give me, O God, to sing that thought!
Give me, give him or her I love, this quenchless faith
In Thy ensemble. Whatever else withheld, withhold not from us
Belief in plan of Thee enclosed in Time and Space;
Health, peace, salvation universal.

Is it a dream?
Nay, but the lack of it the dream,
And, failing it, life's lore and wealth a dream,
And all the world a dream.[2]

2 From Whitman's "Song of the Universal."

Chapter VIII

Several Million Conscientious Objectors

When I have advanced proposals for Christian revolutionary action, including if necessary unilateral disarmament, the question is often put: "Then you believe that the Kingdom of God will have to be realized or we cannot have peace and ward off atomic war?" One is expected to deprecate such a suggestion, or side-step it somehow. Nothing so extreme and unattainable as this! But I trust I have made it clear that something of this sort is precisely what I do mean. No ordinary device will enable us to meet the extraordinary situation in which mankind finds itself. Unless men are prepared to a significant degree to accept the laws of God and the spirit of Christ as the way of life for nations as well as individuals, there is no hope for us. It seems to me that any other view is based on the assumption that we still live in the pre-Hiroshima age.

I do not think, however, that this implies that virtually all Americans must individually become deeply committed and informed pacifists before the program we have been presenting has some hope of adoption. But two things are necessary. In the first place, there must be many more individuals than there now are who not only renounce any voluntary participation in war but by the grace of God live in that spirit which taketh away the occasion of all war and thus become reservoirs of a new kind of power. There must be several million conscientious objectors. In the second place, there must be a decisive change in the religious leadership of the nation; the churches will have to live up to the faith they profess and call upon the nation to act on the assumption that "this way of life which Jesus taught and lived is practical—now." The first of these conditions we shall discuss in the present chapter, the second in the succeeding one.

To say that the nation must make up its mind to rule resort to war completely out of its plans—unless it is merely making sounds—must mean that individual citizens make up their minds to refuse any voluntary participation in war and preparations for war and to exert all the power they have to keep the nation from engaging in war. It is the individual who has a mind to make up and a conscience to honor or to betray. He cannot shift the responsibility for decision to other people—officials, for example—much less can he pass it on to an abstraction, such as "the nation." If the nation must rule war out of its calculations, the citizen must first rule it out of his. What we need is, instead of a few thousand conscientious objectors, many hundred thousand, a few million of them. One of the ways in which we shall be able to test whether there is really ground for hope that World War III will be prevented is by such a growth in the number of determined, active, uncompromising pacifists.

One of the big reasons why war keeps on happening in spite of the fact that there is no longer any rational justification for it and in spite of the fact that the overwhelming majority of people do not want to go to war, have no heart in it and do not expect any good to come out of it, is precisely that in the showdown they will go to war, submit to being drafted, go through it all again, in defiance of reason and their deepest convictions. Governments are aware of this. Military and political leaders are aware of it and consciously or unconsciously are always taking it into account in their deliberations. They figure, and justifiably so, that they do not yet have a mandate to strike resort to war finally and completely out of their calculations. How then can they be expected to give themselves wholeheartedly to finding an alternative? How can they even seriously consider an alternative? They go on building up their armies, manufacturing their bombs, carrying on research in more effective ways of slaughtering human beings. The cannon fodder will be available when the crisis comes and the inevitable war breaks upon the world. In spite of all the idealists, the utopians, the pacifists, the multitudes of plain people say against war, all but a tiny minority will go along. It is when that tiny minority becomes too big to be ignored that the political and military leaders, the technologists and the scientists, will know that they have indeed a mandate to abandon war, that they must find an alternative. It will not be too difficult then to find that alternative.

This necessity of going beyond making speeches, passing resolutions and casting votes is so important and urgent that we must pause to emphasize it. It will do us good to recall some of the things Thoreau said under this head in his great essay on "Civil Disobedience." It is a great American document and should be taught in all the schools. There might well be a requirement that every holder of office in the country read it once a year. Certainly all pacifists should be thoroughly familiar with it and return at frequent intervals to meditate on its profound teaching.

Thoreau was writing at the time of the Mexican War and the agitation against chattel slavery. He says:

There are thousands who are in opinion opposed to slavery and to the war, who yet in effect do nothing to put an end to them. . . . They hesitate, and they regret, and sometimes they petition; but they do nothing in earnest and with effect. They will wait, well disposed, for others to remedy the evil, that they may no longer have it to regret. At most, they give only a cheap vote, and a feeble countenance and God-speed, to the right, as it goes by them. There are nine hundred and ninety-nine patrons of virtue to one virtuous man.

All voting is a sort of gaming. . . . The character of the voters is not staked. I cast my vote, perchance, as I think right; but I am not vitally concerned that that right should prevail. I am willing to leave it to the majority. . . . Even voting *for the right* is *doing* nothing for it. It is only expressing to men feebly your desire that it should prevail. . . .

Those who, while they disapprove of the character and measures of a government, yield to it their allegiance and support, are undoubtedly its most conscientious supporters, and so frequently the most serious obstacles to reform. . . . Let your life be a counter-friction to stop the machine. What I have to do is to see, at any rate, that I do not lend myself to the wrong which I condemn. . . . A man has not everything to do, but something; and because he cannot do *everything*, it is not necessary that he should do *something* wrong. . . . Cast your whole vote, not a strip of paper merely, but your whole influence. A minority is powerless while it conforms to the majority; it is not even a minority then; but it is irresistible when it clog with its whole weight.

How, then, shall the minority which is through with war "clog with its whole weight?" How cast more than a "cheap vote" against war? How withdraw "allegiance and support" from war and the state which makes war? It is, obviously, in so complex and highly integrated situation as the citizen of a modern state finds himself, very difficult to extricate oneself from the wrong it is doing. It is indeed impossible to free oneself completely; and endless discussions will arise as to where to draw the line. But precisely for that reason it is of the utmost importance to draw a line, to dissociate oneself from war to as great an extent as possible. Otherwise it would never be possible to remove a strongly entrenched evil or to alter in any wise the course of events.

What the individual must do first of all is to put himself on record, to stand up and be counted as a conscientious objector and pacifist. In some way he must make a plain and unequivocal public declaration of his position. For most people one of the simplest and most effective ways in which to do this is to join one of the organizations which commits its members to a clean-cut refusal voluntarily to participate in war or war preparation.

There are individuals who have an extreme distaste for joining anything and I am not here insisting that for them enrollment in an organization is an essential. Some of these people make their stand unmistakably clear in other ways. It is those who do not do so who fall short of performing their public duty and perhaps even expose their integrity to question. An opinion or conviction which is a purely "private" one and which never in some way affects one's relations with others is nonexistent except perhaps as an expression of hypocrisy.

When I emphasize, as I do, the importance of taking a public stand, I am not forgetful of the fact that in the end it is not professions and pledge-signing which count but deeds and above all the quiet witness of a life lived in "that spirit which taketh away the occasion of all war." We shall have occasion to return to this point. However valid and fundamental it is, there is good ground for the insistence of all churches and religious teachers on public confession of faith. Public confession of pacifist faith is essential today.

Some persons object to joining an antiwar organization on the ground that they do not believe it is right to "sign a pledge" as to what they will do in the future if war comes. There is of course a sense in which no one can commit himself to a certain course of action in a radically new situation which at the moment he is unable to envisage. That simple fact does not keep us from feeling morally committed to do or refuse to do certain things which are part of a consistent pattern of life. As a matter of fact, people who say they do not want to commit themselves as to what they will or will not do in the future with respect to such issues as war mean that they are not clear in their thinking and firm in their conviction now. They ought to face that. The whole objection under discussion has, it seems to me, ceased to have any meaning. The question when it comes to taking a public stand today does not relate to a contingency, i.e., a war which may occur in the future and present radically new problems. War is on now—hidden war, an armed armistice, an atomic armament race. When it breaks out into the open, it will be atomic war. Are you for that or against it or a neutral? Will you continue to acquiesce in and support it or will you publicly be counted out of it? That is the real question. People are "signed up" as citizens of the nation, as those who at least passively condone what is going on, unless they publicly repudiate that stand.

This observation serves to remind us that it is not enough to join a pacifist organization "once and for all," as some people join a church. Numerous occasions arise in connection with public issues, in church debates, in intercourse with our neighbors, in our union or farm organizations, when one is in effect counted for war unless he stands up to be counted somehow on the other side. Not to let such opportunities go by has become extremely important in the supreme crisis in which we now find ourselves.

In this connection membership in an active pacifist organization is useful, provided of course it is not a mere "paper membership." We shall be reminded of issues as they arise and of what may be done about them. It provides opportunity for corporate witness and action. Furthermore, it provides the sense of fellowship and the support of like-minded people which is so essential as the crisis sharpens, as the war propaganda is stepped up, and fidelity to a minority position becomes more costly and perhaps dangerous.

Randolph Bourne, the brilliant young intellectual of World War I who was so profoundly shocked when his fellow intellectuals of that period gradually gave up their socialist and pacifist principles and be-came apologists for and participants in it, has left a searching analysis of the process by which this defection occurs. It is in an essay on "The War and the Intellectuals" written in 1917 and included in a volume entitled *Untimely Papers* published in 1919. Incidentally, if these essays were "untimely" then, they are amazingly timely now, includ-ing the "Unfinished Fragment on the State," which might well be placed next to Thoreau's essay from which we have already quoted, on the list of required reading.

Bourne points out how terrific are the forces which bring their impact to bear on the individual as war approaches and how irresistible, for most, becomes the impulse to jump into the vast procession, to join in the shouting and the delirious action, how utterly painful to refuse to join in, to stay on the side lines. The intellectual stops think-ing objectively and critically: "Simple syllogisms are substituted for analysis, things are known by their labels, our heart's desire dictates what we see," and then:

The American intellectual class, having failed to make the higher synthesis, regresses to ideas that can issue a quick, simplified action. . . . War was seen as the crowning relief of their indecision. At last action, irresponsibility, the end of anxious and torturing attempts to reconcile peace-ideals with the drag of the world towards Hell. An end to the pain of trying to adjust the facts to what they ought to be! Let us consecrate the facts as ideal! Let us join the greased slide towards war! . . . Hesitations, ironies, consciences, considerations,—all were drowned in the elemental blare of doing something aggressive, colossal. The new-found sabbath "peacefulness of being at war." . . . The American university is a brisk and happy place these days. Simple, unquestioning action has superseded the knots of thought. The thinker dances with reality. . . .

In a time of danger and disaster we jump desperately for some dogma to cling to. The time comes, if we try to hold out, when our nerves are sick with fatigue, and we seize in a great healing wave of release some doctrine that can be immediately translated into action. . . . With war the world becomes motor again.

The reader who is too young to remember World War I would have taken for granted, had he not been told in advance the author and the date of this quotation, that it was written in 1939-41. Remember that urge for action, the pain of seeming just to stand by and do nothing about it. Even many pacifists were seized by it and felt that they must suddenly be "doing something real and worth while." And what a reflection that was upon what they had been doing before!

Recall the course of the intellectuals as the crisis deepened—the professors who were troubled about the souls of their students, especially the men of draft age, "the age that war prefers," because these students still believed what the professors had told them about war and propaganda and hysteria in the late twenties and the early and middle thirties. They will go through it all again—their successors, that is—if the atomic armament race continues. Think, you who do not want to see an atomic war and who hesitate to go on record now irrevocably against taking any part in it, hesitate to burn all bridges and be marked a conscientious objector and a pacifist. Think what thé pressure will be when the hour approaches for pressing the push-buttons and getting ready to slaughter forty million here and forty million there.

It is because indecision will be fatal then, can indeed lead to but one decision, that a clear, uncompromising decision must be made now. It is to prevent that hour from ever breaking—if it may be—and in order to be able to withstand if it does come, and "having done all to stand," that we must now decide and begin to discipline ourselves and build an unbreakable fellowship that will be so precious and rich that nothing will be able to carry us out of it.

Those who make the decision personally to break with the war system must, then, be alert for ways in which they can make effective public confession of their faith and can dissociate themselves from the evil of war. The references from Randolph Bourne remind us how important it is that those who are recognized as leaders and as molders of public opinion, keepers of the conscience of the nation, should do this.

This applies to the intellectuals and especially to those of the Left. They know better than anyone else, perhaps, that war plays into the hands of reaction and totalitarianism, that it cannot possibly carry the world forward to the goal they desire. They believe that we must depend upon the workers and farmers largely to achieve that basic change in the social order without which there cannot be well-being and peace and cultural and spiritual advance. They must see now, if they did not before, that we can never have social progress but will move certainly toward social catastrophe if ever again the masses can be duped into mutual extermination in atomic war. On the other hand, is it not clear that an exploiting imperialist regime could not possibly be maintained if it were deprived of its war machine and of its ability to resort to war in order to evade the solution of its economic contradictions? Surely there is a chance—a chance which men who feel and can still reason must eagerly seize—that if we spent as much time, energy, devotion, sacrifice in trying to persuade the farm and labor organizations and all progressive forces in the nation to adopt an uncompromising antimilitarism, rejection of all war, civil and international, as we have devoted to other revolutionary strategies, we might succeed in winning mass support for such a course. But is there any reason to suppose that the masses would have any confidence in those advancing such a proposal unless the latter personally were on record as renouncing war and all voluntary participation in it?

In one issue of a progressive magazine which appeared shortly before these words were written there were two articles containing such sentiments as these. The first: "The question is not whether Germans deserve decency. We need decency. It will save us. . . . Some one has to stop the disintegration of our civilization. We must break the vicious circle of an-eye-for-an-eye-for-an-eye-for-an-eye. . . . What shall we do about Germany? First, what shall we do about ourselves?"

The second article contains these words: "We could use a radical in Germany to say to that lost and wandering people, 'I am your friend. You expect me to be your enemy. You have given me cause to hate you. But I do not hate you. . . . I am a guy who doesn't kick my enemy when I have knocked him down. I lift him up.' . . . We could use a guy who'd stand up there and say, 'The choice is simple, friends. Christ on the Mount or a sophisticated sage on the microphone. A doctrine of love—or a doctrine of hate.'"

Magnificent sentiments these and brilliantly expressed. Can they be reconciled with war? And is there anything more truly radical today, more certain to lead to fundamental changes in the whole range of life, than abolition of war? Is there indeed in the outward order anything which stands in the way of a New World other than the threat of war? Will these men then join the ranks of the conscientious objectors, the pacifists? If not, what holds them back? Fear of the label of pacifism? What shall be said of teachers of the people who are afraid of labels? And if a label can frighten them now, how shall they be able to stand in the day of testing which is to come?

There are other groups whose members exercise an important influence on public opinion and help to set ethical standards, personal and social, to whom the challenge to renounce war, and to put themselves unequivocally on record to that effect, comes at this crucial moment. The leaders, clerical and lay, of the various religious bodies are included in this category. However, the whole question of the position to be taken by these leaders and by the religious fellowships, the churches as churches, in view of their own creeds and professions and the teachings of the Judaeo-Christian Scriptures, requires somewhat detailed consideration and will accordingly be postponed to the next chapter.

A word must be said here about the educators though to a considerable extent of course there is overlapping between them and those we have called religious leaders. Next to the home, the schools, colleges and universities play the greatest part in determining the thought patterns, the ethical standards, the habits and character of the youth of the nation. It may even be questioned whether in our contemporary culture the schools do not exercise greater influence than parents and the home environment. And this is true in a special sense with respect to adolescent attitudes toward war and participation in it. It is now the accepted thing to conscript youth for war at eighteen, and that means enlistment at seventeen in many cases. But it is common knowledge that this is precisely the time when young people feel the psychological need to break away from dependence upon parents and to play their own part in the larger world outside the home. At the same time they are by no means mature enough, mentally and emotionally, to play a truly independent adult part. The need to "belong to" and be accepted by their contemporaries is overwhelming. But this means for the most advanced of our youth that it is the standards and environment of the schools and colleges that largely determine their conduct. Not a few pacifist parents have seen sons, who up to the age of fourteen considered themselves pacifists because their parents were, change their views under school influences—even Quaker schools, unfortunately. Or if the sons' views were not entirely altered they were still not emotionally mature enough to take a conscientious objector stand in face of the pressure of the school environment.

Teachers and administrators in both public and private educational institutions are, furthermore, confronted with the fact that if war is not abolished, if the present atomic armament race goes on, military influence and control in education will increase enormously. At the moment of writing, although the leading educational, church, labor and farm organizations are practically without exception opposed to the enactment of peacetime compulsory universal military training, i.e., conscription, in the United States, the national administration, the Army and the American Legion are still engaged in a high-pressure campaign to secure the enactment of this measure. The American Legion makes no attempt to conceal the fact that preparation of the minds of our children for such military training must reach all the way back into the elementary schools and be intensified in the upper grades. A great extension of R.O.T.C. work in the high schools, colleges and universities will be an important part of the conscription program. If universal conscription should for the present be defeated, then the pressure for increased military training in high schools and colleges as an alternative will simply be intensified. This will be true, even though not a few experts—and it is rumored even top military figures including General MacArthur, who at the time of writing has not appeared before Congress to testify in favor of conscription nor has he uttered a word in public in support of the proposal during two years of agitation for it by the War Department—hold that the atomic bomb has made the measure obsolete. Those who think in terms of another war want conscription and the militarization of the schools for purposes of indoctrination, to overcome the reluctance on the part of normal human beings in modern times to wage war, i.e., commit national and perhaps race suicide. From their own point of view they are right. In preparation for atomic warfare an immense amount of regimentation will be necessary. What the people, and in particular the educators, must decide is whether the military are to decide national policy at this crucial point.

Teachers, we are told, must be objective and unbiased. Teaching is not indoctrination. In a democracy children and youth must be taught to think and make decisions for themselves and not be subjected to undue emotional pressures. Let us accept this as a starting point. Several observations may be made.

In the first place, this does not mean that we can be indifferent to ethical standards, that honesty, decency, sound sex relationships, cooperativeness, hatred of deceit, theft and murder are not essential. Specifically, truthfulness, a passion for truth, acting upon truth as we are given to see it are essentials of objective education, of democratic citizenship. Furthermore, personal integration and responsible functioning in the community are impossible where there is a cleavage between the professed standards and the teachings of school and community on the one hand and their practices on the other.

The mere statement of these elementary requirements of a sound training in morals is enough to make it patent that modern war, as we have experienced it in the two great conflicts which have already marked the twentieth century and in the atomic battles with which we are now threatened, raises the most serious problems for educators in a democracy. One set of moral standards and social ideals is inculcated in home and school in so far as they embody Christian and democratic values and concepts; an entirely different set of standards and aims is required of those who take part in total warfare. Under modern conditions, if war remains in the picture at all, the nation must be permanently on a war footing, must be militarized from top to bottom, as the totalitarian regimes have recognized. For educators the issue is clearly drawn: they must choose between war and education as we have known it, or at least the educational concepts and ideals we have professed. We can have one or the other, but not both. What choice will educators, the individual educator, make?

A recent development casts an ominous light on this problem and suggests that under the pressure of modern mechanization, regimentation and war we have already lost ground. Recent polls by the big public opinion testing agencies seem to show that a large majority of people in this country still favor peacetime military training and that of this majority a substantial majority in turn say they want compulsory military training, even if it is not needed for "defense," because of its value in inculcating discipline in our young people! What does this signify? It can only mean that the home, the church, the school, the local community have in the opinion of a majority of our people failed in developing democratic self-discipline in our youth. Instead of inquiring how these institutions, which are at the very heart and center of a democratic society, may once more discharge the function they should and in the past measurably did perform, people would have them abdicate their ancient place. The parents, educators, religious and civic leaders who would turn to military training, to conscription, favorite technique of dictators, abdicate their own place and function. They admit defeat. They are tired. At bottom they no longer believe in democracy and its potentialities. They are voting for authoritarianism, for a Fuehrer type of discipline and education. It is out of this mood of tiredness and of disillusionment with democracy that fascism grows.

At the very time when this mood is prevalent, the newspapers announce that we are destroying "the roots of German militarism" by forbidding military training, any form of conscription and the wearing of military uniforms. Take the uniforms off the Germans and Japanese, in other words, and put them on American youth. The fact that multitudes of Americans do not see the contradiction only serves to emphasize the responsibility of educators, every single educator in the country, to make his choice between democratic education and war, and to act upon his decision.

We started with the suggestion that education must be objective and unbiased. A second comment arises out of that assumption. It would seem clear, if academic freedom is to prevail, that pacifist teachers who meet the requirements of good teaching should be treated in the same way as nonpacifists who meet the same requirements. It is well known that for the most part this is not the case even in peacetime, and that in many communities the situation becomes extremely delicate and difficult for pacifists when open war breaks out. It is true fortunately that the situation was much better in this respect during World War II than World War I. But to a considerable extent this must be ascribed to the fact that teachers with pacifist convictions refrained from outspoken pacifist utterances during the war, as was the case also with many preachers, while nonpacifists were not only permitted but encouraged if not required to be outspoken and vigorous in support of the war. Again, as the issue becomes sharper, what position is the individual educator going to take? Will he insist upon academic freedom, equal rights for his pacifist colleagues, or will he permit a situation to develop such as exists in totalitarian lands, where it is virtually impossible for anyone who does not passively if not actively support militarism to find a place in the educational world?

In the third place, the bias against which it is most important to guard in the teaching of history, current events and other social subjects is the nationalistic bias; and the nationalistic bias is nowhere more clearly and flagrantly in evidence than in the teaching of the causes, the conduct and the results of war. Every educator of any standing knows that the difficulty is serious enough in peacetime though here in the United States the version of World War I which was taught in the postwar years differed materially from that which was taught during that war. Encouraging as this may be from one point of view, it serves on the other hand to emphasize that in the period leading up to a war and during the war years the truth is not taught at all. For one thing, many facts are deliberately withheld on the plea of military necessity. Others are as deliberately colored. It is several years after the event that we learn from Sumner Welles, then Under-Secretary of State, that when Roosevelt and Churchill met on a war vessel in the Atlantic the possible and probable war with Japan was discussed. Churchill wanted a statement issued which would give some indication of what had been discussed and would serve as a warning to Japan. Roosevelt wanted a general, idealistic statement. His view prevailed and thus the Atlantic Charter was born and announced to mankind. Some years later when some people insisted that the provisions of the Atlantic Charter ought to be applied in armistice negotiations and peace settlements, Mr. Roosevelt explained at a news conference that the Charter must not be taken as too binding a document; he and Mr. Churchill happened to be together in the Atlantic; he made some notes on pieces of paper; there never was an official copy made—this though the United Nations had in the meantime solemnly pledged allegiance to the Charter. It is perhaps not out of keeping under these circumstances to recall a wag's version of what Mr. Roosevelt said on another occasion, namely, that the name "Atlantic" was of no special significance in connection with the Charter; it just recalled the fact that he and Mr. Churchill were at sea when the document was promulgated.

Such important political—not military—facts are not known during the war. Even if they are known, they are ordinarily not taught, certainly not given due importance in schools and colleges during wartime.

Similarly, the picture of what fighting in modern war is like which children and youth get in school is very different from actual fighting as the G.I. knows it. Surely it would be very hard to exaggerate the responsibility which this imposes upon the educator, man or woman— noncombatant—standing before boys who presently will or may be combatants and will have to face what the teacher will not face, very likely never has faced. It were better perhaps that "a millstone be tied about his neck. . . ."

Again and again, then, we face the dilemma: we can have free, democratic education compatible with the Judaeo-Christian world view, or we can have atomic war. What are educators going to do under these circumstances? Or rather, since it is individual responsibility and decision we are emphasizing all along, what is the educator going to do? He must choose. In effect he will be expressing his choice in his daily work, even though he may hardly be aware that he is doing so. Will he insist on being unbiased and presenting the whole truth? Will he insist on complete freedom of discussion among teachers and students? Will he resist the overt or subtle badgering of teachers and students who hold an unpopular point of view? If military training becomes a major factor in the institution with which he is connected, will he continue that connection and thus run the risk that he is helping to create the impression that the institution is still in the true sense "educational"? If he remains, will he insist that no one shall be forced to take military training? If he teaches men in uniform nonmilitary subjects, will he make his own position clear to them? Will he take part in organized efforts to banish compulsory military training from the institution? If a pacifist colleague is victimized, will he "pass by on the other side" and hang on to his own job?

Furthermore, it is well known that it is the spirit and method of teaching, rather than its content, and even more the character of the teacher, which plays the chief role in determining the standards, values and character of the students. In his capacity as an educator, then, as well as in his capacity as citizen or in other categories that might be named, the educator in our day must answer the question whether he will personally take the pacifist, the conscientious objector, position. Our thesis is that civilization cannot survive atomic war and that if war is to be abolished a large number of people, and particularly a considerable percentage of those who mold public opinion, must personally break with war, make it utterly clear that they will never again support war. The educator as educator insists upon respect for human personality, freedom, the elimination of compulsion, fidelity to truth, the power of mind and spirit as against material forces—all integral to the pacifist philosophy of life. He must answer the question whether he will carry this basic philosophy through to a rejection of war, which negates all such values, or whether he will stultify himself and his profession and capitulate to the forces which will destroy education as we have known it or at least envisioned it.

But the responsibility for a personal decision with respect to participation in war does not rest exclusively on leaders or molders of public opinion. It rests upon every individual. The time must come when ordinary human beings refuse by the thousands and millions to have any more part in war or preparation for war. That is in a sense the whole burden and the message of this book.

It is true that the masses of plain people, and especially the youth who are drafted for war, are victims—victims of bad education, of an environment where faith in democracy has grown weak, of a religious leadership that is weak and conformist and unfaithful to the teachings and spirit of Christ, of a "kept press," of government propaganda, of an exploiting economic order. Those who are in positions of leadership and power certainly cannot escape responsibility and will not escape the penalty for their crimes. Yet as *Time* stated in its issue of August 20, 1945, the first to come out after the atomic bomb was dropped on Hiroshima: "When the bomb split open the universe and revealed the prospect of the infinitely extraordinary, it also revealed the oldest, simplest, commonest, most neglected and most important facts: that each man is eternally and above all else responsible for his own soul, and, in the terrible words of the Psalmist, that no man may deliver his brother, nor make agreement unto God for him."

It is basic and central in both Christian and Jewish and democratic philosophy that each human being is a person, a being of moral dignity and worth, who makes his own decisions as to the ultimate issues of life. It must be so or democratic society is impossible. If another can decide and vote for me, then I am not free, and, if I acquiesce in that, I have renounced democracy. I have embraced the Fuehrer principle. If, on the other hand, I, everyman, want the rights and privileges which are associated with democracy, I must accept its responsibilities as well. I cannot in fact escape them.

Recently I came across what seemed to me a clear and powerful statement of the truth in a little magazine entitled *Humanity*, published and edited by Mr. Morton Alexander of Arvada, Colorado, who describes himself as "a tiller of the soil." He writes of receiving a letter from a friend who somewhat proudly describes himself as a "front-line veteran of World War I" and goes on to say that he knows "the filth and brutality of war" and that "wars are caused by capitalism." Mr. Alexander replies that this last statement is not altogether true:

Wars are put into operation and carried on by deluded men, just like my friend, who was willing to go out and shoot and slaughter and destroy other human beings whom he had been told were his "enemies." . . . There is no place to fasten the final guilt for war—except on those who perform and carry out the black and bloody deeds of war. My friend did not possess the moral courage to refuse to go to war. He weakly surrendered his body . . . marched away as an obedient slave to the State to do its bidding—however villainous and brutal the job might be. . . . True, "the Capitalists" were behind the guns—but they were a long way behind. . . . We had better stop trying to hide our shame behind silly subterfuges and stupid lies. The reason we have war is because men are still willing to go out, like wild beasts, and hunt and slay and destroy other men. And sadly enough, our jungle civilization hails them as heroes and decorates them with honor badges.

There is, of course, in one sense more, even much more, to be said about how to abolish war, but what is here said is essential and indispensable. It is ordinary people, fathers, mothers, boys of draft age, the girls whom they want to please, the G.I.'s of World War II, who must recognize and accept their responsibility, must each make his decision about war before God and conscience.

It is the lack of this sense of responsibility in the ordinary person which constitutes one of the gravest maladies of our time. It is both a cause and a symptom of the decline of democracy and the onset of totalitarianism. It is the prophecy of our doom.

Mr. Dwight Macdonald in a supplement to the magazine *Politics* entitled "The Responsibility of Peoples" cites an instance which brings home with terrific force what happens when the sense of personal responsibility is lost and each individual no longer "behaves as a whole man (hence responsibly) rather than as a specialized part of some nation or profession (hence irresponsibly)." Says Mr. Macdonald:

If every one is guilty, then no one is guilty. The dialectics of this are wonderfully illustrated in an anecdote quoted by Hannah Arendt ("Organized Guilt and Universal Responsibility," *Jewish Frontier*, January, 1945) from *PM* of Nov. 12 last. An American correspondent interviews an official of a "death camp" who had fallen into the hands of the Russians:
Q. Did you kill people in the camp? A. Yes.
Q. Did you poison them with gas? A. Yes.
Q. Did you bury them alive? A. It sometimes happened.
Q. Did you personally help to kill people?
A. Absolutely not. I was only paymaster of the camp.
Q. What did you think of what was going on?
A. It was bad at first, but we got used to it.
Q. Do you know the Russians will hang you?
A. (bursting into tears) Why should they? What have I done?
What have I done? These words ring true. One feels that the worthy paymaster—imagine the civilization that has produced the job of paymaster in a death camp!—is sincerely outraged by the proposal to hang him for his part in killing several million human beings. What had he done indeed? Simply obeyed orders and kept his mouth shut.

In principle, the soldier in the American Army, assuming that he accepts the military regime, has no more choice as to what actions he will or will not perform than the soldier in the Nazi Army. Soldiers may not discriminate, "on the frivolous grounds of personal conscience, between one military order and another." If Dachau is a crime, Hiroshima is a crime, as we have already contended. Germans perpetrated Dachau and much else—under orders. American soldiers perpetrated Hiroshima and much else—under orders. We have to abandon as evil and the source of evil the notion that the individual is not responsible for what is done in war and under orders. We must, rather, arrive at the conviction that war must be abolished and that pending its abolition the individual must refuse to participate in it, precisely because it demands of him that he put his conscience in the keeping of the state, that he let another decide for him whether to kill, how many, and under what circumstances.

Evil practices and customs, such as racial segregation, evil laws, evil institutions, such as war and the power state, whose chief and well-nigh exclusive function it is to wage war—all these flourish because men conform and render obedience and keep their mouths shut. Those who rule and give orders are guilty; but so are those who conform and obey. There is no government save where there are those who consent to be governed.

In this age of mechanization, regimentation and authoritarianism perhaps nothing is more important than that the individual should again learn to disobey evil laws, learn the tremendous power of refusal, of saying no. "So long as the superstition that men should obey unjust laws exists," says Gandhi, "so long will their slavery exist." And he calls attention to an old proverb of India which, translated literally, means: "One negative cures thirty-six diseases."

Even among pacifists there is too often a tendency to minimize the importance or validity of this no-saying, of conscientious objection, of refusal to go along, of non-co-operation. It is said to be "merely negative" perhaps. From the moral standpoint those who advance this objection need to be very certain that they are not in effect co-operating with the evil which they profess to condemn. Often, all that the beneficiaries and defenders of entrenched wrong want is that people should keep still, should not point the finger, should "go quietly about their own business." How simple and pleasant things would probably have been for Jesus if he had gone about healing the sick, feeding the hungry and perhaps forgiving sins—if only he had not been a conscientious objector to Jewish Sabbatarianism and nationalism, Roman imperialism and the use of the Temple for commercial purposes and exorbitant profits. Those who hesitate to be noncon-formists and non-co-operators need to make sure that their attitude is not due to a childish dread of doing something that is not respectable, a desire to move in "good society," a reluctance to pay the price of an uncompromising severance of relations with an evil order of things.

Practically, nothing is more clearly established than that somehow tremendous forces are released when a few individuals appear who are not afraid to refuse, who will not conform. There is an ancient Hebrew tale symbolizing that truth. It is of three young men who were told to worship the king's gods and the image he had set up. And the young men said: "Be it known unto thee, O King, that we will not serve thy gods nor worship the golden image which thou hast set up" —be it known unto thee that we will NOT. So the king threw them into the fiery furnace which he had prepared—which usually is pre-pared—for such contumacious and dangerous characters. But pres-ently the king was astonished and dismayed, as the mighty have so often been in similar circumstances. He said to his counselors: "Did not we cast three men bound into the midst of the fire? . . . Lo, I see four men loose, walking in the midst of the fire, and they have no hurt: and the aspect of the fourth is like a son of the gods."

The need of our day is for conscientious objectors, no-sayers. We must find ways to disassociate ourselves from war and from conscrip-tion for war, ways to withdraw our support from the atomic arma-ments race and from the authoritarian power state which engages in it.

If peacetime conscription should be enacted in this country, that would be a major turning point, a sinister development, which would sharpen this issue. It would be a decisive move in an atomic armaments race, virtually a declaration of preparation for atomic war against Russia. It would be part of an unmistakably militarist and fascist pattern for American life. In that case the question would, I think, have to be seriously considered whether those who were determined not to support war preparations would not finally have to resort to that technique for which there are notable precedents in American history, of refusal to pay taxes or such portion at least of federal taxes as was avowedly being used for war preparation. This is not the place for a detailed discussion of the problems this raises. It is desirable that all conscientious spirits should recall at this time the noble words spoken on this subject by Henry David Thoreau in that essay on "Civil Disobedience" to which reference has already been made:

> If a thousand men were not to pay their tax bills this year, that would not be a violent and bloody measure, as it would be to pay them, and enable the State to commit violence and shed innocent blood. This is, in fact, the definition of a peaceable revolution, if any such is possible. If the tax-gatherer, or any other public officer, asks me, as one has done, "But what shall I do?" my answer is, "If you really wish to do anything, resign your office." When the subject has refused allegiance and the officer has resigned his office, then the revolution is accomplished. But even suppose blood should flow. Is there not a sort of blood shed when the conscience is wounded? Through this wound a man's real manhood and immortality flow out, and he bleeds to an everlasting death. I see this blood flowing now. . . .
>
> I have never declined paying the highway tax, because I am as desirous of being a good neighbor as I am of being a bad subject; and as for supporting schools, I am doing my part to educate my fellow-countrymen now. . . . I simply wish to refuse allegiance to the State, to withdraw and stand aloof from it effectually. I do not care to trace the course of my dollar, if I could, till it buys a man or a musket to shoot with—the dollar is innocent, —but I am concerned to trace the effects of my allegiance.

Thoreau is sometimes spoken of as an anarchist, though it seems to me that in this essay he takes issue not with government as such but with a state which rests on slavery and war. It is not against government in any case but against war and against the modern "sovereign" power state whose function is war that we are contending here. It is these which produce anarchy in the modern world, undermine all free, that is, all genuine, government, substituting dictatorship for it, rend civilization in pieces and threaten to transform the fair earth into a slaughterhouse. They will not be stopped and deprived of their diabolical power to do evil until men stop obeying them, say a final no to them. We need above all else a few million conscientious objectors who will not bow the knee to Caesar, to the modern Anti-Christ. And it shall be they who seem to divide who will in fact provide the power which shall bind the society of mankind together again and insure that "government of the people, by the people, for the people shall not perish from the earth."

Chapter IX

What the Spirit Saith to the Churches

Thoughtful men and women no longer doubt that another war must be prevented and the war system must be eradicated or civilization is doomed. Our survey has driven us to the conclusion that this cannot happen unless a profound psychological and spiritual change takes place. The nation or people which experienced such a change would be convicted of the sin involved in making war rather than frightened by the thought of what would become of them if war should be waged against them. Such a people would renounce war, disarm, become pacifist—and be prepared to accept the consequences. Our argument led us also to the conclusion that the kind of reorientation of mind and conversion of spirit which we have found necessary could conceivably take place in time to avert a global catastrophe only if the spiritual leaders and the religious forces of a nation were to embrace the pacifist faith and lead the nation in renouncing any further participation in war.

The thesis that the Christian Church or churches are called upon to do just that has recently been stated in a most eloquent manner by an Englishman, Howard Spring, not himself a pacifist, in the book to which we have already made reference, the autobiographical *And Another Thing*. Mr. Spring's discussion of this matter, which, incidentally, occupies a minor portion of his delightful book, is so significant that we cannot avoid commenting on it at some length.

Mr. Spring is the author of a number of best-selling novels including *My Son, My Son!* and *Fame Is the Spur*. He is a distinguished newspaperman, one of the few who accompanied Winston Churchill on the occasion when the Atlantic Charter was drafted. He served in the British Army in World War I and in the Cornwall Home Guard during the recent war. His book is dedicated to two of his sons who died while in the armed service of their country during that war.

If the churches were to give a pacifist lead to the nations, their proposal would not at first be accepted, Howard Spring surmises, and the churches would have to pay a heavy price.

I think that if success came at all, it would be only after a long and fluctuating struggle. It is probable that the churches acting as I have suggested would at once lose large numbers of members, and almost certainly, these would be the richest members. . . . Once war had broken out, all the allurements that draw men to the national cause, away from the cause in which there is neither Jew nor Greek, would be felt with the accustomed force. But if the churches as churches stood firm, if the banner remained, no matter how few saw the matter to an end, then, once the war was over and the inevitable frustrations and disillusions again sent their chill winds rattling through the hollowed minds of people, once the sad eyes of humanity again pondered the stone it had received instead of bread, there would be a flocking back, and this time in large numbers.

So it would go, with the Church of the Prince of Peace swelling in peacetime, losing numbers in war-time . . . until *in a very long run*, it would be a force too great for the temporal masters of the world to ignore. Long, tedious and exacting as this process would be I see no other which offers a chance of ultimate peace on earth.[1]

Mr. Spring goes on to express his firm conviction that the one hope the churches themselves have of survival is that they should embrace pacifism. Basically this is so because if they fail to do this they will be betraying Christ himself:

Whether Christendom cares to face the fact or not, Jesus was a pacifist and would have had no part or lot in this bloody shambles which besets us. . . . I see no logic in an attitude which on the one hand insists that Jesus was . . . "very God of very God," whose word was literally the voice of God speaking in the world, and on the other tells us that a follower of this omnipotent and omniscient and all-wise God may with a clear conscience act in flat contradiction to God's teaching on a vital matter.[2]

[1] *Op. cit.*, p. 89.
[2] P. 33.

He makes a further interesting observation:

It is significant that, although Christendom is founded upon the conception of God which was brought into the world by Jesus, it is not to Jesus that the martial Christian appeals. Nelson's last words were not "Jesus and my country" but "God and my country"; and Cromwell did not urge his troops to "Trust in Jesus and keep your powder dry." He, more than most others, would have seen the incongruity of that. There are occasions when we unconsciously slip back two thousand years to the pre-Jesus view of God: the view that he himself examined and put aside. "It has been said by them of old times. . . . But I say unto you. . . ." [3]

The churches would lose members if they followed Jesus' teaching about war "but we should then know who were Christians and who were not. The Church would discover that its first function was not to enlarge but to purify its membership, for the cause of true religion is advanced not by churches becoming full of men but by men becoming full of God."

In answer to the suggestion that neither a pacifist nation nor a pacifist Church might have "survival value" in a non-Christian world, he gives deeply moving and unforgettable replies in two paragraphs which also we cannot forbear recording here:

What is survival value? Does nothing survive when our blood and bones are dissolved? I imagine that the Roman soldiers, dicing at the foot of the Cross on Good Friday, had little belief in the survival value of Jesus. But what survived—and from small beginnings—was the whole conception of life resting within the scope of the word Christendom that haunts these pages like a ghost doomed to disappear at cock-crow. And the cock will be the one that announced Peter's betrayal of his Lord. But the Church lasted a long time; and it can continue to last on a condition; and that condition, I suggest, is that no matter what the odds against it, the "survival value" of a complete acceptance of the teaching of Jesus should continuously be put to proof as the story of mankind unrolls. . . . The man who would follow him, said Jesus, must "take up his own cross." The Cross is still upon the hill, and our "lesser calvaries" avail. These, too, have "survival value." . . .

It becomes increasingly difficult for an effective "opposition" to be staged to any State activity in the modern world. For the Churches to stage one against the Moloch of our supreme and suicidal devotion would be to court

[3] P. 35.

almost certain extinction. But what a death! "For whether we live, we live unto the Lord; or whether we die, we die unto the Lord: whether we live therefore or die, we are the Lord's." What could not spring from the ashes of such a phoenix! [4]

It is difficult for the present author to see how anything more needs to be added or how Mr. Spring's words can fail to carry conviction to any sincere disciple of Jesus Christ. Perhaps the more so since Mr. Spring feels that he cannot claim such discipleship since he has not personally accepted and practiced the pacifist way. Surely he cannot be far from the Kingdom, or fail presently to turn to divine grace to enable him to overcome the contradiction between his own position and the position to which he so persuasively and passionately calls all who name the name of Jesus and profess to be his followers.

Since in our presentation of the arguments for religious pacifism in this work we have devoted little time to the specifically Christian emphasis and since what the Christian churches in this country and other lands do in this supreme crisis is so important, we shall, however, devote a few paragraphs to emphasizing how unassailable the pacifist position seems to be on Christian grounds and how weak the arguments which nonpacifist Christians such as Reinhold Niebuhr and his followers advance against Christian pacifism.

The position of Niebuhr was dealt with some years ago by G. H. C. Macgregor, Professor of Divinity and Biblical Criticism, and Dean of the Faculty of Theology in the University of Glasgow, in a booklet entitled *The Relevance of an Impossible Ideal*. No Christian minister or church school teacher, now that the war is over and Christians must obviously evaluate the war experience in the light of Christian teaching, should fail to study Macgregor's book. What is here said is largely a paraphrase of a few of his points.

The foundation of Niebuhr's theological attack on pacifism rests on two grounds, his doctrine of human depravity and his view that Jesus' teaching envisages a wholly transcendent and future Kingdom of God and that his perfectionist ethic has no immediate relevance to the practical problems of national and international life.

[4] Pp. 83, 94.

The first is a one-sided and unscriptural view of human nature. To cite but one illustration, Niebuhr regards grace as forgiveness rather than as power, as "enabling grace." Man is depraved and impotent in himself but the Holy Spirit frees him from the power of sin and he produces and is under obligation to produce the fruits of the spirit. The depravity of human nature is not invoked when men steal, lie and kill in ordinary circumstances. Certainly the Church does not condone them. Why invoke this doctrine when the question of theft, deceit and murder in war comes up for consideration?

As for the second point, Niebuhr himself pretty much knocks the props from under his own contention when he says in his *Interpretation of Christian Ethics*, speaking of the "perfectionist" demands of Jesus: "The note of apocalyptic urgency is significantly lacking in many of the passages in which the religio-ethical rigor is most uncompromising. The motive advanced for fulfilling the absolute demands is simply that of obedience to God or emulation of His nature, and there is no suggestion that the world should be held in contempt because it is soon to pass away."

The Kingdom of Jesus' teaching though transcendent is manifested in the world. We are bidden to pray that God's will be done on earth. In Christ it is God's will to redeem a sinful world order. As the great New Testament scholar, Dr. C. H. Dodd, has put it in his *History and the Gospel*: "We are wrong in confining [the New Testament promises] to purely spiritual experience. They declare that as *any situation* is brought within the context of sacred history, with its creative centre in the Gospel facts, it is exposed not only to the judgment of God, but also to possibilities of transformation and renewal which we can neither define nor limit, because they lie within the immeasurable power of the mercy of God. It is to this transformation of *an actual situation* that the prayer of the Church refers, Thy Kingdom come."

When it comes to the issue of war itself, the charge that Niebuhr makes, that pacifists unjustifiably isolate war from the ethical position as a whole and "demand with reference to this one moral issue an absolute obedience to the perfectionist ethic," is the one which has undoubtedly been most damaging. It may be readily admitted that some pacifists, especially in the past, have erred in this regard. They are, however, increasingly aware of the need of applying the non-violent way and its principles in every relationship. Though there are rare exceptions, the pacifists in the churches are not those who are generally insensitive to other ethical issues and many of them are deeply troubled by their involvement in a sinful economic order.

Macgregor aptly turns one of Niebuhr's own oft-repeated arguments against him here. A characteristic Niebuhrian sentence reads: "If we think that the moral and religious judgment, which discovers us all to be sinners in the sight of God, means that we have no right to act against an acknowledged evil because we are not ourselves pure, we are delivered into historic futility." If that can be used as an argument to justify support of war, it can obviously also be used as an argument for refusal to take part in war by those who are convinced of its evil, even though they may not be "pure" and may not see as clearly how they can dissociate themselves from other evils.

Furthermore, Niebuhr's frequent insistence that we cannot take the place of God, that we must make relative choices, suggests there will be, as history unfolds, issues with respect to which the "tension between the historical and the transcendant" reaches the breaking point. So the Church must take a final stand. Slavery became such an issue at one time. As for the present moment, is it really possible for anyone to question that it is war? To quote Professor Macgregor:

The obligation laid upon us to accept the laws of the Kingdom is absolute; yet, in a world not yet wholly redeemed, it can never be completely fulfilled. Hence the "tension" of which we speak. Now if this tension is indeed to contribute to ethical progress, then from time to time it will become particularly acute at one point or another. And this has, in fact, happened in history. Under the guidance, we believe, of the Holy Spirit the Christian conscience has become particularly sensitive upon one particular issue, because it has seen there an eruption-point of the forces of evil in their invasion of the Kingdom of God. And at that point Christians have been driven to make a stand, even if that meant at least a temporary withdrawal from solidarity with the community with respect to that particular issue. So it was when the early Church felt compelled to withdraw from collaboration with the State at every point where idolatry was involved. As Dodd puts it: "It was not that this was the only thing in the

Graeco-Roman world which was contrary to the principles of the Kingdom of God; but this was the point at which the opposition to the Kingdom of God seemed at the time to be concentrated; and the Church drew the line firmly, not counting the cost of such non-cooperation." Now the Christian pacifist believes that, at least since modern war revealed its true nature in the years 1914 to 1918, the crucial ethical question has been that of war. In it is concentrated everything that is fundamentally antagonistic to the principles of the Kingdom of God, and consequently it marks the point at which the tension between the worldly order and that transcendent Kingdom reaches the breaking-point, and where the Christian Church must make its final stand.

If, nevertheless, there are Christians who cannot accept the pacifist position today, this will not release them from having to face the question whether they and their churches must not, on other grounds, refuse any further support to war. When Christians have, on the one hand, refused to embrace pacifism but have not, on the other hand, simply adapted themselves to current standards and practices with respect to war, they have taken the position that war may be the lesser of two evils and might, therefore, be supported, provided that certain rules or standards for a "just" war are observed.

The contention that something could be more evil than a total, global, atomic war—and that is what the next war will be if and when it comes—seems so obviously absurd that we do not need to spend time discussing it. The most sober and responsible scientists, those best qualified to speak, tell us it will be the end period!

The other point, about the limits which must be observed in war if a Christian is to countenance it, requires scrutiny. On this matter twenty-six leading Protestant theologians, only seven of whom were pacifists—Reinhold Niebuhr being included among the nonpacifists—made a solemn and unequivocal pronouncement in 1944. It appears in a report of the Federal Council of the Churches of Christ in America, published over the signature of a commission of Christian scholars appointed by The Council and entitled *The Relation of the Church to the War in the Light of Christian Faith.* On behalf of the Federal Council its general secretary expressed "grateful appreciation" for the work and heartily commended it "to the churches for earnest study."

This pronouncement is so fundamental and crucial that the relevant paragraph, though a lengthy one, must here be quoted in full. The Church, say the theologians,

must resist, by open criticism and persuasion, the theory and the attempted practice of "total war," and its counterpart, a Carthaginian "peace." Total war is suited only for a totalitarian society, which as we have said is irreconcilable in principle with Christian faith in the sovereignty of God and the responsible freedom of man. No matter what the provocation, however great the extremity of military peril—even to the imminence of military defeat—the Church dare not approve a supposition that military expediency of necessity can ever rightfully become the supreme principle of human conduct. We are acutely aware how difficult it is to apply in practice this principle of resistance to claims for the supremacy in war time of military demands and to the elevation of war even temporarily into a status of unconditional domination of human behaviour. All of us agree that in war some practices cannot be regarded by the Church as justifiable: the killing of prisoners, of hostages, or of refugees to lessen military handicaps or to gain military advantages; the torture of prisoners or of hostages to gain military information, however vital; the massacre of civilian populations. Some of the signers of the report believe that certain other measures, such as rigorous blockades of food-stuffs essential to civilian life, and obliteration bombing of civilian areas, however repugnant to humane feelings, are still justifiable on Christian principles, if they are essential to the successful conduct of a war that is itself justified. A majority of the commission, moreover, believe that today war against the Axis powers, by all needful measures, is in fact justified. Others among us believe that the methods named are not justifiable on Christian principles, even though they are now practiced or defended by great numbers of sincere Christians and patriotic non-Christians, and even if they be essential to military victory for the United Nations. If it be true that modern war cannot be successfully waged without use of methods that cannot distinguish even roughly between combatants and non-combatants, or between perpetrators and victims, that fact seems to a minority in the commission to raise the question whether in modern war even the more scrupulous side can meet the conditions hitherto held by the Church to define a just war. On these specific issues, then, the commission is divided. *On the basic principle that the Church cannot acquiesce in the supremacy of military considerations even in war time, nor in the view that modern war may properly, even in case of extreme peril to nation, church, or culture, become total war, we are agreed.*

Substantially the same group of theologians, including Reinhold Niebuhr and still limited to seven pacifists out of twenty-two, later made a unanimous report to the Federal Council of Churches, and again at its request, on *Atomic Warfare and the Christian Faith*. Its publication was authorized as an expression of the opinion of the signers. This report included the following statements after extended comments on the problems raised by the resort to atomic warfare:

We would begin with an act of contrition. As American Christians, we are deeply penitent for the irresponsible use already made of the atomic bomb. *We are agreed that,* whatever be one's judgment of the ethics of war in principle, *the surprise bombings of Hiroshima and Nagasaki are morally indefensible.* . . . As the power that first used the atomic bomb in these circumstances, *we have sinned grievously against the laws of God and against the people of Japan.* Without. seeking to apportion blame among individuals, *we are compelled to judge our chosen course inexcusable.* At the same time, we are agreed that these two specific bombing sorties cannot properly be treated in isolation from the whole system of obliteration attacks with explosives and fire-bombs, of which the atomic raids were the stunning climax. . . . *In the light of present knowledge, we are prepared to affirm that the policy of obliteration bombing as actually practiced in World War II, culminating in the use of atomic bombs against Japan, is not defensible on Christian premises.*[5]

Several reflections arise upon the reading of these statements. One is that Christian thinkers are, certainly in modern times, confronted with curious dilemmas and capable in some instances of making curiously fine distinctions. Thus, among the practices which the Church can under no circumstances regard as justifiable is "the massacre of civilian populations." We are reminded of the distinguished and greatly respected Dr. J. H. Oldham of England writing in the *Christian News Letter* in October, 1940: "Christians can take part in war only if the distinction can be maintained between war . . . and murder. The deliberate killing of non-combatants is murder. If war degenerates into willful slaughter of the innocent, Christians must either become pacifists or give up their religion." But the American theologians— some of them—though absolutely ruling out "massacre of civilian populations" could still in 1944 during the war justify "rigorous block-

[5] Italics are mine.

ades of food-stuffs essential to civilian life." It makes a difference presumably how civilian populations are massacred!

More than that, the reader will note that in 1944 during the war these theologians in the first document referred to actually justified "obliteration bombing of civilian areas, however repugnant to humane feelings," as "still justifiable on Christian principles, if they are essential to the successful conduct of a war that is itself justified," and a majority of the commission made it clear that by this they meant the war then being waged against the Axis powers. What does it mean under these conditions that "massacre of civilians" is not justified? Does it perhaps depend on who does the killing?

However, in 1946 after the war the same men "affirm that the policy of obliteration bombing as actually practiced in World War II . . . is not defensible on Christian premises"! We are entitled to ask what they learned about obliteration bombing between 1944 and 1946 which enabled them to justify it in 1944 "on Christian principles" but required them to condemn it in 1946 "on Christian premises."

Whatever may be the verdict about the past, I submit that the average person would take it as a matter of course that the theologians, having had to pronounce judgment on obliteration bombing and atomic warfare as actually practiced in World War II, would announce that these practices could not be justified in the future either and that consequently no future war could be justified on Christian grounds, since it is bound to be more atrocious than past wars. Alas, this is not the case. Again it is essential to quote fully. Referring to the judgment about obliteration and atomic bombing in the last war, the report on *Atomic Warfare and the Christian Faith* continues:

Some who concur in the foregoing judgment find their grounds primarily in the circumstances under which particular raids were carried out rather than in the practice of obliteration bombing or in the nature of the weapons employed. They agree that what has been done is wrong, and that it would be wrong for any nation in the future to take the initiative in using such measures for its own advantage; but they believe that the way should be left open to regard the use of atomic weapons under some circumstances as right. For they believe that in the present state of human relations, if plans for international control of aggression should fail, the only effective restraint upon would-be aggressors might be fear of reprisals, and that this possible restraint should not be removed in advance. Others hold that even if belligerent action be regarded as, in extreme circumstances, unavoidable and justifiable, obliteration bombing and the atomic bomb as utilized for that purpose cannot be justified. Still others hold that the atomic bomb has revealed the impossibility of a just war, and has shown the necessity for repudiation of all support of war by the Church. They judge that since in fact belligerent powers are virtually certain to use any means that seems needed to insure victory condemnation of obliteration bombing or of surprise attack with atomic weapons entails condemnation of all war.

Note first of all that "the practice of obliteration bombing" as such is still justified on Christian grounds. What can this mean? The condemnation of atomic bombing is, furthermore, not based on "the nature of the weapons employed." Might germ warfare also be justified on Christian grounds at least in respect of the nature of weapons employed? Why not? The condemnation is based on the "circumstances under which particular raids were carried out." Under these circumstances what was done was wrong and of course doing the same thing in the same circumstances in the future would also be wrong. Can any sane person think for a moment that the circumstances under which atomic war will be waged in the future will be "better," whatever that adjective may mean in this case? If responsible people are going to say such things, they rest under a very solemn obligation to say just what they mean. Otherwise, they are handing a blank check to the militarists.

The specific situation which those who "believe that the way should be left open to regard the use of atomic weapons under some circumstances as right" envisage is this: "Plans for international control of aggression" may fail. Then "the only effective restraint upon would-be aggressors might be fear of reprisals" and "this possible restraint should not be removed in advance."

The hope is that an arsenal of atomic weapons in the hands of the United States will be an effective restraint upon a would-be aggressor, since naturally the United States would not be the aggressor, and so there would not be an atomic war.

This program neglects the point which we elaborated in an earlier chapter, namely, that the United States with its vast wealth, on the one hand, and its arsenal of atomic weapons, on the other, is the main aggressive and disturbing factor in international relations today. But let us forego stressing that point now.

The hope is that the mere threat of "reprisals"—a word which has somehow an ugly and sinister sound, especially when it comes from Christian lips—will suffice. The nation would have to be ready and willing to use atomic weapons "if need be." The nonpacifist theologians whose position we are analyzing are realistic at least at this point, for they make it plain "the way should be left open to regard the use"— not the mere threat—"of atomic weapons under some circumstances as right."

A gigantic effort must of course be made to secure "international control of aggression" and of atomic and other weapons. However, the possession of atomic bombs by the United States is one of the major causes for that lack of trust which blocks even the most moderate plans for international organization. The theologians recognize this and so they call upon the churches to urge "that all manufacture of atomic bombs be stopped, pending the development of international controls." But are they, since they will not unreservedly rule out even atomic war on the ground that it is sin of the most hideous kind, on sound ground in making this recommendation? Is it not quite possible, as the military think, that the only effective restraint on further Russian aggression right now is the atomic bomb? Shall we throw away that one source of security? If they mean that suspending the manufacture of atomic bombs for a while would not seriously alter our power vis-a-vis Russia anyway, do they not think that the tough-minded men in the Kremlin know that too, and hence would be unimpressed? If, on the other hand, they are proposing that we should try the way of trust and divest ourselves of our military preponderance, do they think that kind of thing can be done halfheartedly and piecemeal—trust God but keep a few old battleships and bombers around?

We dwelt at considerable length in a preceding chapter on the futility of the efforts to set up "international control of aggression" under present conditions, the hopeless impasse to which these efforts have led. We pointed out, among other things, the stultifying role played by the very idea that dominates the thinking of these theologians, namely, that efforts at international control may fail, therefore we must plan to be able to take care of ourselves in case the worst befalls. The atomic armaments race and the talk about international organization go on side by side: the actions count, the talk does not.

Still another aspect of the matter should be noted. The supposition is that if international control fails, the United States will have its atomic arsenal, with the blessing of the theologians, since fear of reprisals may be the only effective restraint left on the aggressor. But, presumably unwittingly, the theologians have here given the green light for an atomic attack initiated by the United States. They themselves tell us why, "The new weapons," they point out, "alter in two nearly fateful ways the balance between aggressive and defensive war. If two nations are armed with atomic weapons, both the incentive to strike a crippling blow first and the possibility of doing so are incalculably increased. . . . A premium is therefore placed on swift, ruthless aggression by any power that may believe itself in danger"— in danger from an aggressor, of course.

It may be worth while to emphasize this risk of resort to preventive offensive action by quoting the military expert of the New York *Times*, Hanson W. Baldwin, writing in the May, 1946, issue of *Harper's Magazine*: "The best way to defend America is to be prepared to deliver a smashing offensive against any nation on aggression bent. Here is the basic paradox of the atomic age. Until now, non-imperialist democracies have had no occasion to build up large offensive forces in peacetime. But now the best 'defense' has become the capacity to retaliate—not in kind, but in a bigger and more terrible way. . . . In my opinion, therefore, the great emphasis in our military planning should be upon *offensive weapons*, offensive tactics, and a military organization geared to deliver a swift and terrible blow to any aggressor."

Mr. Baldwin virtually says here what the theologians apparently do not face, but what is most certainly implied in their position, that the "defensive" offensive blow will under the circumstances have to be struck first—if possible. No political or military leader faced with the possibility that an enemy known to have atomic weapons may strike soon and wipe out, as Dr. Oppenheimer suggested, forty million people in the United States, would dare to let that happen and be charged with having failed to take the proper "defensive" measures first. No foreign government will believe, and it is hard to imagine that we can make ourselves believe, that a nation which did not shrink from unloos-ing the atrocity of atomic war on the earth when there was no military necessity for it whatever, on the eve of certain victory, would hesitate to shoot first under the conditions of frightful tension which will exist in the world when plans for international control have failed and the atomic armaments race nears its climax.

Under these circumstances, having specified that "the way should be left open to regard the use of atomic weapons under some circum-stances as right," the theologians nevertheless urge "that the Churches call upon the government of the United States to affirm publicly, with suitable guaranties, that it will under no circumstances be the first to use atomic weapons in any possible future war." Merely to "affirm publicly" would, they tacitly admit, mean nothing. What would, then, be "suitable guaranties"? Not to have any bombs or facilities for mak-ing them might be. But this the theologians, who insist the way must be left open to regard atomic war as right under some circumstances, have ruled out. Nonpacifists sometimes indulge in calling pacifists unrealistic and sentimental. But nothing could be more utterly senti-mental than this proposal that the United States be equipped with atomic weapons and promise not to use them first.

But the basic ethical implications of the position are much more serious. For it is suggested that there is a profound moral difference between dropping some atomic bombs, in such a situation as existed on the eve of Pearl Harbor, a split second or two before the "aggressor" does, and "retaliation"—retaliation, to quote Hanson W. Baldwin, who is far more realistic than the theologians and has the history of what we did to Germany and Japan in World War II to back him up, "not in kind, but in a bigger and more terrible way." To strike first is sin to be condemned and shunned, but to invoke, not the old jungle law of an eye for an eye, a tooth for a tooth, but the law of Christian nations in modern war, of fifty eyes for an eye—that is right, that may expect to receive the blessing of Christian thinkers. At any rate, the way should be left open to regard this as right!

The theologians cannot take shelter behind the assertion that they do not mean this, that all they would approve would be a strictly dis-ciplined and just reprisal, and that if the nation went beyond that they would have to condemn it again—as they condemned, after the event, obliteration bombing "as actually practiced" in World War II—and begin once more with "an act of contrition." They have witnessed two world wars. They have witnessed Hiroshima and Nagasaki and confess that they stand aghast. They have no excuse for cherishing any illusions as to what war and retaliation are, in the very nature of the case, in this twentieth century of the Christian era.

If they persist in this course, the objective result—I am not speaking of subjective motivation—will be that the guilt which rests upon these Christian leaders, for human beings slain, demoralized, degraded, will be far greater than that which rests upon the Nazis.

If the limit which must not be overpassed in warfare lest it be utterly repudiated on Christian grounds has not now been reached, it never will be reached. War displays the fatal tendency to resort to ever more destructive and atrocious means. That is its nature. The Christian who still clings to the view that a war may, on his nation's side of course, be justified is driven to condone in one war what he would have condemned unhesitatingly in an earlier. And, having after the second war condemned the means actually employed, he is relentlessly driven during the third to condone what he condemned in the second after it was over. The process probably cannot go on indefinitely but only because the race will be exterminated.

Why should Christians not draw the conclusion at last that war itself was evil, sin, and could only, therefore, lead to sin and ever more hideous sin? Even to those who have nothing but relativities to go by, it would seem that it might be clear now that having further truck with war is suicide, that it is more sensible to try anything else. But Christian leaders, Christian people, who read the Sermon on the Mount as the word of God, who worship the Crucified Christ, who sing

> In the cross of Christ I glory,
> Towering o'er the wrecks of time!

O, my fellow Christians, has not the time come when we must "cease to rely on horses, and trust in chariots because they are many" and in battleships and rocket bombs and poison rays? The time to take off the uniforms of Caesar forever and to take up the Cross? The time to believe in the power of love, prepared to suffer and lay down its life, to overcome evil?

After World War I a great revulsion against war swept through the Christian churches. It is instructive now to read the pronouncements made in that period. Thus the Lambeth Conference in 1930 declared: "If God has revealed to this generation the fundamental inconsistency between war and the fact of His Fatherhood, the more tremendous is our responsibility for witnessing to this truth. We dare not be disobedient to the vision of a world set free from the menace of war." In the United States the Methodist Church in 1936 General Conference declared that war was "the greatest social sin of modern times; a denial of the ideals of Christ. . . . The Methodist Episcopal Church as an institution does not endorse, support, or purpose to participate in war." The statement with but slight alteration was reaffirmed in the 1940 General Conference. The Congregational General Council in 1934 said: "We of this Council are convinced that we must now make this declaration: 'The Church is through with war!' We of this Council call upon the people of our churches to renounce war and all its works and ways, and to refuse to support, sanction or bless it." The great Ecumenical Conference at Oxford in 1937 declared: "Wars . . . are marks of a world to which the Church is charged to proclaim the gospel of redemption. War involves compulsory enmity, diabolical outrage against human personality, and a wanton distortion of the truth. War is a particular demonstration of the power of sin in the world, and a defiance of the righteousness of God as revealed in Jesus Christ and Him crucified."

The churches receded from these positions during the war. Yet their support of the war was much more temperate than in World War I. They never gave it the virtually unqualified blessing which they gave it then. Especially in the Protestant churches the ministers who maintained their pacifist witness were much more numerous and influential than in 1914-18.

It is clear that the issue of war and pacifism will have to be faced again now. The mighty and tragic events which have occurred, the situation in which the world now finds itself, the prospect of atomic war all make this imperative. The very fact that a pacifist or near-pacifist position was taken before the war and not adhered to may for various reasons have the effect of holding back a thoroughgoing and honest re-examination of the whole problem. But it is in my opinion unlikely that it can be long delayed. Failure to carry through this re-examination will mean that the churches will remain bogged down in the position of the theologians which we have been criticizing, and that will be fatal.

The chief danger is that the Church will not give any distinctive utterance but simply echo the views of current liberalism. The reader may recall the widely discussed article which appeared in the magazine *Fortune* some years ago complaining that "the voice of the church is not inspired. The voice of the church today, we find, is the echo of our own voices. The result of this experience is . . . disillusionment. The way out is the sound of a voice not our voice, but a voice coming from something not ourselves, in the existence of which we cannot disbelieve. . . . Without it we are no more capable of saving the world than we are capable of creating it in the first place."

The business of the Church is to declare what is right and wrong by God's absolute standard, not what is expedient or possible. Men are waiting to have the Church tell them in Christ's name whether making atomic war is right or wrong. Simply that. The ethical evaluation of atomic bombing is what they ask for. Not the effects of being bombed, but whether it is right or a sin to bomb others. Not whether it is so now but not yesterday, under these circumstances but not those. But a plain answer. Any hesitation, any qualification they will take as conclusive evidence that nobody knows; relativity rules; therefore, anything goes. By the same token a clear and unequivocal answer, a command coming out of pulpits and church schools and confessionals saying, "War is no longer, if it ever was, distinguishable from murder. If you claim to be a Christian, you can no more take part in it than in chattel slavery"—this men would recognize as the sound of a voice not their own, "in the existence of which we cannot disbelieve." For it would be God speaking as of old through the prophets and through His Christ.

The Christian churches have since World War I and the revulsion against war which followed it very generally recognized that there is a place and a very important one in the churches for the pacifist. The

pacifist has a vocation which comes from God. The nature of that vocation was stated in the following terms by Professor William Ernest
Hocking in a pamphlet issued by the Federal Council of Churches.
Professor Hocking distinguishes between "the mind which fights and
the mind which remembers." He is not a pacifist and he believes that
these two minds may be in one person. "Commonly," however, "they
are dominant in two persons, and have two functions." The mind
which fights does not and cannot remember and therefore hates. The
mind which remembers cannot generate the necessary passion to fight,
and therefore has to find another way to act. I am reminded of that
moving comment which the Talmud makes on the scene that followed
immediately on the crossing of the Red Sea by the fleeing Israelites and
the drowning of the pursuing Egyptians. The Israelites, says the Talmud, were shouting with joy and exultation; and the angels too were
rejoicing. Suddenly they thought of looking for God and when they
turned they saw that He was weeping. When He was asked the reason
for His seemingly untimely grief, He said, "How should I not weep
when so many of my children have perished in the waters?"

Most men, Professor Hocking continues, "have no trouble in being
good fighters, and in acquiring a dramatic hate for the purpose of
maximum efficiency. But the man who has a genius for remembering,
and temperamentally retains a love of his enemy, is a rare treasure. *He
is the only one who in the end can heal the wounds of the momentum
of acquired hate.* Whether or not he supplies all the intelligence for
peacemaking, he supplies its necessary guiding spirit." [6] He concludes,
therefore, that "the Church must cherish and protect its pacifists. Without their spirit, there can be no lasting peace."

But the pacifists in the churches, small in numbers and spiritually
also all too feeble, surely are not equal to the colossal task of achieving "lasting peace" over against "the momentum of acquired hate" and
of disintegrating forces with which the Church and the world have now
to contend. Is there really any hope unless the Church—the churches
which name the name of Christ—puts aside "the mind which fights"
and gives itself wholly and exclusively to "the mind which remembers,
. . . and temperamentally retains a love of his enemy"? Is not the
vocation of the Church to be the pacifist, the Body, the incarnation, of

6 Italics are Professor Hocking's.

Christ in the world? Has it ever been anything else? Surely Walter Marshall Horton spoke of and for the ecumenical Church when he said that its primary function is "so to wait upon God, so to allow its life to be molded by His power, that it becomes a living cell of the new Divine order that is to be. Its greatest service is to be alive in a higher order of life than that of the secular society about it or even the order of creation."

If the Church does not undertake this vocation I question with Howard Spring whether there is any hope for mankind; but if the Church did become a "living cell of the new Divine order," what might not happen? Then the kingdoms of this world might also become the Kingdoms of our God and of His Christ. Thus hope might be reborn in the multitudes who are hopeless and power would come to the faint and to him that hath no strength. A spiritual movement of truly mighty proportions could be launched by such a Church. Led by such a Church a people, as Professor Tillich suggests, "could renounce power by a common decision and thus become the Church—a people seized as a whole by the transcendental idea—in an unexpected historical moment . . . one of the great turning points of history."

It remains to comment briefly on certain practical questions which arise in connection with this appeal to the churches. When we speak of a nation undertaking a redemptive mission, we are met with the question, But what chance is there that the United States would undertake such a mission? Similarly, when we suggest that the churches take the leadership in calling upon men and nations to renounce forever the sin of warmaking, we are met with the warning—sometimes spoken derisively and sometimes tearfully—that in view of the complacency, the self-centeredness, the timidity of the churches, their involvement in the very economic and political system and attitudes out of which war grows, we are pinning our hope on what is as likely to happen as that the camel should go through the needle's eye.

We can only answer: "That is exactly what has to happen. Why should it not, O ye of little faith? With God all things are possible. If ye had faith as a grain of mustard seed . . ."

There is also this to say, the recurrent theme of this book, to the individual Christian and especially to Christian leaders: You have to make your own decision before God in the awful forum of conscience. "Each man is eternally and above all else responsible for his own soul, and, in the terrible words of the Psalmist, . . . no man may deliver his brother, nor make agreement unto God for him." When you have made your decision, then you have to testify to it publicly. Thus, though you cannot answer for your fellow minister or fellow Christian, any more than he can for you, you can set him on fire if the spirit has been kindled in yourself. That is the way such movements always grow.

Those who have thus heard the call must, and indeed inevitably will, be drawn together in their various churches and communities into small but growing fellowships.

These fellowships, as they obey the Master's command, observe the laws of the spiritual world, will experience Pentecost. We recall how Pentecost came to the first Christians and how thus the Christian Church came into existence. The Master had told his disciples "not to depart from Jerusalem," that is, not to run away from the tough problems, the impossible task. So have we to stay by this problem of war today.

Having accepted the hard assignment to remain in Jerusalem, at the scene of their so bitter defeat and humiliation, there were three conditions to be observed so that they would be ready to accept the gift of the Holy Spirit.

They were to "remain together." That is, they were to be fused into a fellowship. Let us observe in passing, since we devote too little attention to this vital matter in the present study, that fellowship, as was the case with these early Christians, always finds expression in the economic as well as in other spheres of life. There is no communion where there is no community. And there is no community where there is not some genuine form of economic sharing.

They were, secondly, to "wait." We must not be tempted by the urgency of the situation to rush into "doing something about it—anything." Now of all times the wrong thing must not be done, and the right thing cannot be done until the soul is flooded with new power. That which is well done is not done by main force of the human will; it is done out of the overflow of a heart that has waited for "the promise of the Father."

They were, in the third place to pray. To pray means to confess our need and our inability to fill it. It is there on our knees that every good work begins; in the recognition that we are weak so that we may be strong. That we are ignorant and foolish, so that our minds may be filled with knowledge and our hearts with wisdom. That we are impure so that we may be pure. That we all in subtle if not crude and open ways hate so that we may love.

To pray means also to be ready to do what God says is needful in order that the prayer may be fulfilled. St. Augustine once prayed, "O God, make me pure, but not yet." He was an honest man. If we were as honest as he some of our prayers would go, "O Lord, give us peace but don't ask me to become a pacifist. O Lord, take the burden of war from the bent backs of the peoples of the world, but don't ask us to give up the atomic bomb."

When ordinary people face the hard problem, remain together so that they are fused into a fellowship, wait and pray, presently God is poured out upon them, their hearts burst into flame, their tongues are eloquent. They are the Church, to which the word is spoken, "Fear not, little flock, it is your Father's good pleasure to give unto you the Kingdom."

In other portions of this book I have, I trust, made sufficiently clear my views about the essentials of the Judaeo-Christian faith and world view. It will also be clear, therefore, that I believe that the things I have just been saying about Christians apply equally to Jews who give heed to their prophets. Even in this hour of anguish—aye, supremely in this hour of suffering—they are summoned to be the Servant of Jehovah by whose stripes the nations are healed so that the word of their prophet may be fulfilled: "They shall beat their swords into plough shares . . . , nation shall not lift up sword against nation; neither shall they learn war any more."

I shall not dwell further, therefore, on the role of Jewish leaders and the synagogue in the task of achieving peace; but since I have been writing primarily from the standpoint of one with a Protestant background and to Protestants, I do want to add one word about the responsibility of the Roman Catholic church. That church has recognized that the individual may have a vocation to lead the pacifist life. There have been outstanding pacifists among its members, including one whom most would characterize as after Jesus himself the most outstanding, Francis of Assisi. All that we have said, therefore, about the challenge of pacifism to individual professing Christians applies to the priests and the members of the Roman Catholic church. But the claims which that church makes for itself present it and its head with a special problem. The members look to the church and Pope for direction in matters of faith and morals. What, then, are their priests, what is the Pope, to say to them about participation in war?

The Roman church has made a distinction between "just" and "unjust" wars. Whether that distinction was valid or not we do not here discuss. On it has in any case been based the prevailing practice of Christians and churches, including the Protestant, throughout most of the Christian era. The Roman church is certainly bound now by the law which it has laid down, unless of course it is prepared now formally to repudiate it.

Under the accepted formula a war to be "just" must be essentially defensive in character. A brilliant English Roman Catholic essayist, E. I. Watkin, has recently charged that commonly the Catholic clergy have counseled members to follow their respective rulers in going into war even when it was one of "the most glaring aggression. . . . History records no single instance of a national hierarchy, or, we believe any member of it, pronouncing any war declared or waged by his own government unjust. . . . No German bishop attempted to prevent German Catholics taking part" in the attacks on Norway and Holland, "which, however, as unjustifiable wars, were mass murders." In practice, therefore, the Catholic church's own rules "whose observance would have made the Catholic Church a mighty bulwark against unjust war, have been and are nothing more than a window-dressing display."

Mr. Watkin goes on to point out, in the article in the *Catholic Peacemaker* for August, 1945, from which we are quoting, that in the past it has often been difficult to determine whether a war was in fact waged for a "just" object according to the church's standards and so it might be difficult to make this determination in the future. But it is no longer necessary, for the church has another criterion for a justifiable war: "Even a just war must not be waged by unjustifiable means." Mr. Watkin's next observation and his conclusion are so important that they must be quoted at some length: "Under modern conditions, however, war can be waged only by such aerial bombing as must involve the slaughter and maiming of innocent civilians. This, however, is plainly immoral. To kill the innocent is not a lawful means to any end, however good. . . . Under modern conditions no war can be waged without employing immoral means. Therefore it must be unjustifiable."

Mr. Watkin goes on to bemoan the fact that Roman Catholic bishops have usually not condemned such bombings except when practiced by the enemy. It is true, however, that Roman Catholic interpreters have often been more consistent than Protestants in insisting on the validity and importance of the distinction as to means used in war. In this country when Vera Brittain and a number of well-known American Protestant religious leaders protested during the war against the obliteration bombing of German cities by the British-American forces, and Protestant nonpacifist spokesmen were disposed to dismiss the protest as a pacifist one, Roman Catholic theologians with considerable gusto took them to task and pointed out that no Christian, whether pacifist or not, was absolved from drawing the line against certain methods in war. Mr. Watkin continues:

Now there has arrived the ultimate diabolism. The atomic bomb can obliterate in a moment an entire city, its men, its women, its children, its heritage of art and history. I marvel that any priest of Christ can be found to give even tacit approval to such indiscriminate slaughter. No method of war known to human history has approached it for ruthlessness. . . . Violating so flagrantly the rule forbidding immoral methods of warfare, the atomic bomb violates also with equal evidence the rule . . . in the past often so difficult to apply, that the evil wrought by a war must not exceed the possible good to be secured by victory. *Our course, therefore, is plain. If the rules laid down by Catholic theologians in the past are true, no war can in future be justified on whatever issue.* (Italics are Mr. Watkin's.)

Catholics, that is to say, must either trample the traditional rules underfoot or refuse to participate in any war by conscientious objection if conscribed, in any case by prayer and according to their opportunities by spoken or written protest.

A Protestant might leave the matter there at the bar of the individual's conscience but, as I have suggested, it seems to me that the Roman Catholic position requires something more. When the church has spoken so authoritatively and over so many centuries, when its' standards are now so flagrantly violated and continued violation threat-

ens the very existence of the race of man on this planet, surely the
church must speak. The Pope must speak.

The Pope has indeed often expressed his concern about the matters
in deeply moving language, but not yet—I venture humbly to suggest—
with that precision which the present moment requires. There was a
pope, Nicholas I, who said, "War is always satanic in origin." Is it not
necessary to say that again? Furthermore, in earlier ages, I understand,
there were occasions when a ruler embarked on a war the church
deemed unjust, whereupon the Pope absolved the subjects of that ruler
from participation in that war. Has not the time come for the Pope to
say unequivocally that no modern war can possibly meet the standards
of the Roman Catholic church and that, therefore, all Roman Catholics
are henceforth absolved from any participation in war and no longer
bound to accept conscription for war and military training? In that
case, still in accordance with Catholic doctrine, the bishops and the
priests would have to instruct the faithful, including boys and girls,
young men and women, that if Caesar attempts to conscript them, they
must refuse and if need be, joyfully accept martyrdom instead.

One of the critical tests as to which course the churches are going to
take in this country may come—and now I am speaking to all who give
any allegiance to the Judaeo-Christian faith "Whate'er their name or
sign"—before these words appear in print. Very powerful elements in
this country are exerting every effort to force the adoption of peacetime
conscription, universal compulsory military training. It is too much to
expect boys of seventeen and eighteen to refuse conscription for military training or for war if they have to stand alone or more accurately
be surrounded by a massive public opinion demanding willing acceptance or, at best, acquiescing in reluctant and mournful acceptance
of conscription. With rare exceptions, young men at that age cannot be
expected to have the intellectual or emotional maturity to be conscientious objectors not only over against the nation and the secular
culture but over against their own spiritual counselors and their own
churches. By every available means our children and grandchildren
have to be assured by the latter that the only decent, human, Christian
and thus also in the only valid sense patriotic thing to do is to refuse
to go to war. They need to have in their very bones the assurance that
only in this way can they continue to belong to the fellowship of true

and brave men—including those who in the past, in honor and in fidelity to the light as they saw it, went to war—which is also the fellowship of God. How shall they have this assurance unless their spiritual leaders give it them?

There is a sense in which the Church of the Living God will never die. "The gates of hell shall not prevail against her." But any branch or embodiment on earth of that Eternal Church, if it betrays its faith and becomes a "synagogue of Satan," will have its candlestick removed from its place. If it be merely insipid and neutral, refusing to make an absolute choice, speaking in no distinctive and unmistakably divine voice, the most shameful judgment of all will be pronounced upon it: "I know thy works, that thou art neither hot nor cold. I would that thou wert hot or cold; but now, because thou art lukewarm and neither hot nor cold, I will spew thee out of my mouth."

Chapter X

Conscience and the Atomic Scientists

Shortly after the war against Japan came to an end the nuclear physicists and other scientists who had been mainly responsible for the production of the atomic bombs which were dropped on Hiroshima and Nagasaki embarked upon what was for them a radically new course. They emerged from their laboratories and mounted the public platform. They invaded Washington and began buttonholing congressmen from Ox Bow and Oskaloosa, Vermont and Arkansas. They entered pulpits and, at least figuratively, climbed upon the housetops to proclaim in words of the ancient Gospel, "Nothing is hid that shall not be revealed."

The burden of their message was, all are aware, that the bomb was not just another weapon, that humanity now had in its grasp the means to destroy itself, that there was no defense against atomic weapons, that we must do away with them, in short would have to find means to abolish war itself.

The change in orientation and attitude which led to this action by leading scientists is potentially revolutionary in its nature and effects and is in a real sense more important than their material discoveries and inventions. The prevailing attitude among the physical scientists for the past two centuries has been that it was their business to penetrate the secrets of the physical universe and guide the technologists in perfecting the inventions made possible by the findings of pure science; but whether the end products were beneficent or maleficent in their effects on human beings as individuals or on their societies was not something for scientists to be concerned about. Indirectly, if not directly, the scientists contributed a good deal also to the gradual domination of thought in the Western world by the notion that reality consists of things that can be observed from without—"objects" that can be measured, weighed and dissected. The human being also gradually became in the thinking of himself as well as others merely an object in an impersonal and mechanistic universe rather than a responsible and creative spirit. Thus a materialistic and essentially amoral world view developed which in its effects was eventually antimoral and disintegrating. This philosophy or pseudo religion was not implicit in the method of science strictly understood, and of course scientists in general did not intend the effects which I have just mentioned. Furthermore, in their respective fields they displayed a stern and often sacrificial fidelity to "pure truth" or the facts which, if its implications had been understood, might have prevented much error in both theory and practice. Many of them must nevertheless assume some of the blame for the false and dangerous philosophy which was encouraged by the amazing triumphs of the physical sciences and of modern technology, for the reason that they were not always careful to point out the limitations of the scientific method. As individuals they took part by sins of omission if not of commission in creating in the universities and colleges adherence to a relativistic ethics and a supercilious if not hostile attitude toward all religious thought and life. Specifically, by their very concern since the summer of 1945 about the ethical implications and the social results of their work, the physical scientists convict themselves of having been remiss in the past. All too few of them, all too infrequently, were in the habit of acting on the truly moral and religious principle enunciated by their Austrian colleague in nuclear research, Lise Meitner, who said after the bomb had been employed in the slaughter of human beings, "I, like any other responsible person, hoped that its practical realization would not be possible. . . . The scientist is ever awe-struck at the discovery of the laws of nature, and to use these laws for the construction of weapons which might lead to the annihilation of mankind, must seem blasphemy to him."

The physical scientists and the top-ranking technologists have an intellectual and spiritual prestige in our day which certainly far surpasses that of the ministers of religion and of the intellectuals who are not expert in the physical sciences. If the scientists now become convinced that their studies not only are limited to one phase of reality and of human experience but are fraught with the utmost danger to mankind unless attention is paid to aspects of reality and of man's nature which science cannot comprehend—if, in other words, those who have in fact, though often unwillingly, been the high priests of the pseudo religion of modernity are now going to plead that men concern themselves about the things of the spirit and search for stable moral values—we may be about to witness an epoch-making change in the intellectual and spiritual climate in which men live, comparable to that which occurred when the pioneering Greek philosophers and scientists did their work, or in the early Christian era, or when the Middle Ages came to an end. If we were engaged in a general study of contemporary religion, philosophy or culture, it would be necessary to devote major attention to this possibility. As it is, we shall confine ourselves to the consideration of what is implied for the scientists themselves in their new-found concern about the social and moral implications of the thing they have produced. If as citizens and human beings they have a moral responsibility, what is its nature and extent, and how shall they discharge it?

As we have often stated in the course of our discussion, when one speaks of moral responsibility, he is speaking about what it is right or wrong for him to do. He is not concerned about what is being done to or inflicted upon him, but about his decision and consequent action; not with that which goeth into a man, not even the bullet which plows through his brain or the atomic bomb which dissolves his mortal frame, none of which can defile him, but with that which goeth out of him and does defile him if it be vile. Furthermore, he is speaking about what he personally intends and does, regardless of what other men do. On the plane of moral life decision and action are unilateral. If then the atomic scientist is to accept moral responsibility at all, the question he must in the final analysis face is whether he shall go on making atomic bombs or in any way or degree support or condone their production and use. In a sense it is the only moral issue he has to face. Certainly he is in no position rightly to deal with any other until he has dealt with this.

It may be useful to begin with the fact that the scientists did make the bomb in the first place and the considerations which impelled

·them to do so. It would appear that the responsibility for taking initiative in the whole business rests upon them rather than upon the military and the politicians. The publication *One World or None,* to which most of the leading nuclear physicists and their colleagues contributed, states: "Albert Einstein, winner of the Nobel Prize in 1921 and perhaps the greatest of all living physicists, started the government's work on the uranium project with his letter to President Roosevelt in the fall of 1939, in which he outlined the possibilities." A report was presented to the Secretary of War June 11, 1945, by a "Committee on Social and Political Implications" appointed by the director of the Metallurgical Laboratory in Chicago. The committee consisted of three physicists, three chemists and one biologist under the chairmanship of Professor James Franck. In this report, as given in the *Bulletin of the Atomic Scientists* for May 1, 1946, occurs the statement: "One may point out that the scientists themselves have initiated the development of this 'secret weapon.'"

What, then, motivated these scientists, who perhaps despite themselves exercised so vast an influence not only in their own special fields but over the mind-set and character of our educated youth, to develop this awful weapon? In the *Bulletin* from which we have just quoted, following immediately upon the sentence in which the scientists formally and unequivocally accept responsibility, the statement is made: "The compelling reason for creating this weapon with such speed was our fear that Germany had the technical skill to develop such a weapon, and that the German government had no moral restraints regarding its use."

The first observation to be made here is that the scientists clearly assumed political responsibility as individuals for helping to precipitate a possible atomic war between Germany and the United States. The motive was presumably that of "defense": the Germans might have the bomb, their government would have "no moral restraints regarding its use." Certainly, therefore, if the Germans launched an attack with atomic bombs or somewhat similar weapons, the United States would have to "retaliate" in "defense," and the scientists would co-operate to the fullest extent. In view of the length to which obliteration bombing of Germany with pre-atomic weapons was carried in order to "win the war" and in "retaliation" for the blitzing of Rotterdam, London and Coventry, it is fair to assume that in our atomic struggle as many German cities as seemed "necessary" would have been wiped out. But it is now clear that in all probability atomic war would have been launched against Germany even if the German military had uncovered no weapons other than those they actually did use. For if the United States bombed Hiroshima and Nagasaki under the circumstances which we have already described when there was clearly no "military necessity" for it and victory was within the grasp of the Allies, it is no longer credible that atomic bombs, had they been available, would not have been employed in the tense weeks and months following the Battle of the Bulge, for example.

Putting aside for the moment consideration of the ethical quality of the reasoning, "The other fellow will certainly develop an atrocious weapon if he can; therefore, I must beat him to it," we may point out that the scientists have entangled themselves in the same practical or political dilemma as the theologians with whom we have dealt in the preceding chapter. If war is accepted as a pattern of national behavior, competition in making ever more destructive and atrocious weapons must also be accepted. At this very moment, for example, not the slightest effort is made to conceal the fact that experiments have been made in the production not only of more deadly atomic weapons but even of more destructive and atrocious instruments for "biological" warfare.

Once the bomb had been put together at a time when no clear military necessity for its use existed, many of the scientists, admittedly "frightened" by the nature of the weapon they had constructed, made an attempt to keep the weapon from ever being used. One is tempted to ask in passing whether this was any different from the inventor of the slingshot, the cannon, the submarine and the bombing plane proposing that his new product should never be used. When a young nuclear physicist in great trepidation in July, 1945, approached a young social scientist with the query what could be done now to stop the use of the atomic bomb, the latter replied, irreverently but with, surely, a large measure of justification, "What in hell did you think you were making the thing for?"

It is instructive to study the arguments the scientists used in the report to the Secretary of War to which we have been referring, to support their proposal that a demonstration first be made "before the eyes of representatives of all the United Nations, on the desert or a barren island." They warned that unilateral resort to the use of the bomb, especially on an inhabited city, might deeply shock other nations. Furthermore, "it may be very difficult to persuade the world that a nation which was capable of secretly preparing and suddenly releasing a new weapon, as indiscriminate as the rocket bomb and a thousand times more destructive, is to be trusted in its proclaimed desire of having such weapons abolished by international agreement." At this golden moment, the scientists suggest that the United States has this weapon but has not yet used it and is thus in a position, presumably with little if any risk to its own security and might, to perform the unprecedented act of refraining from unilateral exercise of its power, capitalizing on its advantage of possessing the new weapon and thus opening the way for the abolition of war. The weapon is so frightful and the prospect of an atomic armaments race would be so horrifying that the United Nations will undoubtedly want to accept the proposal that it be internationally controlled. "Only lack of mutual trust, and not lack of desire for agreement, can stand in the path of an efficient agreement for the prevention of nuclear warfare." The proposed action by the United States would, the scientists go on to suggest, create "the best possible atmosphere" for engendering mutual trust and thus achieving international agreement. To the objection that this may not be practical politics they respond that their plan "may sound fantastic, but in nuclear weapons we have something entirely new in the order of magnitude of destructive power, and if we want to capitalize fully on the advantage their possession gives us, we must use new and imaginative methods."

Failure to adopt some such plan at this extremely favorable moment will mean, they warn, that "the race for nuclear armaments will be on in earnest not later than the morning after our first demonstration of the existence of nuclear weapons." Thus even from a completely unsentimental, hard common-sense point of view, they counsel, use of atomic bombs on centers of population might be most unwise for if "one takes the pessimistic viewpoint and discounts the possibility of an effective international control over nuclear weapons at the present time, then the advisability of an early use of nuclear bombs against Japan becomes even more doubtful," for it will mean taking "a flying start toward an unlimited armament race. If this race is inevitable, we may have every reason to delay its beginning as long as possible in order to increase our head start still farther."

We do not know and probably shall not know for a very long time what discussions relative to this report of the nation's top scientists took place in the fateful summer of 1945 in top military and political circles. We do know that the counsel of the scientists was not taken. We know, also, that there was no clear "military necessity" for disregarding it. Much was made in the first months after Hiroshima and Nagasaki of the claim that the war had been materially shortened and myriads of American lives had been saved. At least occasionally the claim is still advanced. There seems very little ground any more on which to base it. In any case, war leaders who are constantly making decisions that so many boys' lives shall be expendable for such and such a future objective can hardly claim to be exempt from facing the question whether some lives might not be properly expendable to forestall the launching of an unlimited armaments race with the consequences that would entail.

The counsel of the "frightened men" who had made the bomb went unheeded. The unlimited armaments race is on. The scientists were right in thinking that a golden opportunitiy existed. If national leaders had been ready to think "new and imaginative" thoughts, if they had been humble and repentant, perhaps even if they had been able to exercise some restraint and to practice hard common sense, they would have given heed; the opportunity would have been seized.

What the scientists did not reckon with in that fateful crisis was the mentality of warmaking, nationalism and power politics. War has its own logic. The drive for victory and the power it is expected to bring with it generates a terrible momentum. The mutual trust, which the scientists rightly pointed out was all that was needed, is exactly what war destroys and destroys not only between enemies but between allies as well. Dr. Einstein himself has made the statement that the desire to keep Russia from playing an important part in the victory over Japan probably had much to do with the decision to bomb Hiroshima and Nagasaki. Instead of mutual trust, war and power politics beget suspicion and fear, as they are in large measure begotten by them. By their work on the atomic bomb—undertaken, it is proper here to recall, on their own initiative—the scientists had placed themselves in bondage to war and power politics and had tremendously heightened the elements of suspicion and fear. If the weapon was indeed as terrible as the scientists now frantically contended, could we really trust anyone else with it? What if the Russians, who are so secretive about their affairs, have the bomb and contemplate using it after the defeat of the Axis powers?

The same considerations and attitudes today stultify the various efforts to achieve world organization, the control of nuclear weapons and the rest. So far as we can see they will continue to do so, as long as war is accepted as a possible instrument of policy and war preparation consequently continues. The war preparations supply the suspicion and fear which make steps toward effective control impossible even when the opportunity seems golden and even the hardest common sense seems to dictate plainly the course that must be taken. There will probably have to be organization, machinery for inspection, and the rest when the spirit of mutual trust has been achieved, though the machinery will probably seem less important then than it does now. But the mutual trust will have to be there before even moderate steps in the right direction can be taken, and war preparations will banish that spirit. Therefore, renunciation of the sin of war and the willingness to take unilateral action to disarm are now the initial requirements. All this we argued at length in an earlier chapter and we do not propose to go over that ground again. It should help, however, to carry conviction that once again we are driven to the same inescapable conclusion.

It follows, also, that when men refuse to seize one horn of the dilemma—that of renouncing the sin of warmaking—they necessarily have to accept the other, namely, that of committing themselves to fresh wars and unprecedented atrocities. In the preceding chapter we showed that certain nonpacifist theologians are already in effect giving a blessing, though reluctantly, to atomic war. The atomic scientists are doing the same thing. On May 26, 1946, the Federation of American Scientists made a statement in which, among other things, they deprecated the Bikini tests of atomic bombs and said that although they were co-operating they did so "with heavy hearts and without enthusiasm." The reasoning was as follows: "Scientists seek by education to teach men that they must abandon atomic weapons to preserve civiliza-tion." But men have not yet learned this. Consequently, the "military" still "have a mission, fantastic and shortsighted as it may seem to reason-able men." That is to say, war preparation, Bikini tests, competition in nuclear weapons have to go on until men do learn that atomic war will put an end to civilization and perhaps to the human race as well. There may actually have to be an atomic war to "teach the lesson," which seems to come very close to saying that civilization has to be destroyed in an atomic war in order to prove that civilization will be destroyed by atomic war. In the meantime, "reasonable men," the scientists among them, have to co-operate with the "fantastic and shortsighted" men, that is, the military, in preparations for such war. By the same token, the scientists in each nation will presumably collaborate fran-tically if not enthusiastically with their respective national govern-ments and forces in waging the atomic war. On the part of American scientists the efforts in that war to discover the ultimate weapon will of course be motivated by the knowledge that Ruritania has "the tech-nical skill necessary to develop such a weapon, and that the Ruritanian government"—in contrast to our own which has always been most fas-tidious in such matters—"has no moral restraints regarding its use."

From the political angle there is no end short of annihilation to this process, unless a radically new course is adopted; but on this we have sufficiently dwelt. In this chapter we have still to point out that if scientists are human beings at all and if human beings are in any significant sense spiritual beings subject to a moral law, then the indi-vidual scientist at some point in this process has to be confronted by his individual conscience—in the presence of God—with the atomic bomb and its implications and in that solemn court ask himself whether he can go on, whether he must not dissociate himself to the utmost extent possible from any voluntary participation in atomic war and in preparation therefor. Furthermore, if there is a point at all where a morally responsible being must decline to use certain means, however noble and important he may deem his end to be—a point where he can no longer hide behind the excuse, "If I don't do it, somebody else will" —then surely that point for the atomic scientists is now. If he can in good conscience go on from here to super-atomic weapons, to biological weapons, to X, then there simply is no limit. The scientists themselves have admitted that they do have a moral responsibility for what is done with their discoveries. In the report to the Secretary of War which we have been analyzing occurs the statement: "In the past, scientists could disclaim direct responsibility for the use to which mankind had put their disinterested discoveries." One wonders how accurate that word "disinterested" is in this connection. One recalls also a well-known and highly respected journalist's remark that this disclaimer of responsibility by scientists reminded him of a Borgia who would put poison in his guest's cup and then contend that it was none of his responsibility if the guest drank it. However that may be, "we feel compelled to take a more active stand now because the success we have achieved in the development of nuclear power is fraught with infinitely greater dangers than were all the inventions of the past." Note, from the pen of persons accustomed to speaking accurately and with restraint, those words "infinitely" and "all." The scientists, then, do have to behave as if they were whole men, responsible beings, not specialists and automata.

I have by correspondence or in conversation raised with a number of atomic scientists and others who have been closely identified with the work on the bomb, including some of the most important, this question whether they should not become conscientious objectors against war, and specifically against taking any further part in the manufacture of atomic weapons or similar instruments of indiscriminate destruction. The answers are extremely interesting.

I am almost invariably told at once that a very considerable number of men have already withdrawn from the bomb project. Some are simply impatient to get back to basic research problems. Some have been motivated chiefly by resentment against military censorship and the effect that may have on scientific research and the basic freedoms. Some, I am told, are moved by genuine conscientious objection against any further production of atomic weapons. None, so far as I know, up to the moment of writing, has publicly gone on record as a conscientious objector; and this is what is of course required if the action is to have an adequate effect, whether from the practical or the ethical point of view.

Another argument is that it would be "undemocratic" for the scientists to take things in their own hands, so to speak, by depriving the nation through the withholding of their services of the means with which to wage atomic war. It is the duty of scientists as citizens to try to get the nation to make an honest and vigorous effort to secure adequate international control; but in the meantime they must not do anything to "weaken" the nation and in practice this means, as we have seen, that they continue to co-operate with the military in such further developments in the instrumentalities of warfare as may be deemed proper and necessary by the duly constituted civil and military authorities. So far as I have been able to discover in the course of a continuous and vigorous pursuit of the subject, the viewpoint which I am describing would also lead the scientists to collaborate in an actual war if the United States were to enter such a war. As one of them put it in a personal letter: "I personally believe in obeying the laws of this country and in aiding its efforts in whatever direction my own government and responsible officials believe that we should go. I exercise my right as a citizen in attempting to change the rules, not in frustrating the rules as laid down."

Now this argument about democratic process by the atomic scientists is interesting for a number of reasons. For one thing, these scientists, on their own admission, approached the government secretly during the war, not only without the knowledge of the people but without the knowledge of Congress, with the proposal to make atomic bombs. What the implications were of adding this secret weapon to the arsenal of war we have seen. The scientists themselves, once they had made the thing, stood aghast. They were then instrumental in persuading hundreds of lesser scientists and technicians to enlist in an enterprise the nature of which the latter did not understand. Furthermore, thousands of workers were in their turn enlisted—and in view of the existence of the conscription act, virtually drafted—to work on this project; and two billions of the taxpayers' money was spent without the latter or their elected congressmen knowing anything about it. Consider the helplessness henceforth of the common man, the plain citizen in a democracy, if in the atomic age the technical experts will lend themselves unquestioningly to working in enterprises the nature and purpose of which they do not understand. What is left of democracy, of policy decisions made by the citizenry after adequate discussion? I can see no reason to suppose that any safeguard is left against the perpetration on mankind of such outrages as are pictured in works like Aldous Huxley's *Brave New World,* if the pattern set by our leading minds in the past war is allowed to stand, especially if the individual scientist is at no point to assume the role of conscientious objector.

In the present context it is perhaps a minor but nevertheless not a negligible factor that the scientists who feel they are bound to observe democratic processes submitted to a military censorship over their work and the publication of its results. Again on their own admission, they continue in some measure to do so. The intensity with which they are contending for civilian control now and the bitter criticism some of them have made of the military censorship are undoubtedly an indication of how genuine and severe this censorship has been. But military censorship is one of the most vicious instruments of dictatorship and totalitarianism.

It seems to me that the scientists may rightly be charged with being highly selective about the violations of democracy which they will allow themselves, assuming for the moment that conscientious objection to war or the production of atomic weapons is a violation of democracy. The idea of this particular violation they reject, but the egregious violation of democracy involved in the secret production of the most expensive and destructive weapons, submission to military censorship, acquiescence in the use of their products by the military for unnecessary and essentially irrational purposes, these violations they either practice or submit to.

We quoted a leading scientist as saying, "I personally believe in obeying the laws of this country and in aiding its efforts in whatever direction my own government and responsible officials believe that we should go." He was of course giving expression to a very common attitude, held both by ordinary people and by the most sophisticated. What it really comes down to is "My country, right or wrong." But this is that deification of the state against which we were supposed to be fighting. On this basis, what ground was there for criticizing the German scientists who in many cases also felt that they had no choice but to obey the laws of their country, at least where the national existence seemed to be at stake, and in aiding its efforts in whatever direction their government and responsible officials thought they should go?

If it is argued that the cause of the United States was just and that of Germany not, the atomic scientists have now to answer the question whether they believe an atomic war can possibly fulfill the requirements of justice. If not, will they be conscientious objectors to it?

Or if the point is raised that it is right for American scientists to go in the direction laid down by the government and responsible officials because theirs is a democratic government, whereas the German was not, they must certainly face the question how democratic this government was under war conditions or will be in case atomic war threatens or occurs.

Furthermore, we certainly cannot in a democratic country accept the proposition that the majority is always right and that provision must not be made for conscientious objection by a minority. It is, rather, part of the very essence of the democratic way of life that provision should be made for conscience. A democracy can function only if the common man can be trusted in a substantial measure to judge between right and wrong and to choose the right. If someone has to tell him what is right and make him do it, then the Fuehrer principle and not the democratic is operative. When a democracy, then, fails to make provision for conscience or violates it, it is destroying its own foundation.

One of the scientists in conversation advanced the interesting suggestion that if he and his colleagues were to become convinced that they must in conscience sever all connection with atomic warfare and were to act on that conviction, the effect might be the opposite of that desired since people would resent having the scientists virtually assume the power to decide for or against war—the national "defense"—instead of leaving it to the people or Congress "where the decision belongs." Winston Churchill, perhaps not the highest authority on democracy, rebuked a British scientist who wanted his colleagues to refuse to produce atomic weapons by telling him to "stand for Parliament" if he wanted to decide national policy. It might well be that a good many people would have this reaction if the scientists were to take drastic action on the basis of conscientious objection; we can be certain that the military spokesmen of ultranationalist and reactionary interests would give voice to such sentiments. It would, therefore, be necessary to try to guard against this danger. For the scientist whose conscience once came under conviction this danger would certainly not constitute a valid ground for violating conscience.

However, this danger is in my opinion more than balanced by an opposite one. The scientists warn against the fearful evils of military censorship and level the most biting criticisms against the brass hats who think they can decide policies relating to the atom. Then they publicly accept decorations for their share in making the bomb, and their pictures with Major General Graves, the head and front of the censorship, pinning medals on them appear in all the papers. Will not ordinary people consciously and unconsciously draw the conclusion that the military censorship cannot be so bad after all, and that Urey Bethe, Szilard, Fermi and the rest, on the one hand, and Major General Graves, on the other, are good pals now as they were during the war?

The scientists proclaim that it is their purpose "by education to teach men that they must abandon atomic weapons to preserve civilization." But how can scientists who accept decorations for having made the bomb in the first place and who are aiding or acquiescing in the building of a stock pile of atomic bombs, especially in the present state of international tension, "teach men that they must abandon atomic weapons to preserve civilization"? Ordinary folk are surely bound to conclude that the thing cannot be so serious after all. Is it not entirely possible—perhaps we might say likely or probable—that the only way in which the danger which threatens mankind can really be brought home to ordinary people is for those who know what that danger is to give notice that they will have nothing more to do with atomic weapons and will appeal to their fellow scientists in all lands to join them in slaying the Frankenstein monster of their own creation and thus atoning for the evil they have wrought?

At least one top-flight atomic scientist has given notice that he is contemplating such action. In an interview reported in the New York *Post* of June 15, 1946, Frederic Joliot-Curie is reported to have asserted that scientists would have the right to declare a strike against further atomic research if the United Nations fails to outlaw atomic weapons. He expressed hope that the U.N. Commission would achieve this objective but added: "If, however, after discussion no agreement is reached, I express the personal opinion that we scientists should refuse to continue our work in this field. That last word should rest with the scientists."

One of the reasons which Professor Joliot-Curie gave for his anxiety over the present state of affairs was that secrets were being kept in this field of nuclear physics long after the end of hostilities; this might lead to secrets being kept in other fields too; "and in the end, it may diminish the productivity of scientific investigation altogether."

An English publication, the *New English Weekly*, of August 30, 1945, has suggested a danger to science itself and to the whole fraternity of scientists from another direction, unless the scientists act soon and effectively to help resolve the present crisis. It quotes the remark of the well-known Professor C. E. M. Joad, who called the splitting of the atom "the greatest single disaster in the history of mankind, not even excluding the invention of the internal combustion engine— will nobody stop these damned scientists?" and opines that he was expressing just what "the great majority of people instantaneously and spontaneously felt." I am not at all sure that this was true in the United States. But I am sure that the scientists and all leaders of thought will do well to consider carefully the main thesis of the *New English Weekly's* article. It suggests that "the direction of scientific enquiry has been distorted by certain unconscious illusions (not only by wrong motives in the use of its findings) and that in consequence we have been finding" things out in the wrong order. "The scientific fanatics are dangling before our eyes the promise of controlled atomic energy —and the promise is thankfully received by the little-minded, who immediately think of it as something for themselves . . . warmer houses in winter or a motor car that will run forever without requiring any more fuel." Meantime the motivations and the skills of various kinds which are needed if human life is truly to be enriched and deepened, with the help of new inventions and new sources of power, are lacking. The result is destruction on an ever larger scale and a sense of doom hanging over mankind which, it is suggested, may lead to a revulsion against science and the scientists. Therefore

with the production of the atomic bomb the scientists had better take warning. If they do not look into the matter, find out what is wrong and make a sort of revolution within the scientific faculty itself, the world will sooner or later revolt against the scientists. They will be the next scapegoats. They may not, in reality, be the most responsible for what has occurred, but revolutions and movements to "purge" scapegoats do not nicely discriminate. That a time may come when everyone suspected of possessing the most powerful but efficient kind of knowledge will be spied upon and hunted down, may seem highly improbable just now; but such a phenomenon is by no means unknown to history. We suspect that humanity does not, at bottom, want its life and its life-purposes to be frustrated, and that therefore, unless there is a re-orientation of Science, revolt against it is ultimately certain; moreover, revolts can take all sorts of curious, obstinate, irrepressible forms. Indeed, we suspect that the revolution against Science began, as a psychic disposition, on this last August Bank Holiday, and you could hear it in every pub. And why not? Science is the nearest thing we have at present to a universal world-cult. Suppose that there were a cult, whose brilliant progress in its theology, whilst accompanied by undoubted advances in social morality, brought about a steady increase in, for instance, human sacrifices; and imagine further what would happen if the last and professedly "highest" development in this theology was one that made necessary the periodic sacrifice of several thousand worshipers at a time, the victims to be selected by lottery. We could confidently expect—could we not?—either an irrepressible anti-clerical and anti-religious movement, or else a vigorous "heresy" to reform that religion into a considerably different one.

I for one would regard it as a vast calamity if such a revulsion against science and the scientists were to occur. It would in my opinion be a further manifestation of mankind's deterioration and failure, not an indication that men were finding a way out to a better life. But the scientists themselves, as we have seen, have recognized that a grave social and moral responsibility rests upon them. The situation is such that intelligent persons will realize that small and tentative measures are bound to be inadequate. A reorientation of a revolutionary character and actions which will be very costly and may expose those who take them to hardship and, what may be harder to bear, ridicule—these are needed now.

Among the first and most important requirements is that the scientists should give leadership in the movement to abolish war. They cannot do it so long as they continue to be involved in the production of war materials. It is bound to keep them in bondage to the military and to a nationalistic political leadership. Presently, as we have I think demonstrated, they will be participants in the very atomic war which they plead must not be permitted to happen. Warmaking and peace-making represent two completely different systems of social organization. Men cannot work at both at the same time, any more than they can serve both God and Mammon. A complete about-face is required of the scientists and the great technological leaders. They have to re-nounce all part in war preparation or warmaking. Each must do so, whether or not his colleague is prepared to join him. He must do so now. They are the people who have assured us there is no time to lose. Joliot-Curie's strike against making atomic weapons should not be put off until the United Nations Atomic Energy Commission has failed to set up international controls. The time when it has admittedly failed may be a long way off and then it may be forever too late. Furthermore, some such action as this on the part of leading scientists is necessary precisely in order to bring home to the peoples the reality and extent of the danger and thus to provide the impetus, which is now so obviously lacking, for prompt action in the organizational field.

Except for the fact that admission of blame for past actions is in-volved and the evident danger that some people will call them traitors and—most terrifying of all—"queer," the scientists who become con-scientious objectors and go on strike against war as Joliot-Curie sug-gested need take little risk. The universities, industry, government cannot get along without them. What good would it do to "fire" them?

On the other hand, if the scientists—even a few of them—were to take such a stand, the American people and others would at last realize that they were deadly serious in what they were saying about the fright-ful dangers of atomic war. What is infinitely more important, the American people, and presently others, would be shaken out of moral lethargy and despair and would become capable of inspired action to abolish war and build a democratic society, because they would behold the spectacle of men who do not try to shift the responsibility for their actions onto the military or the state, and who refuse to make con-science subservient to the state. They would see men who understand that if a nation loses its soul, it has lost all, even though it seem to have gained the world; men who fear God and who know, therefore, that it is far worse to make and drop atomic bombs on others than it is to have them dropped on you; men who are also, therefore, delivered from fear, including the fear of fear which is driving men, as if they were possessed of unclean spirits, to the edge of the precipice.

The entire history of Western civilization, rooted in the Hebrew-Christian tradition, which is now imperiled, testifies to the truth that it is such men who lose their lives and find them, and who incarnate in the moral and social sphere the power comparable to that of the atom in the physical. They and they alone can quiet and stabilize the souls of their fellows, and stop the decay of civilization or build it anew when it has been shattered.

There is, as has been often pointed out, a deep cleavage in our souls and in our society because our moral and social development has not kept pace with technological advance. That cleavage must be healed first and basically within the morally responsible human being. It will be healed in the scientist who becomes a prophet—that is, a man who assumes responsibility for what he creates and what is done with it, a man whose words and actions are in true accord. "Mankind's destiny," as the scientists say, "is being decided today—now—this moment." It is being decided by the scientists who take, or fail to take, upon themselves the awful responsibility of being prophets, conscientious objectors, persons, whole human beings, and not technicians or slaves, albeit heavyhearted and unenthusiastic ones, of a warmaking state.

Thus the whole spiritual climate and character of our civilization might be changed. Men might find their way to God and in a new way His Kingdom might be revealed and realized among men, if those who in splitting the atom have learned to "unbuild that miracle of dynamic architecture upon which, as a mere foundation, the Eternal Wisdom has fashioned the miracles of the mineral, vegetable, animal and human Kingdoms" were now to take the lead also in redirecting "our thirst for truth towards that Wisdom by which we ourselves come into existence, and under whose strict mortgage we enjoy any good we have or any powers we exercise—including the cleverness that can destroy its works."

The Apostle pointed out many centuries ago that the Eternal Wisdom has a way of choosing the foolish to confound the wise of this world. Albert Einstein some years ago was a leader among the antiwar forces of Europe. At that time he said that if 2 per cent of those eligible and called upon to take part in war were resolutely and at whatever cost to refuse to be conscripted, war could be abolished. There were those who considered him foolish then and his suggestion just a rash and chimerical proposal of a man who did not stick to his own last. There were also those who regarded him with veneration and believed that here was a man who could combine in himself the roles of the creative scientist and the inspired prophet.

One wonders whether the leading atomic scientists now think that Albert Einstein was wise when in the fall of 1939 he wrote to President Roosevelt the letter starting the political chainreaction which involved Los Alamos, Hiroshima, Nagasaki, Bikini and much besides. Perhaps it was then, when he sent that letter from his study into that other realm where nationalistic political leaders decide the fate of cities, of nations, perhaps of mankind, that he was foolish.

He may have overestimated some years ago what 2 per cent of the average run of the world's youth might be able to do to end war. It is certain that if 2 per cent of the members of the scientific fraternity of our day, including such leaders as Albert Einstein himself, were to raise the banner of conscientious objection to war, multitudes would repair to it. The effect would be great—perhaps revolutionary, "atomic."

Chapter XI

Pacifism in the Atomic Age

In this closing chapter we must deal with the implications of what we have been saying throughout this book for the broad strategy of the religious pacifist movement in the world today. The details of the program of this movement must obviously be worked out and presented elsewhere.

First a word may be said about the historical background of the present-day religious pacifist organizations. Since 1914 there have been two general tendencies or sets of forces that have increased in vitality and importance in a world where many things are in process of disintegration. One of these is totalitarianism in its various forms; the other is religious pacifism. As for the former, it is not necessary to say anything here except to observe that the war has not put an end to or sensibly diminished the trend toward totalitarianism, nor has it weakened the totalitarian forces in society as a whole, though the Axis powers suffered defeat in the war.

As for religious pacifism, probably few are aware that this movement as we know it today dates its beginnings no farther back than World War I and the years immediately following that war. Before World War I the membership and the leadership as well of the Christian and Jewish churches were hardly aware of the fact that their Scriptures and history contained a possible basis for a pacifist attitude toward war and the state. I can personally testify to the fact that it was possible before 1914 to graduate from two theological seminaries and to be ordained to the Christian ministry after a more than casual study of theology, Church history and the Bible without having been given a hint of the pacifist strain in the Hebrew and Christian heritage. In the United States, though the prevailing theology and social ethics always have been Calvinistic, when war actually came nearly all church people acted on the Lutheran conception that once the state had decided upon war it was the duty of the Christian man to obey its mandate. Conscientious objectors were assumed, with little or no argument, to be heretics. There was a vague idea of the existence of such pacifist sects as Quakers, Mennonites and Dunkards, but it was largely built around the picture of the man on the Quaker Oats box; since these people wore broad hats and long hair, they might be expected to be queer in other respects also!

Since 1919, as we have already observed, virtually all important denominations and the historic Oxford Ecumenical Conference have recognized that the pacifist position is at least one of those a Christian may take in conformity with the Scriptures and the Catholic tradition of the Church. It is very generally recognized that "God is the sole Lord of conscience," and that even in so great a matter as war, the Christian should not automatically accept the edict of the state, but must make his own decision as to the proper course to follow. Hence the general recognition of conscientious objectors by both Church and state. Where in World War I the author of *Preachers Present Arms* found less than a hundred American ministers outside of the historic peace churches who maintained anything like a clear-cut pacifist position, during World War II there were at least thirty times as many.

Even among the peace churches, it may be noted, their historic "peace testimony" was in 1914 largely latent, something of which they were aware only vaguely, since it had not been challenged on a large scale for a century. The American Friends Service Committee did not exist in 1914, nor the Brethren Service and Mennonite Central Committees.

Such organizations as the Fellowship of Reconciliation, the Women's International League for Peace and Freedom, the National Council for the Prevention of War, and the War Resisters' League are all post-1914 products.

Another illustration of this point is provided by the list of writers on whose books much of our pacifism is nurtured: Gandhi, C. F. Andrews, Kagawa, Aldous Huxley, Gerald Heard, Kirby Page, John Haynes Holmes, Richard Gregg, Vera Brittain, Laurence Housman, Rufus Jones, Charles E. Raven, Allan Hunter, Allan Knight Chalmers, Muriel Lester, Stanley Jones. Nearly all their work has been done since 1914. Gandhi, who of course is by far the most significant single figure in contemporary religious pacifism, began his work in South Africa in 1907, but he was not a national figure in India until after 1914 and it was not until 1919 that he became a figure of world stature or, for that matter, a full-fledged pacifist.

Kagawa, who also had an immense influence for pacifism on Christians in the United States and who is probably personally a pacifist, though there is some question as to just where he now stands as a political personage, is similarly a post-World War I figure.

So well-informed and competent an observer as Dr. F. Ernest Johnson of Teachers College, Columbia University, head of the Research Department of the Federal Council of Churches, has expressed the opinion that seldom if ever has a more effective job of education for a "cause" been done than that which resulted in the inroads of pacifism into the churches in the 1920's and '30's, and the continued powerful hold of pacifism on religious leaders in English-speaking countries during the war.

During the recent war the membership and the activity of such organizations as the Fellowship of Reconciliation and the War Resisters' League, both in Great Britain and in the United States, increased substantially. Similarly, the work of the Peace Section of the American Friends Service Committee has expanded considerably. On the whole the prestige of religious pacifism in the English-speaking countries increased. As for the smaller religious pacifist groups in Germany and in the formerly occupied countries and the adjoining neutral lands, they had of course an extremely trying experience during the war. Yet they were not crushed. Their members seem to have succeeded to a remarkable extent in demonstrating the validity, under very difficult conditions, of a way of life which enabled its practitioners to refuse to collaborate with native or foreign dictators but which also led them to refrain from hate and violence against the violent and tyrannical. In nearly all these countries the prestige of the movement increased.

In India, as these words are being written, an interim government under the Indian National Congress leader, Jawaharlal Nehru, is taking office pending the convening of a constitutional assembly. Whatever difficulties may yet face that land because of religious or other controversies, it appears that independence from Great Britain is virtually an accomplished fact. Nor will anyone deny that this achievement is largely the result of Mahatma Gandhi's leadership and that it has been achieved with a minimum of violence. Thus, again, it seems likely that the philosophy and method of nonviolence based on religious insight and commitment has gained prestige. Now that Nazi totalitarianism, at least in its German embodiment, has been defeated, is there any clean-cut or promising alternative to a possible revival of fascist totalitarianism, on the one hand, and to bolshevik totalitarianism, on the other hand, save the nonviolence and democracy for which Gandhi stands? The Western nations whose democracy is compromised by its tie-up with an outworn and reactionary economic system and who have not broken with the war system certainly do not offer a viable alternative.

Had World War II come to an end without the discovery and the use of the atomic bomb, it appears that the problem confronting the religious pacifist movement on emerging from its first war experience might have been comparatively simple. The term "comparatively" is here used advisedly of course, for the situation would have been terrible and complicated enough without the emergence of atomic weapons. Yet when all due precaution against exaggeration has been taken, it remains true that war, so far as its techniques and probable destructiveness are concerned, has experienced one of those changes in degree which amounts to a qualitative change and that a new urgency has been imparted to the job of eliminating war altogether. Furthermore, if mankind or civilized society survives, incalculable changes are impending in the technological organization of production and consequently also in our entire economic, political and cultural life. What the world will be like fifty years or so from now it is as impossible for us to envisage as it would have been for anyone living in early feudal times to imagine life in Europe and the Americas during the first three decades of the twentieth century. Those who will prove to be most wrong are those who think that everything will be as before.

The one plainly inscribed guidepost which seems to me to emerge in this situation is one which supports the main thesis of this book, namely, the basic and urgent character of the problem of war and organized violence. This reminds us of the phenomenon mentioned at the beginning of this chapter, that the post-1914 period has been marked by the growth both of totalitarianism and of religious pacifism. At first thought it may seem anomalous that two such opposite trends should exhibit simultaneous vitality and growth. A moment's reflection, however, will show that this is rather what might have been expected. In a crisis, the "in-between" organizations and forces tend to disappear; those that take a clear stand with relation to the issue or issues underlying the crisis move to the front. The technological changes of our age have altered fundamentally the character of war and violent revolution. It is no longer remotely possible to have a limited, nice, polite war or revolution. If there be war, it will be total war, regardless of whether its objectives be primarily national, or class, or ideological. The totalitarians saw this and did not seek to evade the implications. "Let it be total war and terrorism," they said, and say. The pacifists also faced the issue realistically and clearly stated that only by renunciation of war and organized violence could mankind escape suicide.

Though the more theoretical sections of this book have made it clear that our position is not a simplistic or political antiwar position but is based on an essentially religious conception of the universe and the nature of man which must inevitably express itself in all relations of life, we shall presently make one or two additional observations to stress the fact that religious pacifists ought not to be what have been aptly described as "one-cause fanatics." For the time being, we shall nevertheless continue to dwell upon the prominence which we believe must be given in our program and activity to disarmament or the abolition of the war system.

Every movement, like every philosophy, must have a principle of exclusion as well as inclusion. It must limit the matters which it places on its agenda and among them some must receive more emphasis than others in a given historical situation.

In emphasizing once more the primacy of conscientious objection and the preaching of repentance for the sin of war and of implementing that repentance by the laying down of arms by individual and by nation, we do not propose to rehearse the considerations supporting those proposals which have constituted the burden of our study. Decisions in the matter will in any event not be made exclusively on intellectual grounds. If, moreover, we have not already made a convincing case in so far as can be done on such grounds, it is not in our power to do more, certainly not at this time. One or two factors which affect the thinking of pacifists themselves with respect to the strategy of their movement require brief comment.

Some pacifists with whom I have discussed these matters question whether there is any sense in appealing to the nation to disarm unilaterally because they believe that the idea will strike the masses of people as utterly foolish. They do not question that renunciation of war at whatever cost is enjoined by the teachings of Christ and is implied in the religious pacifist philosophy. Pacifists certainly must lay down arms, therefore, and they have to make it clear on occasion that disarmament—even unilateral if need be—is what the pacifist stands for. But when it comes to a political program for mass consumption, it is suggested, something that will appear to ordinary human beings as more sensible should be put forward. As we pointed out in another connection, what appeals to pacifists or even to nonpacifist advocates of world government and gradual mutual disarmament as sensible is condemned by many other presumably good and intelligent people as utterly fantastic and, because of its extreme character, preventing the taking of such sensible steps in the right direction as might otherwise be possible.

I become increasingly convinced that the advocacy of setting forth a moderate or sensible program for general consumption is psychologically unsound and that it will defeat rather than advance either the immediate or the ultimate aims of pacifism. For one thing, the masses of the people know deep down in their hearts that the situation is desperate and that desperate remedies are required; that it is revolutionary and that, if there is a way out at all, it is a revolutionary one.

The fact that they are so apathetic about any program whatsoever and so absorbed in their daily occupations and indulgences, in so far as it is not a phenomenon which always exists, does not in my opinion invalidate this analysis. The apathy is the reaction to what are felt to be inadequate proposals, to prophets "who deal slightly with the hurt of the daughter of my people, and cry, Peace, peace, when there is no peace" or prospect of any.

Secondly, in the final analysis it is the moral and spiritual appeal which moves men, if anything can. Even for making war that appeal is indispensable. The psychologically sound thing for pacifists is to make an uncompromising and loving spiritual appeal like St. Francis, George Fox and others. But that involves going down to the roots —the call to repent of the sin of warmaking, the summons to take the Christian, the nonviolent, course. If there is any possibility of evoking a mass reaction, it is in this approach.

Another objection raised by pacifists is that it is unwise and ethically unsound to call upon a nation which is not Christian to follow a Christian course. As one has phrased it, such a nation by definition could not take such a course on Christian grounds; but if it disarmed, for example, for prudential reasons, then its action would be hypocritical, it would not be prepared to accept the consequences of such an action, and thus more values would be lost and greater calamities incurred than might have resulted if a less idealistic course had been followed.

With the general question as to whether a nation can be summoned to observe the moral law, including the law of self-sacrifice, we have dealt in an earlier chapter. We do not believe there is scriptural or other sound ground for believing that a nation is exempt from the moral law. The alternative always is the acceptance in some form and in final analysis of the law that the nation may live for no other object than its own survival. That doctrine bolsters the existence and the profoundly immoral behavior of the contemporary absolutist state. Religious leaders who hold that the nation may not and should not be called upon to be willing to sacrifice in order that mankind may be saved seem to me to share responsibility for the survival of absolutism and totalitarianism.

The fear that a nation which followed some such course as we have suggested would do so without a pretty thorough realization of the costs involved seems to me unfounded. On the one hand, we are told that advocating a straight-out pacifist course is too extreme, ordinary people will not consider it sensible. On the other hand, we are warned that the masses might actually take such a course without realizing that it was an extreme and costly one. Such verbalizations pretty much cancel each other out. If a people were moved to adopt a pacifist policy, they would certainly know that it was revolutionary and would be costly—like a war, for example! The charge that the masses are not given a clear picture of the price of deliverance from their present bondage and terror may much more properly be leveled against the proponents of other programs.

As for the suggestion that the masses might accept a Christian program for prudential reasons and thus be guilty of hypocrisy, there is unquestionably an admixture of evil and hypocrisy in all human action. I am not aware that in other connections, we conclude that the requirements of the moral law may, therefore, be disregarded. I suspect also that a certain type of asceticism and Puritanism in part at least inspires this argument; an action has to be painful in order to be good; it must bring nothing but mortification to the individual or nation, otherwise it is not Christian. We do not believe that what is good for man or society in the sense of conformable to the moral law and what is good in the sense of human well-being, in all senses of that term, stand in such an antithetical relationship. The actual relationship is more complicated, or better, perhaps, more dialectical than that. A man or nation must be willing to face death in obedience to the will of God and must not serve God for a price; but the end of obedience to the will of God is not death but life. The moral law is the statement of the nature of Reality as it bears upon the behavior of responsible persons or spirits. "In keeping it," as the Psalmist said, "there is great reward." If a man would save his life he shall lose it. Unless he is willing to lose it, he shall not find it. That is one aspect of the truth. But if a man will lose—or is prepared to lose—his life for Christ's sake he shall find it. That is the other side of the paradoxical truth, which cannot indeed be worked out in theory and formulas but which can be and in some measure is constantly being worked out in the life of men and of societies.

A people which should rise in action to the height of accepting a redemptive role would hardly do so without having undergone a profound spiritual experience. But if it were also to be clear-eyed enough to see that from a prudential point of view continued involvement in an armaments race was suicidal, that would hardly stultify its action or vitiate its spirit.

On the other hand, religious pacifists will, I fear, suffer from split personalities and their activities will be stultified unless they frankly go to the nation with a total pacifist program. For one thing, they must take note of what they will counsel the nation to do if various other proposals to prevent atomic war, including world government and disarmament by general agreement, fail. Will they then admit that the nation has no choice but to prepare for atomic war and to fight to win? Would that be the "lesser evil"? A few pacifists, perhaps, would say so. I cannot see either the logic or the ethical merit of that position. In any case, the great majority of religious pacifists would say that war was still utterly evil and that it would be better in every way for the nation to refuse to have anything more to do with it. But the time to plant in men's minds the idea that war must be ruled out of national calculations altogether is now. Certainly the moment when appeals for general disarmament have apparently failed will hardly be a propitious one to advance the proposal that the nation should disarm anyway. Having given the impression that all their expectations are built on general disarmament, pacifists will, it seems to me, cut a sorry figure if at that moment they come forward and say, "Of course, what we meant all the time was that men and peoples must have done with war, regardless of what others do."

There is another direction from which the same kind of question comes at pacifists. They seek to win individual recruits, including religious leaders and atomic scientists, for example, to the conscientious objector position. The argument that in the past pacifists have seriously hampered the preparations of the nation for war, have encouraged an isolationist or appeasement policy and so on, we have considered elsewhere in this book. We do not think that it has any substantial merit. But this is, for one thing, because pacifists have not actually been numerous and influential enough to have a substantial effect on any nation's policy. We do, however, want to increase the number of strongly committed and active adherents to our cause. It is conceivable that our numbers might become large enough and our activity sufficiently effective to have a very appreciable and perhaps decisive effect on national policy. Conceivably a nation might thus at a very critical juncture be seriously divided. Our opponents may exaggerate the danger, since it is very likely that if pacifism makes substantial progress in one nation, it will in others also. Nevertheless, the possibility cannot be dismissed. More than one nation might indeed be seriously divided in a crisis. If we believe that a people may rightfully be called upon to follow a pacifist course, then we have a democratic right and a duty to try to win enough pacifists to make this possible. In that case we have also to run the risk of a serious conflict within the nation. If we do not really believe that a nation may be called upon to adopt such a course, then it is surely questionable whether we have any right to win more than a very small minority of individuals to the pacifist position. I do not believe, by the way, that basically nonresistant groups, such as the Mennonites, can escape this dilemma unless they think God authorizes them to limit the number of converts they will make or in His inscrutable providence has actually limited the number in advance. Nonresistant and "passive" as they may be, those who refuse to participate in war are bound, if they achieve substantial numbers, to constitute a problem for statesmen in a war situation.

If, then, we are going to go on to make converts, we have to be willing to accept the responsibility which would be ours if their numbers become substantial. That entails acceptance of the proposition that the pacifist course is the right one for the nation also. And if that is our conviction we shall have more unity in our own spirits, and consequent drive, and we shall also make a stronger appeal to the masses—perhaps especially to the membership of the churches—if we come to them with a total program unequivocally set forth.

There is danger for pacifists in getting involved in the advocacy of partial or diluted programs and arguments: for example, in pointing out in the struggle against conscription that if the government will pay more money, it can get all the volunteers it wants for the armed forces. I confess to having made some use of such arguments myself and to having a deep-seated reluctance to becoming or seeming to become doctrinaire and "narrow." And there may be a limited validity and usefulness in reminding our fellow citizens that on their own non-pacifist assumptions conscription is not needed. Certainly the adoption of peacetime conscription would be a serious further step backward and one earnestly wants to see it put off: Yet the argument that you do not need conscription because you can get volunteers for the business of systematic killing is at best one that can hardly arouse enthusiasm among pacifists. It may play into the hands of military men who chiefly desire a mechanized army anyway. The general run of citizens may just take the argument to mean, "We do not need conscription—yet." Certainly the pacifist has to answer the question, "What if we can't buy enough volunteers?" If his answer is really, "I never was in favor of volunteers anyway and I am still and always opposed to conscription," he should have said so at the outset and all the time. There are obviously many other situations in which the same considerations will be relevant for pacifist strategy.

There is danger in any but a very clean-cut and unequivocal program that the pacifist movement will fall between two stools: it will not generate the inspiration, the daring and the dynamic of a spiritual mission to the peoples and the nations, and at the same time it will be but a poor performer in the political arena in the conventional sense of the term. Even in the latter we shall be more effective if we come into it like the prophets of our faith in all times and lands with the whole word of the righteous and loving God to His people, the sheep of His pasture.

George Bernanos in his *Plea for Liberty* published a few years ago made an eloquent statement of what seems to me the psychologically sound approach for religious pacifists today. Having referred to the way in which the house of civilization is falling apart, he asks,

What would you have me do about it? . . . The most imprudent thing of all would be to poke a little to the right and a little to the left, here repair a section of wall, there readjust the position of a beam. Rather we must tackle the whole job at once. . . . The hope aroused in men's hearts must be proportionate to their present despair. I am well aware that it is fashionable among the bourgeoisie and even among Christians—who could believe it!—to make mock of those who promise the moon. How strange it is to hear such sneers coming from the mouths of certain priests, the same sacrilegious mouths which on Christmas day must repeat a certain promise —a thousand times more daring than the promise of the moon—the promise which assures Peace to men of good-will.

This is not the occasion to try to picture a society or nation which had adopted the pacifist attitude with respect to war and in which, therefore, pacifists were "in power." It is incumbent upon pacifists to face this problem and if India achieves her independence Gandhi will obviously have to make immediate decisions with respect to some aspects of it, though the government itself will, it is clear, not be pacifist. In a good many fields, such as education and the treatment of the mentally ill and of lawbreakers, a pacifist or near-pacifist approach is already and in increasing measure being accepted as sound. On the other hand, we must bear in mind in any speculation as to how certain problems would be dealt with in a pacifist society what we pointed out in another connection: whether the threat of atomic war is actualized or is not, the world is in for colossal changes. Speculation as to the shape of things to come will have to be very tentative. The greatest aid to intelligent adaptation to the unforeseen changes mankind will encounter will be an attitude of experimentation and a determined adherence to democratic, that is, nonviolent methods in dealing with social problems.

Although no effort will be made to deal with the problems which might engage pacifists "in power," it is necessary to comment briefly on one or two items not directly related to war resistance which figure in the pacifist program now. One of these has to do with the economic order. The pacifist who thinks that war can be abolished while everything else remains unchanged, and especially his own comfortable middle-class existence in the U.S.A., is rapidly becoming extinct. It is generally accepted that one of the great taproots of war is economic maldistribution and maladjustment. Prevailing opinion among pacifists holds that imperialistic capitalism leads to war and fascism and must be abolished.

This does not, in my opinion, imply that we have to accept the theory current among Marxist-Leninists and others influenced by Marx and Lenin that war cannot be abolished until after capitalism has been radically uprooted and a communist (or socialist) world order has taken its place. The relation is more dialectical and less chronological than this view implies. It may be noted here that this theory exercises considerable influence in at least two respects on the present policy of the Russian regime. In the first place, Stalin and his colleagues probably to a considerable degree actually believe in the thesis that "war is inevitable under capitalism" and that capitalist war will be directed fundamentally against "the workers' state." On this basis a war policy is assumed to be necessary and justifiable for Russia. But it is hardly open to question that the rulers of the Russian state, having adopted a war policy for the reasons characteristic of expansionist nation-states, then proceed to provide this policy with an idealistic covering and to project guilt upon the other nation by contending that the capitalist nations by their very nature precipitate wars and the Soviet Union is forced—reluctantly, of course, since it is "peace-loving"—to defend itself.

There is a close relationship between imperialistic and monopolistic capitalism and war. Religious pacifists who believe, as the Statement of Purpose of the Fellowship of Reconciliation states, in a "social order which will suffer no individual or group to be exploited for the pleasure or profit of another, and which will assure to all the means for realizing the best possibilities of life" will support in all democratic and nonviolent ways open to them such progressive movements as strive to reduce or eliminate the factor of exploitation in the economic order. But the effort to prevent and abolish war must not wait upon the completion of the effort to establish a new economic order. Basically, the two must go hand in hand. At the present stage those who are primarily concerned about economic reform or revolution need fully as much to learn that war and the survival of the war system will defeat their aims and bring catastrophic evils upon the common people everywhere as pacifists need to be reminded that economic evils must not be neglected. Gandhi and others are right in insisting that, in a subject country like India, independence must be achieved, the foreign tyrant must get off the people's back, before the reform of the economic order can be effectively tackled. The war system plays in other nations much the same obstructive role that foreign domination plays in colonial lands. Certain it is that so long as war remains in the picture, reactionary economic forces will be strengthened in countries like the United States and as the crisis becomes more intense will turn to some type of fascist dictatorship. The survival of the war system will place an eventually intolerable burden upon more progressive movements, such as the British Labor party, and will tend to thwart and corrupt them. Similarly, so long as the threat of war exists, the Russian dictatorship will be strengthened rather than relaxed and the Russian people will remain in the hands of a terroristic police state, which will have war making as its principal objective exactly as other absolutist nation-states do.

It hardly needs to be repeated that there is an urgency about abolishing the threat of war, and therefore a justification for concentrating on that job, which does not obtain with respect to changes in the economic order insofar as these are not themselves an integral part of the war system. On the other hand, if war were removed, a vast burden would be lifted from the backs of mankind, great new energies would be released, monopoly capitalism would no longer be able to resort to an armament boom and war to escape its dilemmas, armies would no longer exist to threaten and if need be terrorize the masses striving to revolt against oppression, and a much more hopeful attack could be made on economic problems.

What is true of war in the usual sense of that term holds good also of organized violence for the achievement of basic social changes. Technological and other factors being what they are, violence will produce reactionary and not progressive results. The inference to be drawn by social progressives has been well stated by an exceptionally able young theoretician, Philip Selznick, in an essay entitled "Revolution Sacred and Profane" appearing in a little magazine, *Enquiry*, for the fall of 1944:

Socialism must adopt the moral absolute of pacifism. If social-democracy was naive about the method required for the transfer of control over the industrial apparatus, it was equally sanguine about the ability of men to choose consistently the method which embodied their own values. The pacifist absolute is such in respect to its function, operating as a hard rule for those groups which have testified to its truth. But the judgment and conclusion which it represents are empirical insights. . . . We are too deeply involved in immediate relationships, too sharply influenced by proximate consequences, to be able to maintain the integrity of our ultimate aims unaided by functional absolutes. Hence the need for an act of collective faith in the enduring viability of procedures which we accept as crucial to the character of our movement. Democracy is one of these functional absolutes; pacifism must be another. The unity of democracy and pacifism as an interdependent set of means and objectives becomes more plainly manifest as each new development in the modern world unfolds. These tenets are more than tools: where they operate they are constituent fundamentals of the movement, referrable only to the moral sources of its being.

Pacifists, we may add, ought to lose the inferiority complex which some of them have over against various types of "revolutionists" they encounter. It is the nonpacifists who lack the essential and decisive ingredient of sound revolutionary philosophy and strategy in the contemporary scene.

It would be impossible to set forth in any detail the kind of economic order we should seek to build even if space permitted and the present author had the qualifications for such a task. For here the point we have made previously is most relevant: It is beyond our powers of thought and imagination to paint the economic and social order which would be possible or actual when war and dictatorship have been removed and atomic energy and other discoveries are harnessed to peaceful purposes. A world in which goods might well be so abundant that money would lose all utility, where leisure and not labor would be the problem and men might be conscripted, if creative uses for leisure were not devised and used, not because there was any need to be trained to fight others but to have drones to feed and to keep drones from boredom and consequent revolt. The principles or values which will guide pacifists as they face problems in this field we have frequently stated. What needs here to be said about their application can be put very briefly.

The principle that an individual or class must not exploit another presumably implies support at important points of social ownership and management as against monopoly by an individual or an oligarchic group. But the "socialism" which religious pacifists would support would be democratic socialism. At this historic juncture the substitution of economic collectivism as such for capitalism may not be a genuine socially progressive step any more than the invention of an atom-smasher as such is. It may be a step in the disintegration of civilization. Indeed the burden of proof is decidedly upon those who think that it is not; for historically, a highly centralized controlled economy accompanied by political dictatorship and geared to making war on a colossal scale has been characteristic of civilization in decline. A considerable number of people are still misled at this point by the traditional Marxist-Leninist conception that the only thing that could replace capitalism would be socialism and presently communism. If only, then, capitalism were crushed and removed, what followed would represent the achievement of the goal of history, men would be free, peace would reign and a rational social order would prevail. We do not think that an objective appraisal of the collectivist dictatorships, whether of the Right or of the Left, can result in the opinion that they represent any such achievement or give any promise of leading men toward it.

Their basic convictions will lead pacifists to attach great importance to freedom of religion, thought, press, speech, assembly and association, and to suspect any form of "security" which involves bartering away the freedoms. They will consequently be drawn also toward "decentralist" economic forms and to co-operatives. The latter are likely to have increasing importance not only as elements in an eventual new economic world order but as providing the way by which an increasing number of pacifists can make a living in such a way as not to be giving needless support to an economic order which contradicts their most cherished convictions. The notion that any individuals or groups can escape completely in such a complex and highly integrated world as ours from implication in the dominant economic order seems to me illusory and dangerous. But the fact that we cannot withdraw completely should not lead to the conclusion that we may as well be completely immersed. Unquestionably a good deal of energy should be devoted to organizing economic life now along lines that are consonant with the pacifist philosophy and that give human beings bread and fellowship here and now.

Even those pacifists who may have to remain in conventional occupations in which they are largely enmeshed in an exploitative economy are not excused from serious, indeed exacting, efforts to bring their economic standards and daily practices in line with professed pacifist convictions. A secularist may logically work, let us say, for socialism while personally behaving as a thoroughgoing exploiting capitalist. Even so he will be deceiving himself. Socialists and Communists of an earlier day were constantly proclaiming that the new order was just around the corner. They never, most of them, really believed it. As soon as socialism seemed imminent Social Democrats ran away from it as fast as possible; and when Communists got political power, they set about building—totalitarianism! For those who had eyes to see they had been making it clear all along that they did not believe their own announcement, for they thought that the stupendous change in the outward order, the revolution, could take place without any appreciable change taking place in themselves at all—as if a fish could live as easily on land as in the sea! In any case, no one can honestly work for the coming of the Kingdom of God without trying to make his life *now* conform to its principles.

We make only a passing reference to another most important item in the religious pacifist program, that having to do with race relationships. Here again, it is not a question of "either-or"—work to abolish war or work to abolish racial inequality. We have to do both. If racial antagonism is intensified and gets out of bounds, war will ensue. The next war might be predominantly racial in character—or the war after the next. Undoubtedly it would be frightful. On the other hand, if war comes, racial antagonisms will be enhanced. As for the colored races, resort to violence might be tempting to them in certain contingencies. The white peoples, warlike and contemptuous of others as they have been, have largely deprived themselves of the power or moral right to protest effectively against such a choice by other peoples. But God and history will not be mocked. Never more surely than in our age will those who take the sword destroy themselves as well as others. Religious pacifists will certainly devote intensive energies to the positive effort to level the barriers that have separated man from man, group from group; to open roads for full intercourse among men regardless of race; to make straight in this desert a highway for our God. As in other realms, so in this they will not wait until society has altered its attitudes and practices before striving to make their own conduct conform to Christian standards.

A brief reference to political activities and instrumentalities must similarly suffice. As Walter G. Muelder, now Dean of the school of

Theoiogy at Boston University, pointed out, pacifists do not regard themselves as a "peculiar" people and they do not claim to possess an "esoteric" knowledge. "Despite the war, non-violent cooperative methods have made a tremendous advance in the world." What pacifists do is to conserve those positive methods of co-operation and noncoercive living and thinking which hold society together. "Pacifists have faith in the constructive findings of social science, psychiatry, counselling, social work, political science, and economics. Where others falter because of fear of state pressure or because of nationalism, pacifists experiment in those forms of community and those social institutions which conserve the finding of science." They will accordingly share with their fellows in many constructive activities of the community—local, state, national and international—having to do, for example, with education, the treatment of offenders against society, and the development of efficient and truly democratic instrumentalities to meet various public needs.

Both in this connection and in connection with their major distinctive work of undermining the absolutist state and the war systems, the question of what political parties to support and how much time to devote to such support arises for pacifists. Not much careful thought has yet been devoted to this problem and it is not entirely clear what course would be most productive. The following points seem clear. In the main, religious pacifists will not withdraw from certain political activities. They will be skeptical of the ability of any political party which does not renounce war and organized violence to fulfill an effective revolutionary role in the present stage of history; and they will accordingly strive by democratic means to commit any party which they may support to such renunciation. In supporting or opposing candidates, especially for national office, they will attach more importance henceforth to their attitude toward war and conscription than in the past.

Pacifists will bear in mind also that a political party seeks to gain control over the national government and this almost always comes to mean control over the machinery of a warmaking power state. But religious pacifists do not want control over such a state; they do not want such a state to exist at all. No party which does not categorically renounce war is likely to solve that dilemma: It may think it will scrap war machinery when it takes office, but it will find that "temporarily" it must take the first step of making a wiser and more restrained use of war machinery than the party it has thrust from power, and that temptation is satanic.

There is considerable doubt whether "power" in modern industrial society resides primarily in political parties as such rather than in the mass organizations of farmers, workers, industrialists and minority groups—to some extent also in agencies such as churches, educational institutions, the press and other agencies of communication. Both for this reason and because in the United States there is hardly likely to be time to build a new political party before the issue of atomic war or peace has to be settled one way or the other, pacifists will probably work largely in and with the organizations and institutions just mentioned, seeking of course to win their members and leaders to acceptance of the spirit and methods of nonviolence.

Thus we come back to a final word about the great mission to which, we have urged, religious pacifists are called—the mission to preach repentance; and the remission of sin and deliverance from fear to those who turn to God in trust; and the renunciation of war by men and by nations, by our own nation.

Irwin Shaw, a soldier who saw service on many fronts, wrote for the *New Yorker* in 1942 a story under the title, "Preach on the Dusty Roads." It is now the first story in a volume, *Act of Faith and Other Stories.* It is about a father, a high-salaried accountant for a great corporation, who says farewell to his son who is off to the war. After leaving his son he has, as a reviewer phrases it, "a blinding moment of apocalyptic vision." The author's description of the content of that vision is as follows:

The war [the father thought] was being fought for twenty years and I didn't know it. I waited for my son to grow up and fight it for me. I should've been out screaming on the street-corners. I should've grabbed people by their lapels in trains, in libraries and restaurants and yelled at them: "Love, understand, put down your guns, forget your profit, remember God. . . ." I should have walked on foot through Germany and France and England and America. I should've preached on the dusty roads. . . .

"Preach on the dusty roads." Yes, that is the call that comes to you and me today from "the trumpet which sounds from the hid battlements of eternity." Everywhere the summons to love, to understand, to renounce war, to lay down the sword must be preached. Everywhere men must be reminded that God wills it. He will give grace to those who trust and obey Him. His will is joy and peace.

Men and women, young and old, must preach on the dusty roads and quietly and persistently witness in home, office, store, factory. A great mission to the churches must be organized. After the manner of St. Francis and the early Quakers, missions must be undertaken to the great as well as the humble, to heads of states and to the outcast.

Religious pacifists in the United States who undertake the mission to call their own nation, so privileged, so sinful, so great in its potentialities, to follow the Christian, the pacifist, way can call upon pacifists in other lands to work for the conversion of their own nations to the same way of salvation. Gandhi in India, having led his people to independence by the nonviolent method, may turn to the great work of seeking to win them now in his old age to set the example of a disarmed nation trusting in nonviolence to guard the freedom that was won by nonviolence. Kagawa and Japanese Christians and pacifists might labor to keep in the constitution of that nation forever the provision which rules out war and armaments. There are already those who believe that for the sake of the "national honor" and in order that the nation may fulfill its "obligations" to the society of nations that provision must be expunged. On August 28, 1946, the then Prime Minister Shigeru Yoshida expressed the view that "the question of the renunciation of war is one that might be taken up after the peace conference." That is, once the peace treaties have been signed, war preparations may begin again, in conformity with universal practice among respectable powers.

Concerted, persistent, powerful efforts by pacifists in all lands to increase the number of conscientious objectors and to bring about disarmament by their own respective nations would mean a movement for universal disarmament brought about by the conquest of fear and by the spirit of love for mankind. In such a movement there is hope as there is not in any movement for general disarmament depending on mutual fear of each nation for the others and on fear of the atomic bomb.

Such preaching as we are advocating is, of course, religious preaching in content, in inspiration, in basis. Advisedly, I have usually prefaced the term "pacifism" with some such adjective as "religious," "Christian" or "Judaeo-Christian." I do not refer to a verbal profession of religion; nor to this or that dogmatic formulation; nor to adherence to this or that ecclesiastical institution. I do mean a pacifism rooted in a certain conception of the nature of life, the universe, God; to a pacifism which is an inner experience, an inner attitude toward life, hence a way of life, and not merely a tool or device which the individual uses in certain circumstances on his environment. One must not only favor pacifism or nonviolence as a policy in such and such circumstances, one must be a pacifist.

As for the further qualification of the term "religious" at various points in this book, for thirty years now whenever I have been or, more accurately, desired to be a true Christian, I have been a pacifist; and whenever I have desired to be a true pacifist, I have also desired to be a Christian. I agree with Nels F. S. Ferré that "the pacifism of radical Christianity confronts our whole actual system with the whole gospel of Christ." But there is nothing of which I am more certain than that the spirit of Christ is not one of exclusion and there is nothing that Jesus himself made clearer than the conviction expressed in the well-known words, "Not every one that saith unto me, Lord, lord, shall enter into the Kingdom of heaven but he that doeth the will of my Father who is in heaven." Therefore, I welcome also Ferré's comment in an as yet unpublished paper: "Our definition of Christianity is not invidious, but inclusive, only partiality and exclusiveness being excluded, or rather, excluding themselves from natural participation. Only what denies or defies a common righteousness and salvation by the forgiveness and power of God's love and total care for all and every good thing is excluded." Since the God and Father of all has, furthermore, not left Himself without a witness among any people, there is both room and need in our approach for concern to promote what Walter G. Muelder has called "the creative interaction of the great world religions."

Since in any event our mission is a religious one, our preaching will bear fruit in the degree that it is an expression of our life and is reinforced by it from day to day. The works of mercy will, therefore, constitute a regular and large part of our program. And daily we shall strive humbly and patiently and courageously where we find ourselves to live in God and for our fellows. "By this we know that we have passed from death to life, because we love the brethren."

It follows also that our work can be done only if by worship in some genuine and deep sense we open our spirits to receive the grace and power which God alone can bestow on His creatures. What we do will be healing and constructive only if it is the joyous overflow of a pure inner spring. We have to be pacifists before we can preach pacifism rightly. We have to be Christians before we can do Christian works. If this means that some among us feel called to withdraw for extended periods of self-examination, renewal and worship, they must obey the summons, and the understanding will not feel that these comrades have "stopped working." On the other hand, the priority of being over doing is not essentially a chronological matter. It is not that in time one first becomes a Christian and afterwards does Christian things. If one truly behaves as a Christian, he is a Christian. It is spiritually that being underlies doing and doing must not seek to outrun being, and in this sense being has priority and worship comes first, also in the further sense that man must place no reliance upon himself but only on the grace and love of God.

Normally, therefore, being and doing, worship and work, will go together and be continuously and creatively integrated. We are called to work in the world. We must "preach on the dusty roads," in chancelleries, in schools, in factories and mines, in churches and synagogues, in jails, in homes. The time is short. The task is overpowering. Yet nothing must stop us, not even the sense of our own weakness and limitation. Not even if we encounter only apathy and experience defeat, if like seed we must be sown into the ground and die before we bear fruit. We have to take upon ourselves the awful responsibility of "the good" described in the immortal closing lines of Auden and MacNeice's "Their Last Will and Testament":

To the good who know how wide the gulf, how deep
Between Ideal and Real, who being good have felt
The final temptation to withdraw, sit down and weep!
We pray the power to take upon themselves the guilt
Of human action, though still as ready to confess
The imperfection of what can and must be built;
The wish and power to act, forgive and bless.[1]

At this crucial moment in human history, in the presence of such responsibility, we "upon whom the end of the age has come" stand humbled yet not cast down. God, who places the responsibility upon His children, gives also in overflowing measure the power to accomplish the work—the God "in whose will," in Augustine's great words, "is our peace" and the peace of the stricken, war-ravished world.

[1] From *Letters from Iceland,* by W. H. Auden and L. MacNeice (New York: Random House, Inc., 1937), p. 259. Used with permission.

Index